The Mystical Universal Mother

The Mystical Universal Mother

The Teachings of the Mother of Yellow Altar

By Hua-Ching Ni
Teacher of Natural Spiritual Truth

The Shrine of the Eternal Breath of Tao
College of Tao and Traditional Chinese Healing
LOS ANGELES

Acknowledgement: Thanks and appreciation to Janet DeCourtney, Frank Gibson and the students in the Atlanta Center for assistance in typing, editing, proofreading and typesetting this book.

The Shrine of the Eternal Breath of Tao, Malibu, California 90265
College of Tao and Traditional Chinese Healing, 117 Stonehaven Way
Los Angeles, California 90049

Copyright 1991 by Ni, Hua-Ching.
Library of Congress Catalog Card Number 90-60709
ISBN 0-937064-45-9

Library of Congress Cataloging-in-Publication Data

Ni, Hua Ching.
The mystical universal mother : the teachings of the Mother of Yellow Altar / Ni, Hua-Ching.
    p.   cm.
ISBN 0-937064-45-9 : $14.95
    1.   Spiritual life (Taoism)   2.   Women, Taoist.   3. Ch'en-mu, 3th/4th cent. I. Title.
BL1923.N54   1991   91-60709
299'.5144--dc20   CIP

This book is dedicated to the love
that the universal mother gives
to all her universal children
and those who are wisely choosing spiritual learning
as the way to reach their rewarding life.

To female readers,

According to Taoist teaching, male and female are equally important in the natural sphere. This is seen in the diagram of Tai Chi. Thus, discrimination is not practiced in our tradition. All my work is dedicated to both genders of human people.

Wherever possible, constructions using masculine pronouns to represent both sexes are avoided; where they occur, we ask your tolerance and spiritual understanding. We hope that you will take the essence of my teaching and overlook the superficiality of language. Gender discrimination is inherent in English; ancient Chinese pronouns do not have differences of gender. I wish for all of your achievement above the level of language or gender.

Thank you, H. C. Ni

Warning - Disclaimer

This book is intended to present information and techniques that have been in use throughout the orient for many years. The information offered is to the author's best knowledge and experience and is to be used by the reader(s) at their own discretion. This information and practices utilize a natural system within the body, however, there are no claims for effectiveness.

Because of the sophisticated nature of the information contained within this book, it is recommended that the reader of this book also study the author's other books for further knowledge about a healthy lifestyle and energy conducting exercises.

People's lives have different conditions. People's growth has different stages. Because the background of people's development cannot be unified, no rigid or stiff practice is given that can be applied universally. Thus, it must be through the discernment of the reader that the practices are selected. The adoption and application of the material offered in this book must be your own responsibility.

The author and publisher of this book are not responsible in any manner whatsoever for any injury which may occur through following the instructions in this book.

Contents

Prelude

"Tao is the destination of all religious, while it leaves behind all religions just like the clothing of different seasons and different places. Tao is the goal of serious science, but it leaves behind all sciences as a partial and temporal description of the Integral Truth.

"The teaching of Tao includes all religious subjects, yet it is not on the same level as religions. Its breadth and depth go far beyond the limits of religion. The teaching of Tao serves people's lives like religions do, yet it transcends all religions and contains the essence of all religions.

"The teaching of Tao is not like any of the sciences. It is above the level of any single subject of science.

"The teaching of Tao is the master teaching of all. However, it does not mean the teaching relies on a master. It means the teaching of Tao is like a master key which can unlock all doors leading to the Integral Truth. It teaches or shows the truth directly. It does not stay on the emotional surface of life or remain at the level of thought or belief. Neither does it stay on the intellectual level of life, maintaining skepticism and searching endlessly. The teaching of Tao presents the core of the subtle truth and helps you to reach it yourself."

**Mother Chern - The Mother of Yellow Altar
(Traditional Drawing)**

Preface

This book's focus is to help men and women learn from the teachings of a woman teacher, the Mother of Yellow Altar. The Mother of Yellow Altar is a woman Taoist who was also known as Mother Chern. Her active time was around 200 - 300 A.D. She probably was the first woman to set up a Taoist jing, a safe, quiet and peaceful place with houses for Taoists to do spiritual cultivation. The Jing was called Yellow Altar Jing. Thus, she was known as the Mother of Yellow Altar.

Many people who have pre-conceived ideas of women's status may ask:

Can a woman be spiritually achieved? Is a woman able to reach divinity?

This book is going out to you, men and women, to help you find the answer. Then you can conclude whether a woman can be spiritually helpful and divine or not.

Correct knowledge can be produced by a balanced mind. Accurate judgment can decide the direction of one's life. The good direction of a life can extend it to eternity. This book wishes to provide you with correct knowledge, accurate judgment and good direction. What else can give this service to you?

By growing the divine nature within yourself, you will see the world much more deeply. Then you may decide to allow the examples in this book to guide you back to the full growth of your divine nature by attaining the great harmony within and without.

Your Spiritual Friend,
Ni, Hua-Ching
February 2, 1991 U. S. A.

Chapter 1

The Doctrine of Harmony

Q: Master Ni, you have written an inspiring book about your father, Eternal Light. Would you please tell us about your mother? Was she a spiritually achieved person?

Master Ni: As the son of a Taoist woman, I learned greatly from my mother's life and cultivation. I was her third child, and now I wish to share with you some of the wisdom she imparted to me. First I would like to tell you something about her family, because that will give you some insight into the depth of her spiritual achievement.

My mother did not talk much about her family, and I never knew my grandparents because they died before I was born. However, bits and pieces of information came to me from relatives or family associates.

Occasionally I heard something about my grandfather. He was an extraordinary person, a very kind person. His interest was art. He especially enjoyed and appreciated the performing art of Chinese opera. His personal spiritual philosophy followed the same viewpoint as the scholar Fahn Tien who served as minister during the Liang Dynasty. At that time, Emperor Liang Wu Ti (reign 502-550 A. D.) was attracted and devoted to the newly developing Buddhism. He lead the whole royal court, ministers and people of the entire country in following Buddhism. Fahn Tien was the sole minister who expressed a different opinion. He said that human life was like lighting a lamp; when you turn on a lamp, there is light and spirits. When you turn off a lamp, there is no light, no spirits; the spirits scatter. This was against the belief of the emperor, who trusted that the spirits of a human being were never extinct. So my maternal grandfather had a different point of view from most people, taking the same point of view as Fan Tien.

My grandfather was a Confucian scholar, because he saw the darkness in Chinese politics. During his time, he became an admirer of Master Lu, Tung Ping. It was personal worship rather than a religion. It was a fashion in

Chinese society for scholars to worship Master Lu. Those scholars may or may not title themselves as Taoists. But, my grandfather's spiritual appreciation opened the opportunity for my mother, his only daughter, to study Tao with a female Taoist who continued the teaching of Mother Chern.

In his personal life, my grandfather put his energy into cultural or recreational work. It was not a business, it was charity. He sponsored four Chinese opera companies. There are many kinds of Chinese opera, because different regions have different folk operas. At that time in the Chinese countryside, few towns had a theater or large building for fixed performances. But stages for plays were built as part of local temples. People watched the operas during the festivals which occurred at different times of the year. My grandfather sponsored groups for traveling and performing.

Opera was a seasonal business. The companies would be invited by villages and towns during special festivals and when farmers were not in their busy season. Some actors were also part-time farmers or had other professions.

My grandfather's support for the four operas consumed all the money he had inherited from his family. Each opera company consisted of a large team of people. That was a large number of people to finance considering that there was income only during the performances during the farmer's slow seasons. When acting season was over, actors and actresses still needed to eat, and they would come to my grandfather for a loan. But they were unable to pay back the loans, so after a period of years, my grandfather's financial resources had become drained. He himself went into debt because he always looked for money to support these poor but talented people, who did not know how to organize their lives and finances.

My mother was my grandfather's only child and was raised with the influence of the opera. When she was older, because of the financial problem, she learned how to manage the opera and the actors. My grandfather had drained the family's resources. My grandfather was still a respectable gentleman despite the fact that he had lost his financial solidity. Because they owed people lots of money, my mother simply took over the business and improved it.

My mother set up a system: when the actors and actresses made money, she paid them only half at that time and saved the other half. That other half was paid to the performers during the time they did not have work. After telling them about it, she made the performers sign a paper that they agreed to this arrangement. They needed to trust this new system that my mother proposed. The performers did not actually have a way to refuse my mother's management, because although they were proficient at acting, they were poor in financial management. However, this new system made the actors and actresses maintain interest in their artistic development. They could concentrate better on the performing arts rather than worry about where their next meal was going to come from.

My mother used to tell me that on a big scale, actors and actresses are poor at being themselves, because they are always acting another person's life story. However, in a certain role of a certain opera, once they touch their own sensitive area, they do well in expressing themselves. Thus, putting the right person in the right role really brings life to the performance of a historical or imaginary character in a drama. So the actors or actresses were a combination: on one hand, they did not know how to manage themselves. On the other hand, they were excellent at self-expression in the arts.

That was my mother's early life. She discovered that actors and actresses, when not performing, have too much time for leisure, and so they will do all kinds of things such as gambling or smoking opium. But no art appreciator, and not even an art sponsor, has a way to discipline them. It takes someone like their direct employer or manager to help them. Such a person is needed to find jobs and constantly sponsor them.

This made my mother, for practical reasons, look for a way to help set up discipline for them. In the whole world, perhaps those performers were the least receptive to keeping good discipline. My mother finally decided to teach them what she learned from her teachers who helped in her search for spirit. She received the deep experience of those teachers who searched through all religions looking for a clearer spiritual vision among confusion. So she developed her teaching from the old religions with a special view of spirituality.

At that time in Chinese society, there were few female actresses. They did not act in men's companies, but there was a women's company in which the only men were in the orchestra or band. In the men's company, the male performers acted the women's roles. It is art, and when they dressed up, their performance was realistic. In the women's company, women acted the men's roles. Because this is an art that requires training, the women in men's clothing look like real men, old or young.

Chinese opera is different from Western opera. In it, the players may paint their entire faces with colorful makeup, giving it a stylized appearance. Ancient clothing styles are revived. Long graceful robes and colorful silk or satin costumes are required for both men's and women's parts. Almost everything, from makeup to accompanying music, is symbolic rather than literal, as in Western opera. Only after three years of successful concentrated training can one become a beginning performer.

The opera performers were a hard group to discipline. They were not responsible and not punctual. To put on a performance, the performers need to arrive backstage at the right time and get ready to do the show. The ones who came early could dress nicely, and put on the elaborate facial makeup evenly and skillfully. Performers who came at the last minute rushed around to get ready and made a mess. They did not have time to put on the clothing right, do their makeup nicely, or put their hair ornaments properly in place. One can learn something from that; it is better to arrive backstage earlier.

Some years later, I had a chance to meet some visitors who were actors and actresses under my mother's management. I heard from them that my mother had a special religion which she taught. Her religion specifically found followers in the four companies of actors and actresses. My mother set up a portable altar, a yellow tent that was carried along to each performance location. That helped the performers do their spiritual practice consistently. This religion made the performers become more serious in their lives and seemed to have a real spiritual effect on them. They began to keep better schedules, stop gambling and drinking too much alcohol, avoid sexual misbehavior and so forth.

After my grandfather passed away, the opera companies were disbanded. Some time later, my mother married. But the influence of the spiritual activities was still there, because they had been deeply affected by it, and so they continued the religious activity long after that.

The worship my mother promoted among the performers was not her invention. It had a long background, but in some way it was a little more organized than the ancient way. Through this, my mother's doctrine was expressed. Her doctrine was derived from what she had learned from her teachers.

I would like to tell you the doctrine of my mother's revelation of the Universal Mystical Mother. It is put into points below for easier understanding.

1. Taoist conventional thought is that the human race was not started by a man. Because men have a different physical nature, they can never give birth. So the first human being must not have been a man, but a woman. Even the first spiritual being had to be female. Male energy is the self-splitting from the Universal Being who is described as the Mystical Mother.

During an earlier period before natural energy became a human being, the universal shape was a spirited being without gender difference. This did not change until the natural spirit formed itself on the earth with a physical shape. For a long period of time, beings had no gender and were not in the process of life and death, or being formed and unformed. They had no reproductive capability. Much later, the development of different natures of beings occurred, and male and female differences developed. Finally, the female and male shapes successfully reached maturity.

By this development, beings could carry on their own reproduction. It was also told that in the second level of subtle nature, male and female were formed. When beings formed themselves with physical energy, immediately the sex difference was determined. In other words, in the subtle form or shape, a male and a female life were decided.

In China, we have the custom of worshipping human ancestors, but nobody knows who the first human ancestor was. Some ancient legends tell of Pang Gu, Tien Wang Shi (the Emperor of Heaven), Ti Wang Shi (the Emperor of Earth) and Lung Wang Shi (the Emperor of People). My mother thinks that they were not necessarily male human individuals, and that it was when men began to have desire for control over other people that this old legend was started. It created the image of a male as the source of authority who was given power over others as emperor.

So the first doctrine of my mother is to point out that the real divinity or real spirit of our human ancestors was above gender. But female or feminine is more suitable to describe the very beginning. Nobody argued with my mother, because there was a historical background to support this.

The ancient Chinese before Shang Dynasty (1766-1121 B.C.) had faith in Neu Wu, and believed that she was the first woman or goddess who created human beings from mud and water.

2. My mother guided me to know that the universe contains or produces everything. The ancient sages thought that the universe is shaped like a valley, so the nature of the universe is feminine rather than masculine, as a conception of space. It gives room for productivity. There is this space called the universal valley. Then a new thing comes in, or comes forth from that universal valley. The conception of a valley is receptive and feminine. Thus, the universal valley is feminine or neutral.

This can be illustrated in modern terms. We know that masculine nature is present as the creative energy of the universe, but the creative universe has to have a field to work in. Thus, masculine energy is like a piston; it is necessary to have a cylinder so that the piston can work. If there is no cylinder, the piston cannot work to produce any energy.

In this view, the universe first offers a cylinder type of energy that is feminine and receptive. Any energy formed like a piston, or something that moves or keeps operating in the universal valley, would be a latecomer.

3. Nature brings about everything. Without doubt, nature is energy itself. It does not remain itself; nature has myriad transformations and becomes different things. Yang describes the motion of natural energy. Yin describes the capacity of natural energy. The motion of energy creates the field of the energy. The range of motion of natural energy is the capacity of the energy. They are one energy. The function of the mind reacts to the motion and the capacity of energy differently. If the feminine nature is the background, then the masculine nature is the changes. Both are changeable, transformable realities of nature.

Masculine energy is applied as an expression in circumstances. The variable circumstances are the stages and changes. Thus, during a change, masculine energy is expressed, but first there is energy, then the transformation comes. In other words, first you have energy; then there is a chance to have masculine expression in a circumstance.

Masculine energy is the energy of change and feminine energy is the energy of constancy and repeating constancy. Whatever is constant and eternal is divine; therefore it is suitable to use feminine virtue to describe the divine energy.

So my mother's third doctrine is easy to understand: nature is feminine, because the feminine can produce and give birth to many things. The feminine is productive; the creative part is the background. It is important to understand and trust that nature is providing and giving. Thus, nature is closer to being feminine. Things can be born and die, but nature itself is a providing and feminine virtuous condition; therefore, it can constantly give birth to new life.

The second doctrine explains differently than the third one. The second one expresses a notion about space, a universal valley. The third one means all life - nature itself is life - is more feasibly feminine than masculine.

4. The commonly accepted concept that God is the image of the masculine is partial. God is also feminine natured. My mother defined that God is a force behind everything; it is behind the universal creative energy. Anything apparent, such as the world and humans, is the fulfillment of the feminine aspect of God energy.

Creativity is expressed through people. God is behind the creative expression of people, so God is hidden. God is not in front, because God does not take name or credit, but humans do. Therefore, God is more feminine natured than masculine natured.

5. My mother's fifth doctrine is spiritual devotion to the Mystical Mother of the Universe. She thought that all existence or entities, whether beings or force, that are expressible or manifestable can fall into the category of beingness because all things and beings come from the impulse of nature. Any projection from nature, as an existence or as a gathering of invisible force, is mortal; it dies. It is momentary. But behind the manifestable beingness or force there is unmanifestable reality. This unmanifested reality is more feminine natured.

The impulsive force or the masculine manifested force is passing or mortal. Human beings are mortal or destructible. So masculine expression is more related to physical reality and feminine expression is more related to spiritual reality. The feminine spirits of the universe are immortal; they have no death. The spirits of human beings or gods are feminine, eternal and indestructible. Although feminine nature and masculine nature comprise the completeness of the universal being, in order to attain eternity all men need to learn to complete themselves with feminine virtue. There comes the hope for the real achievement. The diehard and dare-devil type of male energy is a short flash in the existent world.

6. Male energy alone cannot be a god. The enduring spirits of the universe are the harmonized spirits. The typical male forceful energy is abrupt, sudden, radical action or violence. The feminine energy is gentle, unseeable, unfeelable, and always there. A man can become a god if he refines himself and completes himself with feminine virtue. That is unified refinement or spiritual achievement.

So all people in the manifested sphere who wish to attain eternity must refine themselves. They must refine the coarseness and roughness of nature. Then they have a chance to connect with their true spiritual nature, which has no gender characteristics or discrimination. However, what is behind the active screen of the world is not masculine. It is the gentle, persevering, constant feminine virtue of the universal valley that manifests the spiritual virtues of the subtle universal source.

7. Men, if not balanced themselves, are not qualified to be a divinity or to think about being divine. Nor need one accept an imbalanced masculine image as a god, because that is not real. My mother understood that aggressive male images were mistakes. To correct this mistake, men must give up their pride and become humble about their physical strength. Their shape contains too much coarseness and is their obstruction or obstacle to being spiritual.

The imbalanced masculine force is an obstacle for the achievement of the eternal spiritual substance. Men need to give up pride about their shape and their force, and learn the gentle force of universal femininity. Otherwise, they will become lost in the circumstance they are attached to.

Attaching to material reality and egotistic expansion causes loss of self. It is possible, then, for men to achieve godhood through learning to use the feminine principle in a positive, creative happy life.

8. Conventional Buddhism, which came from India, declares that being a woman is spiritually inferior and that if a woman is a good person for three lifetimes, she can then become a man. However, the truth is opposite. All men who wish to achieve themselves spiritually must learn

gentleness from the virtue of a woman. Women who maintain and develop their womanly virtue have a better opportunity to achieve spiritually because women are close to universal femininity. A man may not need three lifetimes; however, he needs to cultivate himself to contain all good and gentle virtues of woman.

9. The Jewish or Christian Bible states that woman is a rib of man. It means a ready assistant. It is beautiful. The truth of the universe is that man also is a rib from a woman. Man and woman work together, side by side, shoulder to shoulder, hand in hand. This is how to fulfill the mission of universal life. Men and women are assistants to each other in making the world.

Each life is the life of the universe. It continues the universal life. The mission of giving new life cannot be done by only feminine or masculine beings. Each supports the other to accomplish the universal spiritual mission. Therefore, men and women are the side or ribs of each other.

10. Even though that is the reality of the universe, the natural virtue of typical universal femininity allows the man to be boss.

On most occasions a woman remains as assistant, coordinator or follower. That is an expression of wisdom. This is true greatness which can only be found by the universal virtue of femininity. Such greatness cannot be found in some men. Men tend to be competitive. They wish to be bigger, higher than others. Only by learning from the universal virtue of femininity can they change their unrefined or undeveloped quality into a perfect being.

Kindness can be produced by the motherliness of feminine virtue. Men are somewhat selfish unless they learn to be kind. In the family, the woman really supports and gives much to the new life. She gives her own energy. But she still does not own the life to which she has given birth. She does not dominate the life to which she has given birth. This is called the subtle virtue of universal femininity.

11.   My mother described wisdom as feminine nature. Wisdom is something you cannot see. Wisdom is not action, it is the guiding energy of an action. Worldly pursuits, without wisdom to guide them, are meaningless, short-lived or destructive. There are all types of actions or behaviors, but not all actions or behaviors mean something unless they are connected to the guiding energy of wisdom. Because wisdom is not visible, it is not an expressing energy, and it is more assisting than dominating energy. Thus, it is more feminine than masculine.

That was my mother's definition of wisdom, or description of the nature of wisdom. Wisdom can be something that is initiated or performed. It also can be what is gathered from many mistakes or wrongdoings.

However, she went further to say that there are two types of wisdom. Wisdom that is accumulated from error is expressible wisdom. If wisdom is an afterward understanding, although it serves your future behavior and actions, it is not as good as guiding wisdom. Guiding wisdom is an inexpressible energy built into an action or behavior. It does not come after an event but before or with it. It is thus hidden within good action or good behavior. Therefore, because it is hidden and works behind the scene, it is feminine natured.

No wisdom encourages fighting, roughness, crudeness, or taking rash or hasty action. Those characteristics are the nature of men or masculine energy. Therefore, it is clear that without the wisdom of feminine guiding energy, roughness, harshness, violence and suddenness all express the low level of secondary force. The secondary force belongs to men or masculine nature. If a man understands the nature of wisdom correctly, he can give up his secondary level nature of roughness.   (About this, one student said, "Yet, she believes in spanking!" Another student said, "Spanking is an expression of wisdom!" Master Ni said, "It is neither. It was out of circumstance and the sense of duty that it is necessary to correct the wrong habit of the young sons.")

This was my mother's definition of wisdom.   She described that if wisdom lacks virtue of femininity, it is not wisdom.   At least, it is incomplete as raw information or knowledge, or is an unbalanced viewpoint. Wisdom comes from cooperation, consulting, harmony, gentleness, patience, tolerance and a deep wide capacity which can contain and allow things to happen naturally. Wisdom is energy that can participate and join in action and behavior, and at the same time be above actions and behaviors. That is the nature of wisdom. If you correctly understand wisdom, you know that it is wise for a man to learn feminine virtue.

12. The feminine energy in the universe is harmonizing, assisting and accomplishing. Feminine energy can also initiate a project or thing.

However, initiating something without also having accomplishing energy cannot bring about its fulfillment and leads to stagnancy or disorder. Initiating energy without correct support just brings irresponsible behavior, or irresponsible, careless projects, because something is started but not finished. No plan is complete unless there is the constant accomplishing energy to fulfill it.

The accomplishing, harmonizing energy is feminine. It does not need to compete or be in front. It does not need to fight or make a show. It does not need to be a leader, but it is accomplishing. That is subtle virtue. This subtle virtue is feminine.

Precisely, here in my mother's teaching, the words virtue and nature describe a typical spiritual quality. In the practical sphere, there are manly women and womanly men. In married life, there are husbandly wives and also wifely husbands. They are all right if they find the right marriage or a suitable work environment; they will find harmony and positive fruit of life. Otherwise, trouble will be seen. However, balanced individuals will find wider suitability and things will be easier in achieving the right goal. Correctly speaking, a balanced personality is an important direction in which to direct oneself.

My mother choose not to be a leader; she chose to be a helper. She chose to harmonize her life of subtle virtue in meeting the role of being a wife and mother. She choose to be a woman who came to help somebody accomplish something. She chose my father because she felt she could exercise her accomplishing nature in fulfilling his projects.

These were not all of my mother's doctrines, but they were the most important ones. I appreciate my mother's 12 points which are consistent with original Taoism. In the original *Book of Changes*, K'un, the receptive or feminine energy, was the hexagram that led the other 63 hexagrams. It established the teaching of the gentle path of the universal virtue of femininity. It was King Wen of Chou (around 1134 B.C.) who changed the order and put Chyan, the creative and active energy of masculinity, at the head of the other 63 hexagrams. Chyan was more fit for King Wen's revolutionary movement to overthrow Emperor Jow (reign 1150-1102 B.C.) of the Sharng Dynasty.

In my view, it is not important whether Chyan or K'un is the first chapter of the *Book of Changes*. The teaching of the gentle path is elucidated by my mother's work. I just continue the ancient teaching.

Much later, as an adult, I had an opportunity to study Taoism. My particular interest was the ancient original Taoism. When I studied it, then I understood that my mother's teaching is the most original teaching handed down from the ancient ones. Original Taoism existed before the culture became mixed up. Some parts of my mother's teachings were her application of the old teachings towards new times, especially for me, a young man with limited power of understanding.

When she managed the opera companies, my mother established an altar in her father's house with the image of the Mother of Yellow Altar, who was the initiating teacher of her spiritual school. All the opera people went to learn spiritual practice from her there.

After my grandfather passed away, my mother discontinued the opera business, which was really more like a charity. It was not her true interest; it had only been a response to circumstance to help my grandfather. She then went to find her side or rib. This next chapter is the story of how she sided with my father and my father sided with her.

Chapter 2

Spiritual Life Within Married Life

Q: After your mother married your father, did she become his student?

Master Ni: As a young boy, the impression I received from my mother and her distant relatives was that my grandfather never had the idea to marry her out of the family, but that he wished her to marry somebody into the family. That was because he did not have a son. It became a big pressure for my grandfather; he was always looking for someone to marry into the family. If my grandfather had some sons, he would easily have consented to her just marrying somebody's son and he would have let her become a part of their family. But that was not the case. Usually a man who would like to marry into someone else's family had no family or lacked financial independence. He did find many young men, and brought them over to the house and introduced them to my mother. He let my mother interview them. However, the young scholars felt they were not a match for her. They were scared of her because she was smart, perceptive and capable. For this reason, marriage to my mother was not as desirable as my grandfather had hoped.

After my grandfather passed away, my mother naturally disbanded the opera groups. She heard about my father, Ni, Yo San, a country doctor of traditional medicine who had a good reputation, but no money. My father ran a doctors office in a fair sized town. He lived in the back rooms of the office with his son, who was born by his late wife.

Aside from his busy medical practice, my father mostly enjoyed his spiritual practice and study. Because of his devotion to study, his son, my half brother, became somewhat like a free young animal. He adopted many bad habits, like playing ma jiang and smoking. At the time I grew up, around the early part of the 20th century, using matches was quite a modern thing. We used to use a flint stone when we needed fire. However, my brother had a pocket lighter. I liked that lighter, because one touch and crack! immediately fire came. But I dared not smoke because my mother's discipline was strict.

My elder brother was a fashionable, worldly person when he was younger. My mother, with the agreement of my father, could not extend her strict discipline on him, because that would have caused misunderstanding between them. In the conventional society of China, a stepmother's helping heart can easily be misunderstood as mistreatment. Also, my mother was not older than my brother.

My brother adopted his bad habits before my father's remarriage. My mother did her best to keep things smooth with my elder brother to keep my father's emotions calm; my elder brother was the reminder of my father's memory of his love towards his past wife. My mother offered her gentle help towards the young man. This is how in later years my brother could still be a good doctor, even with some of the built-up fashionable bad habits of his childhood.

I would like to tell you how my parents met. My mother heard about my father's reputation as a spiritually achieved person and a good doctor. So she went to visit him as a patient. If I remember correctly, my mother was 17 or 18 years younger than my father. Usually each patient in my father's office needed to wait for his or her turn, and my father took care of them one by one. He would feel the patient's pulse and ask a few questions before deciding what to do about the problem. My mother went in and waited. When the time came for her turn, my father followed his custom and wished to pull the beautiful hand into his to feel her pulse. However, my mother refused, saying, "What I came here for cannot be checked out by pulse. My problem is constipation." My father said, "Oh, constipation. Then you do not need treatment. You only need to tell me about your lifestyle. I will give you some suggestions, such as doing exercise or more household chores. Movement will help you bring more air into the trunk of the body to improve the movement of your bowels. Also drink water, especially in the early morning. Eat more fruit, too." My mother replied, "I will take your advice." She wished to pay my father, but my father refused to accept payment. That was my mother's first visit to my father's office.

After some time, maybe one month later, she went again to see my father. My father told me she came in the afternoon, after his busy hours had ended. He was surprised that she came back and asked, "Wasn't your problem taken care of?"

She said, "This time I did not come for treatment, but to ask some questions. I know you are a spiritual teacher. I would like to know many things. I would like to see if you can help answer my questions."

My mother first asked my father about the general foundation of spiritual learning.

My father answered: "Each individual has three spheres of energy. People cannot easily feel two spheres of energy which are above the physical shape of the body. You have a mind that you can be aware of, but spiritual energy cannot be felt, because it is invisible, inaudible and surely untouchable, unless you are trained to attain delicacy of the mind. Spiritual energy is higher than mind and much higher than the body. Thus, you cannot imagine or control it. This type of study is higher than the service of religion.

"General religions serve people's emotion. Most people who follow religion are not ready for spiritual development yet. However, it is still somewhat important for people to learn from religion. If you learn from a religion, what you learn is the symbol of spirit, not spirit itself. Religion is a tool that you can use to channel the invisible spiritual energy, but religious teaching itself is not the truth. There are many different kinds of religions, most of which are not for the purpose of deep service.

"Basically, all temples, worship and religions serve the same level: to gather the spiritual energy of your life being so that you can channel it. To accomplish this purpose and also for deeper study, you do not need to go to a temple. You can do it directly by yourself. All you need is a quiet room in which you can channel your own spiritual energy. That will bring about truthful achievement. Spiritually, you will attain more and more, step by step. Of course, you need special instruction and guidance to be able to do this and reach the deeper levels. This path is individual spiritual cultivation for personal spiritual development."

My mother asked, "Can a person who does her own special cultivation use a certain religious form?"

My father answered, "Yes. There are three principles for spiritual cultivation. The first is借假修真 'to borrow what is false to nurture what is truthful.' This means, all religious worship is an external expression or set up system which extends its dominance in your life rather than assist your spiritual independence. There are a few religious forms that aim to help you to set your focus upon truthful individual enlightenment.

"The level of form that is used depends upon an individual's spiritual reality. Do not let the form become dominant in your spiritual growth and neglect what is truly of importance: spirit. It is untruthful if any religion states that spiritual energy can only be a certain way.

"In truth, spiritual energy does not have one fixed form. It uses whatever form you give to it. Therefore, if you use an external religion, whatever you set up in your mind and relate to will always help you gather your spiritual energy in your life being. This principle is 'to borrow what is false to nurture or 'to cultivate what is true.' If you can remember this, whenever any religion presents its artistic expression, you can use it to help yourself. Then there is no need to deeply explore all aspects of that religion or all religions. It is all set up by the mind as an artful expression of spirit. The images or forms and descriptions do not carry the spiritual reality. There are different ways of expression; they are totally irrelevant to the deep search.

"However, at the same time that you know the images are false, you can also consider the images as true. If your mind reacts to any system or setup and it works for you, then it is true for you on the shallow level of emotion. Even if something is not true for you, it is true for somebody else.

"The second principle of spiritual-self cultivation from the ancient achieved ones is借他修己 , i.e. to "borrow the other to cultivate the self." It means at some time you need a teacher. The teacher's function is decided by you to help your power. You borrow his spiritual being to support your spiritual being. You must still be objective about your teacher so that nothing occurs between you and your teacher that would cause you to lose your balance. Do not become overly involved with your teacher's personal life such as money matters or sex because that creates the potential for losing your balance. Many people feel lost when they lose the teacher.

"If you do not understand something the teacher is teaching you, do not have an emotional reaction. If the teacher is not clear in the teaching, do not have an emotional reaction. That causes you to feel either happy or upset. In the tradition of spiritual self-cultivation, your position is to borrow the teacher's existence, presence, image, etc. to help your own spiritual cultivation. A spiritual teacher's function is as much as that to help you spiritually.

"It is improper to entrust all your fortune to a teacher, although it is proper for teachers to be fairly paid for their teaching. Never die for your teacher or his teaching; if you do, you are placing your soul in the wolf's mouth. This is also against the principle of "to borrow the other to cultivate the self."

"The world has been twisted in its development and structure. A spiritual teacher does the same thing as a world leader. Some of them will attempt to make you a slave by taking your fortune and your life energy to serve them or their purpose. Worldly religion tends to do that. It is a reality of spiritual undevelopment rather than spiritual development.

"Never expect or think your teacher to be perfect. Never idolize your teacher. Also never bring a complaint or dissatisfaction to the teacher. A teacher is someone outside of you. You use a teacher's image and teaching to help you grow. You must learn to treat your teacher fairly. Be serious and of single purpose to learn whatever the teacher has attained, but never become too deeply entrapped by the teaching or ideology in order to give yourself some room to grow by yourself.

If you are a teacher, do not let people fool you or conduct your life energy towards their worldly emotional entanglements. If you are a student, do not allow people to fool you or to misconduct your life energy towards their end.

To overtrust someone else such as the teacher, or a religious leader to take care of your own spiritual achievement, is spiritual darkness. A student can keep this principle in mind.

If you are teacher, help the students but do not hold them onto you all the time. Do not arrange your teaching as a social scheme to get what you want. Do not make the student adopt your lifestyle or stay the way you stay. Spiritual cleanliness starts with you, so that you have nothing to do with all the problems of the conventional backward spiritual community.

The best way to treat your teacher and the company of your spiritual cultivation is to offer your pure friendship with spiritual love and useful support, but avoid worldly type of emotional fabrication. If you over-love your teacher, then you also hate or dislike your teacher. Then you pull down and come back to your worldly emotional mold again. That is harmful in the path of truthful spiritual learning. Religion and spiritual cultivation are different. Their nature, purpose and level are different, and each one brings about a different reality. If you are truthfully looking for spiritual development, even if you relate with external religion, truthful achievement still comes with your own individual spiritual cultivation. This does not distinguish you in a worldly sense, but you attain a distinct spiritual quality.

A teacher is someone who has something to give. It is not someone who comes to rob your body, to rob your money and to rob your soul. A fair exchange between student and teacher is less material and more spiritual. Learn to respect the teacher who gives you something to support the growth of your life spirit. That is the trade. Truthful teachers also know to use their students as the reflection of their virtue. It means the teachers extend their kind energy. It does not mean the teachers like to control people.

"The third principle is 持志帥氣which means, "to use your mind to control or govern your energy." Life is a gathering of energy; the mind is the center. Health and spiritual cultivation are like gathering money. Money is external; however, the principle of money gathering is to use a small amount of money to look for all different sources of income or different directions of income. The purpose is to change small money into big money. The achievement is to go from being penniless to becoming a person of wealth.

Spiritual cultivation is the same as gathering money; you need to gather your energy. You are already a piece of gathered energy. By governing, controlling and conducting your energy to maintain your health and strength, you can have a long, happy life.

When you understand that, you will discover that spiritual cultivation is easy to do. The principle of spiritual cultivation is that when you keep calm and still, your energy also keeps calm and still. When you move, your energy also starts to move. When you move or become active, you might cause the energy to become scattered. However, you need to know one thing; nobody can avoid being active or doing movement. So the principle is whether you are still or whether you are active, you keep your energy still. You do this by concentrating on the center of your body. If you keep calm in the innermost center, the energy will always be gathered.

There are different practices or spiritual programs. Some pull you out; they are not beneficial. Some can help you gather energy back to yourself. That is the important thing to learn and to do.

The first principle of spiritual achievement is internally to use your mind to govern your energy. People do not know energy, and they also do not know how to apply their mind. This causes energy scatteredness or exhaustion and needs to be avoided."

In learning Tao, these three principles are important. They will help you have spiritual achievement.

I would like to repeat it again. This principle is called, 'Using your mind to govern your energy.' Your energy must be governed, especially your emotion. Once your emotion is stirred, your bodily energy is disturbed. It is either stimulated or suppressed in one of two types of emotion. If you are excited or angry, then your energy suddenly rushes up. If you worry or are sad, your internal energy goes down. The sad or worrying emotion will transform your body energy to be watery, and then you will shed tears, or if you are sexually excited, the internal energy will transform to be watery. It is important to use your mind to keep from being emotional; thus, you can maintain your good energy. It is important to control your energy.

Life is a piece of energy. If you know how to control your energy well, it means in the practical spiritual cultivation in which you engage in each minute, you will reach the spiritual goal. Otherwise, talking about it, reading a book or writing a book, do not keep you centered. You need to stay still and spiritually centered, undisturbed, unexcited, not causing your energy to be dispersed in a wrong direction. Regardless of how we act or do not act, we always need to gather energy. Make yourself as an energy center of the surrounding energy. In this way, you will help yourself.

In ancient times, people who cultivated Tao used a good location or a beneficial spot called blessing land or Heavenly cave. Those spots were not useful to most people who lived there because they did not know anything about energy. Those people tended to be somewhat scattered. A person who keeps going everywhere cannot gather energy. For example, it happens when a person does something like visit a busy section of a city; that person is scattered by all the attractions. People who are spiritually centered, make themselves an energy center no matter where they live. Naturally they will gather good energy.

Governing, gathering and conducting energy are important practices. The mind is the governor of the body's energy. So it is important that the mind learn to be a wise queen and learn to govern and control the energy. Do not be a brutal or foolish leader; if so, your whole kingdom will become corrupt. Governing your energy by your mind is the third important principle in cultivation of Tao.

Some people lack self-control. Lack of control does not reflect a correct way of living or conducting energy. Such individuals need to remember that to cultivate Tao, they do not need a special religious form. If they need to use one, that is okay too, but it is not necessary. If you use your mind to govern your energy, calmly, peacefully and orderly, then you are cultivating Tao.

This was the first time my parents discussed spiritual topics. At that time, my mother started to recognize that my father's spiritual quality was broad and profound. He was not like an ordinary spiritual teacher who is enthusiastic to sell what he does.

Although my father was impressed by my mother, he did not decide to marry her right away. One of his acquaintances or patients acted as a match-maker or intermediary in the marriage. It was a more socially acceptable custom to do that at the time. At first my father refused the whole idea, saying, "First, I do not want to be changed. My life is this way. When I see that woman, I know that she is smart, sharp. She is so managing.

"Second, I am not rich; I would like to stay this way. I do not work for gathering money. I could provide well for her, but I am not interested in accumulation.

"Third, I do not need to be married. I was married once; I have a son, but now I wish to concentrate on my spiritual life, and the simpler the better."

My father was convinced very simply to accept the marriage. My mother accepted the three terms. She said something like, "First, I am not going to change you, you can still be independent. I will give you what I can offer to you in the way of help. I will offer it, and whether you take it or not is your personal choice. Second, I am not going to marry your money. I am not going to marry your profession, either. I wish to marry your open personality and spiritual life. You show much more maturity than other men I have met, young or old. Third, I will marry you not to become your wife, but to become your patron, your benefactor."

My mother continued, "You are a spiritual teacher; I am a student of spiritual self-cultivation. I am not looking for marriage, I am looking for a man for whom I can be his patron or supporter and who will in turn be my patron or sponsor. As a woman, I have the capability of being a patron to the right man. This is not marriage, this is a mutual spiritual patronage. If you do not marry me, you shall never find any other woman who can accept those terms."

My father thought about it. He was not greatly excited about the terms. He wondered how deeply my mother had attained spiritually. He did not know that my mother was the heir to the teachings of Mother Chern, who was also known as the Mother of Yellow Altar. She was also helped by studying many different teachings from various schools of Buddhism for a long time and had attained understanding and achievement in Buddhism. Her interest in spirituality was greater than anything. Not knowing all those things, my father treated her like any other worldly person, with respect but staying a bit away.

The match-making did not go smoothly at all, but sometime later my father decided that he really needed someone to take care of the housework, he might like to have a companion, and he needed somebody to help in ordinary circumstances of life. Thus, he became objective and more open to my mother's proposal. After consulting with her, he realized that she had good understanding and was a deep woman. So he decided to marry her, including her different personality of strong independence.

My mother did not tell my father that she had learned the ancient original Taoism, and was the spiritual heir to the teachings of Mother Chern, the Mother of Yellow Altar. She did not want that to become the support of earning my father's interest or to complicate the situation.

After marriage, my father's life changed totally. It is not that my mother changed my father, but she changed the family condition. First of all, my father did not have any money, because he was a person who could not keep money. He could not turn away people who asked his help when they did not have money. When he saw good art, or finely made things, he would buy them. Or if a situation arose requiring money, he would pay. So to help him meet the expenses of the house and clinic, my mother decided that whatever income he made, he could spend half, but half would be saved. It was not for family expansion, but for safety. It was for dignity. Borrowing money from others is much worse than saving money. My mother already understood financial disaster. This small change helped my father's life.

After the marriage, half the money was for spending and half was for family security and old age. I learned financial prudence from my mother. I also learned something from my father, which was about the things he liked to buy.

My mother's management changed the family financial scene. My father was no longer broke all the time. He wished to be a person of no possession and spiritual freedom, but with my mother's management, we bought a nice house. We had a big enclosed back yard which turned out to be a beautiful garden that nurtured my childhood.

This is how my mother married my father, but I believe after the marriage, they still maintained a spiritually independent life. My mother discussed spirituality with my father. He was open to discussing things with her, but my mother was much younger. Because my father and his friends were older, they were more achieved and talked about deeper things.

In some ways, my mother was much stronger than my father. When my grandfather was alive, she had followers; people needed her help and could follow what she said, because she explained things line by line. Her followers were really serious and did what she suggested, even after she stopped her teaching activity. She did not continue to teach after making the decision to marry.

My father never organized any people as followers or students, but my mother had a group of people admire her and follow her in her past. He would teach, then forget who had learned from him. He would forget who he had talked to, and he did not establish anything. My mother had a more organized mind.

Most interesting is that my mother could adopt all the religious terminologies in teaching me. At that time, most people in China used a combination of Buddhism and Taoism and other religions from the west. My mother could fully use the terminology of each religion. So in expressing herself, she was less academic, but what she said related more to practical life. This comparison was made by some of my mother's followers. After her marriage, she continued learning from my father.

My father was in some ways more spiritual. My mother connected her teaching with real life. I think we need both.

So this was a special model of marriage; two independent spiritual persons learned to offer help to each other yet, at the same time, each one continued growing spiritually. I trust that this spiritual patronage has a different spirit than ordinary marriage. I personally witnessed the benefit. Although my parents were different in age, they worked well together because of the foundation of spiritual patronage. As a team in life, they respected each other's personality and spirituality. They never brought up any difference for fighting, but always remained in a good position as patrons to each other. You need my help, I help you. I need your help, you help me. In that way, each individual is covered in worldly life, and at the same time each individual can accomplish his or her own spiritual cultivation and goals. Spiritual cultivation cannot be done in partnership; each one has to achieve it by oneself. That is important.

By observing my parents, I wished to find a woman who had a high understanding like my mother. I followed my mother's wish to let ancient natural spiritual achievement directly happen in worldly life, and not outside of worldly life. However, women of spiritual achievement were rarely found in the stage of my life then. One must not hold too high expectations of other people or of the world. That became a reason for my marriage late in life.

My mother changed and adapted herself to become a housewife, assistant, mother and was dutiful in accomplishing her tasks because she was helped by her mother. My grandfather passed away earlier than my grandmother. Before my grandmother passed away, she told my mother she must marry a man more mature than herself. She should not declare that she was a teacher and leader.

She also guided her to know that "A man with masculine energy does not like to have a teacher or leader in his house. A wise woman knows to let the man do the talking and express himself fully to her. However, there is no man wise enough to accomplish big or small things totally by himself. He needs help. At the same time, he does not like to have a wife who is his teacher. Therefore, a wise woman allows her man and sons to hold their masculine pride and does not henpeck them in the home. Once their pride is damaged, then there will be more difficulty in the future.

"When you help your man, it should be done quietly and attentively, claiming no credit. This does not create denial of the man's position as a husband or capable man. Never forget to assure your man that his position is respected. Then, you can run the family life without big trouble.

"Marriage is for happiness. Happiness is a delicately natured atmosphere in which the woman shoulders more responsibility than the man, because most men do not know that much. Whatever the man can provide for the family materially and emotionally needs always to be encouraged and appreciated. People encourage their dogs that catch balls which they throw far, so surely encourage what your man has done for the family.

"The woman, in reality, is the center of the family in the sense of being the one who offers the strength to hold the family together by producing the nutritious atmosphere of happiness. No matter how young or old the man is, the woman is usually the one of psychological maturity and moral responsibility. Women can also be otherwise; then human life's good quality changes.

"Your father was not a man of money. He was not a man of political position. He was a man of artistic interest. He squandered his fortune for his interest. In general family life, there is no wife who can provide all interest her man likes to have. However, I did not cause the loss of happiness in life by nasty reactions to what he did. He created an environment for you, a young woman, in which you could exercise your intelligence and talent.

"If your environment is troubled, do not become overly self-determined or bossy. In marriage, being bossy is harmful to the happiness of a couple. Happiness is supported by harmonious cooperation. In family life, it is woman who decides whether the home is a battlefield or a sweet flower garden. The man does not know how his wife will react when he comes back from the outside world.

"It was I who supported your father's interest. When you are married, it is useful for you to support your husband's interests that do not carry him away from the main track of life. Do not fight him, but give help and let your man be aware of your support. Help him find a good and useful way to fulfill his interest.

"Also, a wise woman never angers a mad dog or a man."

My mother was also helped by her teacher, who gave her an envelope and instructed her to open it in the beginning of that year. The paper inside read:

"Ten li (around four miles) from the South City Gate,
At the waterside, you will find Doctor Ni.
He will be your man.
Teach all the things you have learned
    to your third child, the first boy.
Let him go as far as he wishes,
    because for a long period,
    China will become an unsuitable place
    for spiritual habitation."

In this chapter, there is a lot of information about a wife's responsibility to a husband. If you are the husband, you need to learn to take a husband's responsibility to a wife from the suggestions I give to the wives of the world. Also, here are a few more suggestions for husbands:

When you decide to be a husband, you must accept that women have a physical cycle. It affects them emotionally. During the hormonal imbalance, some women have poor control of themselves so you need to be psychologically ready for unreasonable fights or attacks from your woman. During the period when your woman becomes rough and irrational, try not to fight back. Let her have a chance to organize herself, or correct herself to make a reasonable presentation to you. Do not take whatever she says too seriously during that time if it sounds negative.

If you have children, you both need to be ready for at least 20 years of sacrificing your emotional position to help your children have a well-protected and normal environment in which to grow an upright character.

After becoming a father, marriage is not only for sex. Sex is not the only reason for marriage. To be a man, the respectful characteristic of masculine energy is to take care of your family and provide good protection. Work towards the security of a family but do not hold a position as boss. If your woman would like to have a say, always let her talk first. If she says something wrong, do not argue immediately. Later, try to bring the picture to her of the way you see things. There is a proverb which nobody can deny. It is "Harmony in a family is the foundation of prosperity."

Be a dutiful, responsible person towards your family. Maybe you handle your personal desire differently, but be wise to maintain the good condition within the family. Try to avoid making your woman jealous. A woman's jealousy is the same as men's jealousy; sometimes a jealous person will not forgive the other for lifetimes. If it arises, divorce or separation might be considered before a situation develops that is serious enough to force her to poison you or you to poison her.

In family life, because you live so close, an emotional or ideologic conflict can happen easily and often. A calm discussion would help each other. Never hit someone. If you start using physical action, it will become a habit. It is better to walk away or move away, but never fight your woman physically.

Yelling or screaming do not help. A raised voice would not make the other side understand better; rather, you only upset your own purpose. If you feel like yelling, temporarily withdraw. There is still a 50% opportunity for the other person to reflect on what was said and to understand you. Otherwise, if you keep yelling, no understanding will be reached.

If you respectfully established the relationship and then real trouble occurs so you cannot live together, you can also respectfully withdraw yourself and dissolve the relationship. When possible, it is best to avoid using a lawyer or court to argue and further damage each other.

Chapter 3

View What Cannot Be Viewed

Q: Should a woman pursuing spiritual attainment be married? Can a woman of spiritual pursuit have a married life?

Master Ni: Before 1949, I traveled around different provinces of China for learning. This was ten months before the communists took over and held China. During that year, I returned to my hometown and saw my mother and father for the last time. I spent 20 days with them. That was the most precious time I spent with them in my life, because I had become an adult and had greater understanding. Thus, I could learn more from my parents.

During that time, my mother gave me instruction about marriage. I asked her to verify the story I had heard from other people about her first meeting with my father.

My mother said, "The people who told you that I proposed marriage to your father the first time I met him overly dramatized it. Both making friends and beginning a marriage comes in natural, gradual steps, not suddenly. Everything has its cycle or right time.   Only when an opportunity is ripe can the fruit be picked. Such things cannot be hurried.

"Your father and I obviously had a pre-existing spiritual affinity or spiritual closeness. When I saw your father, my internal knowledge indicated to me that he was my man. Although I was instructed by my teacher to come to see your father, my mind still had reservations until I met him in person. Then all my doubt was gone."

My mother continued, "I believe he knew that also, but for a certain reason he did not immediately recognize me. We had many meetings together and talked about spiritual things. Mostly your father wanted to know how much I had attained spiritually, and I wanted to know the same about him."

My mother continued, guiding me to know about more than just her marriage. "Once we discussed that religious help has three levels. The first type is the popular worship of spirits. In other words, it is a religion of spirits. In temples honoring the religion of spirits, people worship to invite or exchange blessing from deities or gods. That is their whole purpose. That level is called spirit worship or religion of spirits. Sometimes it involves superstition.

"The second type is the religion of culture or psychology. That level includes religions like Buddhism, which involves human mental development. You may consider it as a religion of sages. More or less, this type of religion extends itself to ideological establishment. The spirit worship that is included in this type of religion becomes secondary, or serves as an introduction to beginning students so they can participate. Once students are involved in the learning, the teachers have an opportunity to uplift them to the level of ideology. The level of ideology is the main structure of this type of religion. However, ideology or religious structure can also become a trap or limitation.

"In general, the religion of culture or psychology is mixed because it also includes the level of spirit worship. Thus, the difference between the religion of spirits and the religion of culture is that the former is pure idolization, but the second adds an element of emotion or 'faith' along with a specific ideological establishment.

"The artistic nature of this level of religion can make people dependent upon what they do not know. Thus, it creates psychological dependence. The secret of this type of religion is its psychological application upon most people, which may help them change their behavior but does not give them true learning.

"The third type of religion is the natural growth of an individual to the point of understanding that each person is naturally born with spiritual energy.

"To explain this, first let me talk about its opposite. Although undeveloped people deny it, they still have spiritual energy. They are just not aware of it, because it takes special cultivation to closely connect the spiritual level and mental level. Undeveloped people are set apart or separated from their own internal spiritual truth. Thus, most people do not reach the level of spiritual energy because they have not developed their minds sufficiently to be aware of it.

"Even though each person is naturally born with spirits, a person's spiritual root determines if he knows the spiritual level. Some people have a deep spiritual root, but never attain an opportunity in their lives to do something to assist their higher evolution. Some people do not know about the seriousness of bad behavior, so during their lifetime, they do more to cause the divorce or further separation between their physical lives and their spirits. For those people, although their spiritual life and mental capacity still looks capable or complete, spiritually they have already suffered death.

"It is important or helpful for each individual to engage in spiritual cultivation and look for further development. Life is a new opportunity that has come to an old spirit.

"The cultivation of Tao, which is the third level of natural spiritual reality, is totally unrelated to the first and second types of spiritual practice offered by the religion of spirits and the religion of false culture or psychology. Natural spiritual growth is much deeper and direct.

"By this discussion, your father and I knew where each of us had reached. My spiritual background comes from the teaching of Shuan Nu, the Mystical Female or the Mystical Mother of the Universe. The Mystical Female is the spiritual transformation of the Big Dipper. She helped Yellow Emperor. Shuan Nu is the universal spirit. Neu Wu was a mythological description of the Universal Mother and was also a true human woman as the leader of ancient society with great spiritual power. The Prince of Sun was the fruit of Mother Chern's spiritual cultivation. Mother Chern was the first teacher of the School of Yellow Altar. Shuan Nu was the true spiritual source of the teachings of the Yellow Altar. It is a truthful teaching that guides individuals who are seriously doing spiritual cultivation and working for spiritual development.

"After we had discussed the deep sphere of our spiritual learning, we felt more relaxed, and your father came to think I could be his companion. He did not take his choice of 'inner person' lightly - by this I mean, the person who would help inside his house, his environment.

"I also asked your father why he said he did not wish to be married again. I asked him whether it was because he believed that woman is inferior.

To this, your father replied, 'It is not that woman is inferior, but women are sometimes carried away by emotion if they do not live connected with their spiritual center.'

Then I asked your father, 'Don't men also have strong emotion?'

He replied, 'Men also have emotion. How he uses it depends on his spiritual cultivation. You can classify people of emotion on one level, and people of intelligence or intellect on another level. People of spiritual achievement are on an even higher level. There is a lot of difference among people. Some people live for money, some live for fun and some live for personal interest. People's living is the expression of their spiritual reality.'"

Those discussions made my father and mother understand each other better, and helped them decide to choose each other, although they already had a pre-existing spiritual affinity.

My parents continued to understand each other's way of spiritual practice in daily life and real spiritual stage in order to accommodate each other even better after marriage.

Once my mother asked my father, "How do you view emotional trouble? In practical daily life, all people have emotions. Everybody must have emotion while still alive, unless someone is not a real person and is more like a robot or zombie."

My father told her that his spiritual cultivation was to remind himself that he takes his perch on his root, which is the place before Heaven and earth were born.

What did this mean? My father's way was, although he was shaped and lived in the world, to keep remembering that his spiritual root was in the subtle sphere of pre-Heaven. Because most people live according to circumstance, they are upset or annoyed by trivial things in life. A person whose spiritual root is before or above Heaven is never bothered by the world.

Although we have entered the world, there is a certain fulfillment that needs to be done. Although we still have emotional reactions to circumstance, we know they are not serious because we take residence before Heaven and earth were born.

This was my mother's description of a person's life spirit: "Before Heaven and earth was born, at most, we were a little bit of spiritual energy without form. For example, I could not call anything as myself, nor could I recognize another person or separate myself from that person. I did not have a name, nationality or possessions; therefore, what emotion could I create for myself?" She continued:

"Life itself is built up by a group of circumstances. All circumstances are on the level of the skin, the surface. Because they only touch the surface, circumstances can never touch a person's deep soul."

My mother made progress by quietly being at my father's side. She thought that his life made her spiritual reality much deeper. Although she had been in spiritual learning for a long time and had received spiritual education from many profound teachers, she felt she was benefitted by my father. She truly understood that my father was her soul mate.

What is a soul mate? The so-called soul mate is not an interest out of whim or from external attraction. It is a kind of unbreakable spiritual closeness or affinity, which becomes known after seeing another person for a long time. Both sides grow a special feeling. If there is no feeling, no marriage or friendship can be established; the feeling must exist on both sides. Marriage is not a business; a feeling must exist. That feeling was the reason, the true reality, behind why my mother married my father.

After the marriage, it was not only my mother's good policies and good management of my father's income, but also her diligence, frugality and effective work that greatly improved the new life of the two people.

When I was small, none of our clothes were purchased from any store, nor was any tailor invited to make them. All the clothes of the family, including my own and those of my two sisters and brother, were made by my mother. She made not only our clothes, but also all our shoes. Because I was so physically active, I used up about one pair a week, so my mother had to keep making shoes for me. Through many evenings, she sat under the light, which at that time was an oil lamp and did not give a strong light, making the soles of shoes out of many layers of cloth.

So you see, my mother never had any time for a break. She took care of the kitchen and laundry, made all the clothes, and helped in the clinic. She did everything. My mother's contribution to my father and the family was great.

My father had his hair cut in a barber shop, but my haircut was done by my mother, who had purchased some tools from a barber. I did not like my mother to cut my hair, because while she was cutting, I could not move around for fear of the sharp blade by my head. I had to sit quietly. My mother would guide me to do meditation and sit like a statue. I was afraid of haircuts, but every two weeks or so, I sat there for twenty minutes and she cut my hair. She told me, "Do not complain about sitting there. For a young child to have his head touched by a spiritual person is a blessing. They will always pass good spirits to you. This is the reason I do not let you go to a barber shop like your father. Because you are a child, my service will benefit you spiritually. Do not make a face similar to when you drink bitter herb tea."

My mother took care of me personally and watched over all the details of my life. Sometimes she embroidered the front top of my shoes. But when I wore the shoes out to play, the other boys laughed at me and said I looked like a girl. So I came home and used black ink to darken the embroidery so it could not be seen. That made my mother mad. It was from her good heart and good will that she did the embroidery, but I did not like to be laughed at.

I never washed my face, ears or behind my ears well enough. Each day, my mother checked them out and rewashed them. Almost all the details of my life, of my childhood, were cared for by my mother. She was a devoted wife to my father and loving mother to all of us.

My mother emphasized working meditation in her spiritual practice. Whenever she did kitchen work or sewing, her mind was not wandering; her mind was quiet. Because she was familiar with her work, she could keep her mind in meditation. So she had lots of time to meditate, and achieved what she called "internal knowledge." Internal knowledge is the ability to know the outcome of things or situations. Practically, internal knowledge was her pursuit.

When we moved into our new house, the front room on the second floor was my study, and the back room was the family shrine. The twelve diagrams of Tai Chi or the ultimate law with Ba Gua (eight symbols of nature) were hung on the four walls of the family shrine. No other decoration was in the shrine other than one picture of a woman. My father used this room in the early morning for his spiritual practice, and my mother used it when she had some spare minutes here and there from her housework. In this private shrine, on the offering table, we had a statue of the holy baby, who was the Prince of Sun. It is different from the ordinary shrine of Taoist service. (Typically, the images of the Realm of Purity was displayed by pictures or statues, or in another way. If using pictures, the three covers of my first publications in English can be used for this purpose.) In it there were statues of the three realms of purity, presenting the pure spirit, the pure mind and the pure body that is worshipped person to person, or a statue or picture of Master Lu, Tung Ping. Master Lu, Tung Ping is a true model of achievement. He fulfilled his worldly obligations and personal cultivation, and he also extended himself to help others. He is a good, complete model.[1]

Every day, my mother asked me to look at the diagrams to receive their non-verbal instruction. I did so; however, I felt nothing at all. My father smiled and said that if I felt

---

[1](Editors Note: The three realms of purity are represented on the covers of Master Ni's first three books in English: *Tao the Subtle Universal Law, The Complete Works of Lao Tzu and the Taoist Inner View of the Universe*. Master Lu, Tung Ping is pictured on the *Workbook for Spiritual Development of All People*. A poster similar to the cover of the Workbook is also available.)

anything, it would be something other than the spiritual energy the diagram exuded. If I felt nothing, it was correct, because spiritual energy is nurtured subtly and gently. He told me that the diagrams also carried a deep spiritual message which would benefit me and help me grow.

When I understood them, I valued the diagrams as being less burdensome than other spiritual training. Most spiritual training is only applied after people cause trouble or burdens for themselves or other people. Most spiritual training is only psychological help. However, these non-idolizing diagrams truly help one's mind and spirit develop freely. There is no limitation to the growth of a person's spiritual, material or scientific understanding in any dimension. These diagrams might be given in the book, Taoist Mysticism - God and Mankind United as One. The essential diagram is the diagram of Tai Chi. Tai Chi means the ultimate law.

It has recently been discovered that these same diagrams were carved on a stone plate in the wall of Lao Tzu's teaching tower in western China (Chou Tzi County, Shiang She province). Tower temple was the place that the pass official, Kuan Yun, discovered Lao Tzu and made Lao Tzu his teacher to cultivate and achieve himself. I suggest that these diagrams may be made into posters and offered by the book department. I wish to hear about this from my book readers. For now, the most important diagram in expressing the universal nature is

This diagram is also considered as the image of Neu Wu, the Universal Mother.

In China, each family of business or professional people worshipped the god of money or the god of wealth. Rather than do that, my father said that our spirit is our wealth. To correctly establish this type of external worship, it should be the god of wealth of all people. If everybody in society is rich, then naturally, all people can be taken care of. If everyone is rich, then no one needs to worry about income, and everybody can pay their bills. So we wish that everybody could become wealthy.

When I was talking to my father on that occasion, he gave a prophesy. He said, "In the future, nobody will worship or respect the 'God of Wealth of all People.' Instead, the god of poverty of all people will be realized as his replacement." Many years later, I knew that he meant the communist rule of China. He also mentioned that worship or spiritual practice is a privilege. "In the future," he said, "those things will be considered reason for guilt." He also said, "You are young, you shall see it," but unfortunately, he saw it more than I did. I left China and only observed it from a distance. After communism was established, especially during the ten year so-called cultural revolution, things happened exactly as my father said.

As my spiritual practice, my mother requested my father to write a Taoist key word, shuan 玄 , in the shrine. The word shuan was written on a small screen, and behind it was the picture of the Mystical Female. My mother used it as a symbol of the Universal Mother. My mother also gave this practice to me: she asked me to walk nine steps away from the character of shuan, and sit with my eyes open to stare at it.

Whether you are a young or old person, you have an excess of mental activity on the levels of the conscious, unconscious or subconscious. It does not stop for one second. Because of so much activity, your mind becomes like a traffic jam: congested. When that happens, there is no space for your spirit to communicate with you nor can you reach your own spiritual energy. When you can break through this mental jam of thoughts, emotion, and conscious activity, then you can subtly connect with yourself, with the spirits.

Shuan 玄 is the teaching of Tao. In the teaching of Tao, Shuan is something hidden, something mystical. However, at the same time, it is not hidden or mystical. There is no word that can describe it. If you wish it to be explained, then your mind is only continuing to work. If your mind cannot stop, you do not uplift yourself from that level and go to the higher level to achieve spiritual realty.

Let me continue to help your understanding of thought. Worship involves thought. For example, if you worship a god or goddess, there is a certain doctrine; a divinity has a certain formality about how it is shaped, dressed, its posture, its background and so forth. Those are thoughts. Thoughts are still on the mental, emotional and conscious level. If you stay with that, you have not reached the level of Tao, the unthinkable, undefinable and unexplainable. Whenever you look at the character for shuan 玄 , your mind fails, your emotion fails, your conscious action fails and your prediction fails; you cannot go further. Once you come to this level, your true spirit starts to be active. Thus, shuan can be the key word to move you from the general conscious level to the unconscious level, where your real spirit starts to be active. My mother's practice was simple.

My mother taught me in various ways according to circumstances and whether I was receptive to learning. Most of the time, she explained to me what I had experienced from visiting Buddhist temples, and other shrines. Sometimes she talked about the Zen Buddhist practice of the "enlightenment intensive" or "Wu Tao." It is a seven-day meditation for students to understand self nature. It was usually done by a group of students who worked together but were supervised by the Zen master. The master gave a short sentence or question and the students reflected upon that sentence for the seven days. At the end of that time, they are examined by the teacher. One popular sentence was, "Who is the one that prays to Buddha?" During that seven days, the students sat in front of the master, trying to achieve the breakthrough to find the self nature. After seven days, the teacher talked to the students one by one. Many students try to answer the question. Mostly they say, "It is me, It is I." That one and similar answers are denied by the master.

My mother gave the question to me and said she would ask me for my answer after seven days. Because I was trained to view "shuan'" as a lesson of my spiritual learning, it was a puzzle for me.

Who, then, is the one that prays to Buddha? The one who reaches the place where no name can be applied cannot give any words. The one who gives words to explain it stays on the level of mental explanation. Thus, those who try to define or describe it waste words to describe something indescribable. No one can pretend to be the one who has attained. The teacher himself, after years of this kind of difficulty, finally found the breakthrough, so he will know if you had an actual experience or if you are still applying your mind to the answer. If you did not have an experience but only applied your mind to answer the question, you have not reached the breakthrough.

Sometimes my mother told me, "Buddha is the mind; the mind is the Buddha." Why so? There are two explanations. One way is that through your recognition, the idea or conception of Buddha can be established. Western spiritual customs are different from eastern customs; Western people do not recognize Buddha. Thus, the notion or idea of Buddha cannot be established in the west. The contents of people's minds are different, so on this level, the mind is Buddha, the Buddha is the mind. This is one level.

On another level, what reality lies deeply under the notion of the Buddha? If you think that Buddha has delivered you from pain or misery in life, how has that happened? The matter is that you had bewilderment, perplexity and inability to see clearly, so you had pain and agony. Once you broke through the vexation, bewilderment and perplexity, then there was no need to mention if there was a Buddha or not who helped you. The help was your own resolution of the problem. But if you think it was Buddha, that comes from your mind. Therefore, the mind is Buddha, and Buddha is the mind.

My mother also explained the school of recognition in ancient Buddhism. It is a subjective, psychological way of understanding the world. The simplest thing in the world is to observe the world. When you observe it, you recognize certain things as important or unimportant. Clearly speaking, the world is how you recognize it. The reality of each individual is different because the formation of each person's recognition is different. In the learning of Tao, it is not suggested to emphasize the differences of viewing a thing. All viewpoints do not need to be unified to allow yourself to reach your spiritual achievement; then when you view the thing again, a new viewpoint may be established by your developed depth. You know that what is viewed is different by stages. No one stage is the final truth. The truth is not final because everything is in a process of change; all things change stages, conditions, etc. The point is that insisting upon a certain viewpoint shows immaturity.

Here is an example of how the world exists for you as you recognize it. Four people are approaching each other at the intersection of a road. You come from the east, I come from the west, somebody comes from the north and somebody else comes from the south. Each comes from a different direction, so their perception is different, their subjective reality is different, and the description each will give is different. Therefore, reality is different depending upon the perception or viewpoint of the person examining it. So the reality of matter or the reality of the world is as you recognize it, but you cannot insist upon your own viewpoint.

There are two levels or ways to view reality. One level is to project subjectively what you recognize as the truth you reached, such as the matter of life, etc. Yes, it is your level. But you cannot deny other people's recognition or level. Today's physics has made a lot of progress; it has almost reached the same point of view that the Taoist ancient ones had reached long ago. This means, the reality of the material world is what your recognition views it as. That is one way to view reality.

We are talking about how people psychologically view the world according to their subjective experience. Also we are talking about people viewing the world according to some established theories that they have studied.

On a high level, the Taoists say that because people's perception is different, reality must not necessarily be this way or that way, so no argument can be established about whose way is correct. The reality of the world is how each one perceives it. That is the high level; that is how my mother talked about Buddhism.

My mother was not an intellectual. She did not talk much except for when she instructed me. Mostly she did her practice, so her mind became distilled and clear. This is how she attained elucidating, sharp, internal knowledge. She could not be cheated by circumstances or people. She knew many things and could foresee what would happen. She always knew. Her spiritual cultivation really served her and paid off. I would like to give you several examples.

During the Japanese invasion of China, all Chinese people suffered. I was quite young and the family's income depended upon my father's practice, but people could not come for treatment because we lived on the main traffic route - a canal - that went from north to south through town. People did not come because the Japanese might be active on all the main thoroughfares. We could not move away because we did not know where to go. But there were few patients, so my parents were looking for ways to survive and feed all the hungry mouths.

One man, a local person who was a schoolmate of my brother, knew that my father was a moral person and respected for his spirituality. That man joined a meditation club called Tung Shan Sheh, which was popular then in China. He wished to make a business arrangement with my father. He wanted them to work together to bring rice to our town to sell to people, and then split the profit 50-50. My father's part was to buy the rice and bring it from Ping Yang, which was his hometown. My brother's schoolmate proposed to sell the rice, reimburse my father's investment in the rice and then give him half the profit. My father had watched that young man grow up and knew that he was having trouble making ends meet. He agreed to the joint effort. When my mother found out, she immediately told him, "If a person who approaches you knows what you like and speaks your language, and if this person comes around a lot to gain your trust and then talks you into doing a business, he must have a special intention."

My father said, "But we live too close to the main traffic route. Everything is blocked; no food can come in. We live in this town, where many people lack rice and have little to eat. Even if things do not happen beautifully, I think I will still use my strength to bring rice here. Then people will have something to eat." So my father wrote a letter to make the connection to bring the rice to Wenchow.

The unfortunate situation really happened as my mother warned because of the man's intention. The man took the rice and sold it, but no talk about profit, he did not even return the money my father had invested in the rice. It was just as my mother knew.

Fortunately, my mother had suggested that my father invest only an amount that we could afford to lose if it turned out to be a total loss. This influenced me later. Whenever I am interested in an investment but I am not sure it is a good one, I do it as my mother instructed my father on that occasion. This means I am prepared for a total loss.

Much later, the value of money had almost become nothing because of wartime inflation. However, my father's spiritual influence affected my brother's schoolmate, and the capital was finally returned.

This is one example of my mother's internal knowledge which brought foreknowledge and good principles.

Another time, my mother saved my father's life. If my father had any money at all in his pocket, he spent it, but usually for a good reason. If he took me to town and saw something he thought I would enjoy, he bought it for me. He did not carry a lot of money in his pocket unless he went to the city to buy things, but any money that was there, he spent. My mother understood my father's policy, "Money is for using, but in a good way."

During the Japanese invasion, my mother put some money in my father's pocket and sewed it shut so that he could not take the money out easily. We could not afford his spending at this time, so the money was only for important things.

One day, the Japanese army suddenly came to town. They came in motor boats on the canal in the front of the house, so we all ran out of the house through the back door to go to the vast rice fields where we could hide. But my father was out talking with a friend and did not notice the soldiers right away. It was not until they were close that my father and his friend began to leave for a safe spot. Unfortunately, both of them were caught by the Japanese soldiers. Because of the language differences, no communication could be made. My father unconsciously reached into his pocket, broke the thread, took out the money and gave it to the Japanese soldier. The soldier took the money and motioned my father to leave, quickly. So my father left safely. Afterwards, we understood. Because his friend did not have money or anything to give the Japanese soldier, he was killed.

In many things in daily life, my mother did not use her mind in thoughts, but used her energy as concentration. This was why she was spiritually sensitive to things. She worked constantly, but she always kept her mind away from emotion and away from thoughts by concentrating on the invisible shuan  . Her practice was simple, but she achieved beneficially.

Chapter 4

Feminine Nature Is
The Best Spiritual Model for All People

Q: Should a woman live like a man and compete with men? What is the position of woman in a man's world? Not all women are mothers. Nor are women mothers all their lives.

Master Ni: About five thousand years ago, Chinese society moved from being a mother-centered society or matriarchy to a father-centered society or patriarchy. This change had a natural reason. At the beginning, people had not developed competitively in a social sense, so the motherly energy could still hold the world in its care.

The mother-centered society was the original way of human society. Because the masculine nature is more competitive and active, slowly, naturally, women withdrew from any competition. The world became dominated by men, at least outside the family, and was totally under the operation or authority of the male.

Throughout this five thousand years, the woman's position in the family had never been shaken. A woman had always been respected as a good wife and good mother. If you were a woman, actually the only choice was to be a good wife and good mother. The high joy or the highest consolation for a woman at that time, was the honor or the achievement of her sons. If her sons achieved highly in society, the mother was always honored. Her honor came from the son. After a lifetime of hard work, the harvest of old women was their son's achievement.

You must remember one point; the position of a woman in a family will always be respected. But in that society, a woman could hardly find a correct expression after men became competitive and finally achieved dominance. Since then, you could hardly find a woman who could carry out an active role in society until modern times in the United States. Some queens at the side of a king found a chance to gather power and influence politics for a while, but later, they would still withdraw from the front scenes to be a mother.

For the last three thousand years, China was a male dominated society. During this period, the position of mother or wife was never shaken. When you see a Chinese opera, notice that in the family, the position of the mother has almost equal or more respect than the father.

In China, the way of life for women changed when the fashion of binding feet started in about 583-588 A. D. After that, the way of life for women changed again during the Song dynasty (960-1279 A.D.), when the scholars stiffened Confucius' teaching as religious practice. Women totally had no social position, but were only held captives as maidservants, concubines, or as the emotional toys of men. Women were not respected in social activities. The highest position that a woman could have was being a wife.

Unfortunately, good wives and good mothers hardly have a historical name. Only infamous women who badly influenced society were recorded in the history books during the last 5,000 years. One of them was a woman named Mei Shi. The last emperor of the Hsia dynasty (2207-1767 B.C.), the descendant of the Great Yu, become corrupt and lost his empire by deeply loving this woman, Mei Shi.

The last emperor of the Sang Dynasty (1766-1121 B.C.) fell into the same trap because of a beautiful woman. Also a powerful emperor, he lost his empire and destroyed the achievements of his ancestors by his love for one woman. He listened only to her and no one else, and ignored much good advice. The woman's name was Dar Gi.

During the Chou dynasty (1122-249 B.C.), the emperor, Yu Wuan, did the same thing. His obsessive love for one woman also brought his downfall. The woman was called Bao Szu.

When the Chou dynasty was established, there were about five hundred small kingdoms or feudal states in the middle region of China. The Chou dynasty ruled all five hundred feudal lords and their small kingdoms. At that time, a chain alarm type of warning system was developed using bonfires. When one bonfire was started, the neighboring feudal lords would come to the rescue. If the central bonfire was started, all bonfires were started to alarm all feudal lords to bring their armies to the central society for rescue. A bonfire in a certain spot could cause all bonfires, as it was a signal of alarm. Then all the nations, countries or kingdoms would bring their armies to help fight the danger.

Bao Szu was a beautiful woman, but she did not smile or laugh for the emperor. Yu Wuan loved her so much, and wished she could smile for him, but she did not. So he decided to make a bonfire. He thought that Bao Szu had already enjoyed everything and was tired of it, and so she needed some new excitement. He made that bonfire just to please the woman. One by one, all the small kingdoms saw the signal from far away, and came to the rescue. Finally, when they came up to the city wall, they discovered that they had come only for the laughter and smile of Bao Szu. All the feudal lords were angry about that; you can love your woman, but how can you make all armies prepare for war for a woman's pleasure? That was the end of the first period of the Chou dynasty in the West.

The corruption of these three examples was not the fault of the three beauties; it was the weakness of the young emperors. When they felt love, they could not maintain their balance. They could not distinguish between state affairs and personal life. They were mixed up, which endangered the government and the state. Unfortunately, those three women also did not know how to influence their men in a positive way in their position as emperors.

Typically, in the ancient historical records, women were mentioned only if they had a negative influence on a powerful person. Their good deeds or good contributions in society were hardly mentioned.

After that, males holding political power decided that in the future, no woman should interfere with social affairs. This became a common understanding: "Do not allow women to interfere in big business." That was decided, resolved. The fault started from only three women and as I said, it was not their fault, but the weakness of their men.

Later, during the war between the feudal states of Wu and Yueh, (I lived in Yueh, the Chekiang area; Wu is now the Shanghai area), the king of Yueh was defeated by the king of Wu. The King of Yueh did not know what to do to remedy the situation and regain his kingdom. However, the advisor to the king of Yueh started looking for a beautiful girl named Hsi Shih. She was a silkmaker; she washed and dyed silk, but she was known more for her great beauty and charm. Because the king of Wu was so strong and could not be defeated in battle, the advisor to the King of Yueh wanted Hsi Shih to weaken the king physically and confuse him to make him lose control. The advisor trained her to undermine the King of Wu. Hsi Shih successfully accomplished her mission as a spy and the small country of Yueh was restored.

In a competition between two men, when one man is defeated and cannot fly the flags in the battlefield, the loser will chose a woman to do the job. Hundreds of thousands of soldiers, the army of a whole country, are not as strong as one woman. Hsi Shih gave the Yueh people ten years to regather their strength and prepare themselves. Then after she had corrupted the control of Wu, the state of Yueh started the counterattack and succeeded.

Historically, in old Chinese society, a woman's function was to tame the brutal. Beauty was everything. Beauty can be used as a strong weapon; if you have it, see how you apply it.

Now here are a few examples of women who, by their singular performance, helped the nation and society.

Let me first tell you about Chao Chun, a beautiful country woman. During the Hang dynasty (206 B.C. -219 A.D.), the central government already had problems trying to protect the people on the northern Chinese border from the Mongolians, who were poor but strong. In the desert, the Mongolians followed the grazing cycle and always needed to move their cattle according to where there was grass. They admired the life of the inland where the earth was fertile. Thus they always came inland to rob and cause problems. They rode horses to the inland where the Han people lived; they took their possessions, destroyed their crops, and then left. The Chin dynasty (248-207 B.C.) even built the Great Wall to try to stop the Mongolians from coming inland. However, the Great Wall did not always work.

In China there are hundreds of small tribes, all Chinese, but the Han people are the main population. You can call them the descendants of the Yellow Emperor.

During the Han Dynasty, one woman singly carried a great political mission of protecting the central society from Mongolian invasions. She was successful in her mission, so I would like to tell you about her. Her name was Chao Chun. She was a country girl from Fu Pei province who was good at music.

The king of Mongolia wished to marry a Han woman. He threatened that they would invade unless a woman was provided. Of course, at that time, kings did not just marry any woman, but someone of royal blood. The Han people did not have an alternative. They had to comply with the king's request, because they did not have a strong general who would be successful in fighting a war. Even if they fought, they would undoubtedly suffer great destruction and devastation. They finally found a woman who was a servant or unimportant lady in the royal palace who could be taken for a member of the royal family. This woman was Chao Chun.

Chao Chun rode a camel into the desert to marry the king of Mongolia in the year 33 A.D. This one woman was worth thousands of soldiers in an army. This one woman was worth more than the Great Wall. This one woman stood for the safety of the whole empire. She married the Mongol king. Not only did she do that, but she also brought the teaching of civilization to the Mongolian people. She taught them music. Music is a powerful tool; it can change people. It can save people from death, and can change rough people to become gentle people. It can change people's dismay and disappointment into peaceful emotions. She applied her musical talent and training on a locally made instrument, the pipa, which is a type of guitar, and created and taught music. She trained young girls, and thus, through her music creation, she brought the culture of the central society to the border. Her personal effort assured the safety of the Han people during that period of time.

This woman was remarkable. She was a cultural ambassador, a cultural strength who protected the peace of the Han empire.

Another woman in Chinese history worthy of mention is Hua Mu Lan. I already mentioned that there was always trouble in the border, and when this occurred, each family had to send one male to fight. The government always enlisted people to fight the war to protect the villages and cities.

During the early time of the Tang Dynasty (618-906 A.D.) in the Hua family, the father was becoming old. He had one son who was quite young and two daughters in their late teens, one of them named Hua Mu Lan. It was time for someone to leave the family to go fight because there was an emergency on the border. But the father was weak and the family had no suitable male to respond to the demand. The father was worried and saddened about the situation. It looked as if he would have to risk his weakened body to fight the war. Then Hua Mu Lan said to her father, "Let me enroll for this duty under your name. Because it is the obligation of each family to send one man over 16 years old into the army, and because I learned to shoot and hunt, send me. I can do as well as a man, and dressed in man's clothing, nobody will know." The father refused, but he could not find a better solution.

The girl was determined, so she changed her clothes to make her look like a man. She brought her own spear and bow and went to her father. He did not recognize her; he said, "Young soldier, where do you come from?" Because of her good disguise, Hua Mu Lan convinced her father to let her respond to the required duty, and she joined the army.

The war lasted ten years. She started in a small position as a rank soldier, and because she fought hard and was smart, she became a general. When the total victory was achieved, and everybody could return home, she was decorated with honors and had many soldiers, who still believed she was a man, following to serve her. Her father and mother were happy to see her and killed many livestock to treat the soldiers and generals that came with her to a feast.

While everybody was sitting in the feast, she quietly left the hall, changed into her woman's clothes and came back to serve the meal. She filled the cups of wine in the hands of all the generals and soldiers. The guests wondered, "Where is our general? Why did he not accompany us? Only his sister and parents are here." They were looking and looking, waiting and waiting. Finally, they could not stand to be deserted by their comrade, and expressed what they wanted. Then Hua Mu Lan spoke up, "Why can't you recognize me? I fought with you shoulder to shoulder, day and night, for ten years." In that moment, the soldiers and generals suddenly realized that she was a woman.

At that time, if a woman needed or wanted to achieve something, she had to disguise herself in man's clothes. There are other stories about how some women disguised themselves in men's clothing to pass an examination or receive a high position. Those women only did it because of circumstance, to help their wronged husbands who were put in jail or to help their fathers. But this woman fought the war and defended the nation. I think she is extraordinary, and worthy of mention. If allowed, a woman is not a weakling; a woman can fight a war too, as good, maybe sometimes better than a man.

When I was young, I would sit with my mother in front of the stage and watch the actors and actresses perform historical stories. One of the grand operas was the story of Hua Mu Lan. Some of the women included in this chapter are from my recollection of the operas; some are from the great volumes of Chinese history.

My mother suggested that women learn some martial arts to defend themselves and others. At that time in Chinese society, people believed that women needed only to stay home and did not need such skills, but the learning of martial arts and all kinds of exercise was supported by my mother.

Now I would like to introduce a woman who was politically active in China. In ancient Chinese history, although some women were queens who directly ruled or influenced the government, only one titled herself as "empress." She was Wu Tsai Tien. Wu Tsai Tien was the daughter of a low-ranking officer, yet she had the opportunity to seize the power of a whole nation.

Wu Tsai Tien was a maidservant in the royal court of Tang Tsai Tung, a wise and powerful emperor who achieved highly during the Tang Dynasty. The ambition of this emperor was healthy; he wished to be an emperor as wise as the ancient Niao or Shun. Tang Tsai Tung had not only been a great general on the battlefield, but now on the emperor's throne, he ruled wisely. So the Tang Dynasty was a glorious dynasty in Chinese history; all the border tribes came to pay homage to him. He was a wise emperor who gladly took advice.

Wu Tsai Tien was a young woman who served the emperor. She became 'apprentice' to the emperor, but not in a formal way. She was appointed to serve him when he used his toilet. The Chinese term for that is to change clothes or use the dressing room. It was not called a toilet as modern people say, because the toilet did not exist at that time.

I think the emperor made a lot of his decisions when he was in his dressing room. He must have brought his documents there to review in private for the big decisions. This gave the woman a chance to observe or even possibly help. I think she mostly observed or learned indirectly.

During the warring period of the Chou Dynasty (403-249 B.C.), it was an evil custom that any servant of the emperor, male or female, had to be buried alive in the event of the emperor's death. However, by the time of Tsai Tung's death (627 A.D.), Chinese civilization in political circles had made a little progress, and the women were allowed to become nuns and never touch a man. However, when Wu Tsai Tien had been maidservant, occasionally the prince - the emperor-to-be - would come to visit the emperor, and he noticed the beautiful girl at the father's side. Maybe he had an ambition in his young heart to have that woman.

Before Tsai Tung passed away, he choose his son as his heir, but with reservation. He really doubted his son's capability. But because there was no other choice, he also appointed four advisors to help the young emperor.

After the emperor's death, Wu Tsai Tien, still young and beautiful, stayed in the Buddhist temple as a nun. One day she received the summons of the new young emperor. So she was taken back from the nunnery to serve the new emperor. Little by little, she did more and more for him. She used the opportunity to make the emperor marry her formally. Surely the advisors knew about the situation, but Wu Tsai Tien was smart enough to split the unity of the four advisors. She married the emperor and killed those who openly opposed the marriage. After the marriage, she was a queen. Her husband was far behind his wife in intelligence and experience.

As queen, Wu Tsai Tien used the emperor's inadequacy in managing affairs of state and extended her own influence. You know, a Chinese boss is very busy, especially an emperor. If he is a good emperor, he needs to read all the documents, make the decisions and write them on the back of the papers. The emperor was not only weak physically, but he also had weak eyesight. This gave Wu Tsai Tien, who had been the 'apprentice' of his father, an opportunity to exercise her talent. When any decision was made, if any words were needed on the document, she was able to write them better than the emperor himself. The emperor finally said, "Okay, since you really do better than I do, I will just let you do it." Through this opportunity, she earned the opportunity to control the prime ministers and all the other important officials.

After the first five years, the husband was practically a puppet of the queen. At last, in 684 A.D., Wu Tsai Tien simply poisoned him and declared herself Empress.

In total, Wu Tsai Tien spent more than 40 years influencing or directly ruling China. She was a powerful woman, talented and shrewd. She also made some positive contributions to society. She was admirable, but unfortunately, she seemed to have forgotten the wise and kind way of rulership of Tang Tsai Tung, and instead used a different way to govern. She applied the secret police to enhance her control. The worst thing is that in her personal life, she imitated men. For example, a Chinese gentleman, a person of position or even an ordinary rich person who could afford it, often had several women as concubines. Equally, this female emperor had several male concubines. Scholars and historians all comment negatively upon her lust. But a natural view of some of the other aspects of her life showed that she was a talented person.

One thing could be noticed from her example; if a woman comes to a man's world to extend ruling power, she might apply the same nasty practices that bad male leaders use. Tang Tsai Tung was a wise and kind ruler and earned support from all directions. It was unfortunate that Wu Tsai Tien needed to extend her ruling power through the use of underhanded means. It seems more unfortunate when a woman does so; then a woman cannot be what she is. She loses herself and becomes worse or more cruel than men. That was how she succeeded. That was her story.

These historical events show that some women have the talent to become the leaders of a nation or empire. The only problem with that job is it is important not to get caught up in dishonest or immoral techniques of power seeking. To risk losing the great virtue of humanity for the dirty play of politics may not be worth it.

If you have a high position and, even if you are wise, you are subject to temptation in your surroundings. If you are an empress, men change their attitudes to be like a cat. They try to please you, and bow, bending themselves. At that time, you can subtly observe that the one on the throne is no longer a woman, but must be like a strong man in order to fulfill her authority and responsibilities. The entire royal court and all the government officials will serve the woman on the top. In the case of Wu Tsai Tien, her rule was as the same as any negative masculine ruling power.

Is competition worthy for a woman? It depends on how the woman views it. I think it is not healthy for women, also it is not healthy for men, unless the person has a special ambition to use that position to bring benefit and blessings to all people. When most people are put in such a position, they just wish to fulfill their lusty ambition and swollen personal vanity.

Masculine energy and feminine energy both contain positive and negative tendencies. Men can learn from women's positive feminine aspects, and woman can learn from men's positive masculine aspects. It is a must for building a well balanced and complete personality. However, the negative aspects of masculine and feminine energy are detrimental and need to be eliminated from your spiritual cultivation. If you do not eliminate them, your spirit will be bad - like a devil.

I have given a negative example of a woman ruler. Now I would like to give you a positive example of a virtuous and intelligent woman who influenced an emperor in a positive way. It was the wife of Tang Tai Tung, the wise old emperor who ruled before Wu Tsai Tien. He had a prime minister who was a straightforward person. Many times when they argued principles while talking about the right thing to do, the prime minister never gave the emperor a break. He always showed him the correct steps that would help his rule and benefit the people, even if they were not easy to accomplish. Sometimes he made the emperor feel awkward or displeased. However, despite his occasional discomfort, Tang Tsai Tung never changed prime ministers.

There was one very touching episode. One day, after meeting with all his high ministers, Tang Tsai Tung returned to the palace to be with his wife. At the meeting, he had argued terribly with the prime minister, Wei Tseng, who really give him a hard time. The emperor felt that this time he had really taken too much from the prime minister; he was angered and displeased. After entering the garden of one of his beautiful houses, his queen greeted him. She saw that his face color was bad, and she asked him what had happened. The emperor replied, "Wei Tseng (the prime minister) does not respect me. He does not yield to me. He looks down upon me as if I were his son. I am really angered. I would really like to kill him."

His wife, the queen Taang Sun, did not say anything, but withdrew. After some time, she returned wearing a beautiful new dress to formally greet her husband again. The emperor was surprised; he asked her, "What special occasion is this that made you change into formal clothes?"

His wife said, "This occasion is special; I have come to congratulate you."

The husband said, "Congratulate me for what?"

The wife said, "Congratulate you on having a loyal minister."

I tell you, if the woman had liked to please the emperor by saying something bad about the prime minister, I think the prime minister would have been killed or deposed. However, it was the emperor's leadership and the help of his wise ministers that enabled him to create a new, brilliant, glorious epoch for the people of China. Such a powerful man can bring glory to family, glory to people, glory to his nation, and glory to his leadership. No opponent can stand in his way. In general, there was no difficulty in his rule, because all problems were wisely dissolved by his keeping open to all good advice.

Now I would like to tell you about the illustrious princess of Tibet, Wen Cheng. From the enormous volumes of 25 periods of Chinese history, we see the need of a strong and effective central government to provide peace within the entire region of China. However, peace and safety were obtained at a high price under the evil leaders of the monarchy system. Monarchy had large protective armies, but suffocated the organic condition of society and encouraged competition for high governmental positions and sovereignty. Unfortunately, evil monarchies lack the focus necessary to improve the life of an entire society. They do not provide the appropriate atmosphere for the self-expression of society. That caused the Chinese society to fall behind in improving itself. Many talented people died in vain for the unnatural establishment of political systems.

There were only a few opportunities for a wise one to achieve higher than others and make a contribution to society. Most of them were suppressed or sacrificed for the unnaturally established power. I consider that the failure of China was the failure of the political system which caused unnatural bondage for all.

But let me return to my story of a wise woman, Wen Cheng, the princess of Tibet.

The Tang Dynasty was a new epoch. China became so powerful that the neighboring countries bent their heads to bow to the emperor. All the neighboring territories wished to be part of the big territory and have a strong connection to the central empire.

To the southwest of central China lies the high land of Tibet. Tibet is part of China now. Tibet at that time had just become a unified kingdom after the fighting of the smaller tribes, and they now had a centralized king. The king was young and looking for a marriage relationship with the royal court of Central China. He requested that a princess be married to him. This request was turned down by the emperor because of the emperor's pride or whatever reason. But the second time the young king made the same request, the emperor considered it, because he had become a little smarter in politics and more mature. Rather than needing to rely on a strong army to keep peace in the border, a marriage relationship could better serve the purpose of national defense. He choose one of the daughters of a relative, but not one of his own daughters. He called her Princess as though she was his daughter and sent her to marry the king of Tibet.

This woman was not an ordinary woman. Her name was Wen Cheng. She came from a well-bred family, yet faced the misfortune of having to marry a barbaric king. In the mind of the Chinese people, it was better to stay close to one's parents in the inland to enjoy the prosperity and good things of life. Nobody wished to go to the border. That was her great misfortune, but the woman changed her misfortune into her personal spiritual achievement. How? She used the opportunity to bring the whole culture of the inland to the border. Her dowry, in addition to gold, silver and diamonds, included a group of talented people such as Confucian scholars, achieved Taoist teachers and leaders of the new Buddhism. By the way, the new Buddhism was a combination of Hinduism, Brahman, Buddhist and Taoist practice, but it used Buddha as the unified spiritual focus or object of spiritual worship. So all the prayers that had previously gone to Brahma, now went to Buddha using all the techniques developed by other sources.

Also included in her dowry were scholars, artisans, architects and contractors - people achieved in all different trades. Directly or through her influence, she brought the whole group to the new territory.

In ancient times, among the tribes there was only one idea - war. At that time, diplomacy had not yet developed so that both sides could achieve their goals without mass destruction. Instead, people only knew one stage of mind. That was: "I want what I want, I don't care what you want." The only solution was war or fighting. This real situation was clear to Wen Cheng and she wished to improve the mind and intelligence of the people. So she brought the force of culture with her from China to Tibet.

Before Wen Cheng arrived, Tibet had used magic practice or magic religion. It is not fair to call it black magic, because they also had healthy magic, but the type of religion they used was not an ideological, philosophical or cultural attraction as are most religions today in the western world. Human spiritual nature had not yet evolved that much in Tibet, and so the religious practice was still quite primitive. Cultural influence is produced by the human mind looking for a better life. In the new territory, the new queen combined the essence of all the good teachings under the name of Buddhism.

The world at that time was not like today, when political parties are active among people. Two important ruling forces were applied within all general political territories to earn the obedience of people. They were military force and religion. "I conquer you, you must obey me. Those who obey shall survive; death to those who disobey." That was the military way. The other way was religion: using persuasion, a leader could make people accept a new religion, then make it the social and ruling power. A smart leader during those times would use both military power and religion.

Wen Cheng did not bring an army for controlling the people of Tibet and assuring the defense of her own country. Nor was it her mission to go to Tibet to establish a strong country that would eventually threaten the central society that she came from. She helped her new husband, the king, by bringing all the talents to put together a new religion.

Wen Cheng's influence in promoting Buddhism affected almost all later developments in Tibetan religion. There are four main sects of Tibetan Buddhism: red, white, yellow and flowering. The red was the original one, and is called ning ma. Ning ma means the old. That was the sect that Wen Cheng influenced the most. If you were to study the practices of this sect in depth, you would come to the realization that there are some high secret ancient practices of Taoism under the name of Buddhism. By promoting the new religion, Wen Cheng helped the people of Tibet, because the life of the mountain people was not as good as the life of the people of inland China. The Tibetans had more severe weather and poorer land. However, Wen Cheng brought much good influence and spiritual support to them.

She also made a change in the entire world: Tibet was the only kingdom in which the religious leader was also the ruler. Everybody in the country was thus related to the ruling force, not necessary politically, but all people were related religiously, and this was promoted by the government. That was how Wen Cheng saved her country from border problems and how she helped the people of Tibet as an independent border country.

In the great volumes of Chinese history, there are many examples of women who achieved in literature. My mother thought that a woman's nature is naturally more delicate than a man's, and a woman is more sentimental. In literature, sentimentality is the most important element. A woman has this skill and just needs to transform it into writing. But literary skill was not admired by my mother.

Among women, she particularly exalted princess Wen Cheng, the woman who brought spiritual education to Tibet under the name of Buddhism. My mother did not oppose using or establishing religion to bolster a leader's social position. Religion, even if used by a sovereign, comes from the people and is their spiritual expression.

My mother did not admire the position of royalty such as queens, although she understood that each one of us has a destiny or fortune. But she admired the strength and energy of Wen Cheng whom the Tibetans entitled "The Mother of Green Delivery." In this case, green means evergreen or everlasting, and delivery means delivery from men's foolish competition for leadership.

My mother recommended to all of us that the masculine central culture and religion through 3,000 years had not brought benefit to mankind, but only established more contention.   That contention was the fault of the male-oriented religions which were imbalanced or not holistic.   My mother did not say that creating a religion centered around the image of a strong woman would bring progress to human society.   But she believed that a balanced spiritual teaching of original Taoism provided a cooperative direction of the human future.

My mother guided me to know that the future of humankind will not establish a women's religion to compete with men's religion.   She also said that society will not be improved by women supporting and establishing the conventional male-dominated religions which have existed for the last 3,000 years.   My mother believed that certain men and certain women were suitable for spiritual leadership, but that this leadership was not limited to one gender only.   To her, it was most suitable for men and women to work together doing spiritual teaching in response to the need for balanced and harmonious spiritual education and culture.

Chapter 5

Wise and Unwise Women

Q: It is interesting that China has a long history. There were so many examples that we can learn from. We would like to know if there were any other women in Chinese history who influenced the Chinese people. Their example might also have some value in our learning.

Master Ni: In recent Chinese history, the woman who was visible politically was Empress Dowager, Tsi Shi. She was born in 1835 and passed away in 1908. She dominated the Manchu court over the vast Chinese society for 47 years towards the end of the Ching Dynasty.

Once I mentioned that China lived in its own environment and never encountered the situation of world change. Just before the last century, close to the end of the Ching dynasty, western countries suddenly became prosperous and extended their colonialism towards the nations of Asia. The fat land of China, ruled under the Manchurian family system, was one important target. At that time, the male heir to the throne was a youth, so his mother, Empress Dowager, who was the regent, sat on the throne. Practically, all state affairs were handled by her. Unfortunately, she mishandled them and received nationwide blame for that.

If you visit the Peking palace now, you will find a picture of the Empress Dowager in one of the beautiful red painted buildings. She looks quite elegant. She had an artistic nature but narrow political vision. One must not expect too much from any person who was never trained to take care of state affairs and who suddenly receives such a position. That was a fundamental defect of the system of monarchy. Neither men nor women can rule well without training. However, the throne was a family privilege during those times. It was passed down from generation to generation until one of the emperors was defeated by a leader from another family; then a new dynasty started.

So the power of the Ching dynasty lay upon the shoulders of the Empress Dowager, Tsi Shi. Shortly thereafter, the new situation of western colonialism arose. However, Empress Dowager ignored what was happening because she did not know how to respond to it. The nation had lots of money; it had lots of silver. With that silver, a fleet of ships could have been built to defend China from a maritime invasion. Instead, Empress Dowager used that money to build a beautiful flower garden for her own birthday and to develop the Peking opera. She did not choose to defend the nation; she chose personal enjoyment. This happened because power, privilege and authority suddenly came to one person who was not trained or educated and did not know the obligation or mission of such a position. She had the power to tackle or resolve the problem, but used it instead for her personal enjoyment.

Not only that, she ran the nation as a family. She was against improving the social system. In contrast, when her son became emperor of China, Kuan Hsu (reign 1875-1909 A.D.), he learned about the west's achievements in politics and studied the industrial revolution. In the meantime, Japan quickly adopted the model of the western nations and thus improved and strengthened itself. Japanese leaders were inspired by the west and thus that country met the new situation by adapting to it.

China did not adapt; at least, not at the hand of Empress Dowager. She suffocated the new movements calling for social and political changes, beginning what the Chinese people called the hundred years of national disgrace. Among many humiliating events, the beautiful garden that she designed was burned down and destroyed in 1900 by the allied armies of eight western countries. During this time, all the western powers and stronger neighbors extended their power over the Chinese territories, helping themselves to special privileges in the cities and collected customs duty in the harbors. China suffered tremendous disgrace from those powers, and Empress Dowager was to blame because of her fondness for personal enjoyment. Her short vision and selfishness stopped the natural growth of her nation.

Men can be foolish, but women can also be foolish. It does not matter whether it is a man or woman who runs a government. Only wise leaders can bring progress to a society. It is a matter of a society. Only wise people give support to wise leaders.

Unfortunately, the leadership of Chinese society in the last 3,000 to 4,000 years, wise or foolish, came out of the result of military struggle.

Dr. Sun Yat Sen (1866-1925 A.D.) started a revolution to end the system of dynasties and created the Republic of China in 1912 A.D. After his death, Chiang Kai Chek continued working for the same goal: a modernized China with political democracy. The leaders understood that they needed to adopt a better system, something like the ones in America or Great Britain. That was the direction towards which they moved.

Women could not do anything. A group of men also could not do anything. Unfortunately, their measure was too moderate for some of the country's young scholars. Some people could not immediately or objectively see how the new programs could work for Chinese society. This caused some young, strong personalities to choose Russia as their teacher or model. They wished to transfer the model of the Russian revolution onto Chinese society. They used the Marxist book, *Das Capital* and Lenin's theory of revolution as holy books and followed them devotedly. This was already almost a half century after the foolish Empress Dowager was no longer on the throne. During that half century, there was no political coherence in China but endless struggle for sovereignty by different groups.

The young leaders who studied the example of Russia successfully revolted against Dr. Sun Yat Sen's vision of learning from an open society such as the United States. They replaced it with the model of Russia. Now, in 1990, we can see the collapse of communism in Russia. The communist system is totally against human nature and can bear no fruit. Empress Dowager did not rule well, but the communist party leaders did much worse, because they had the strength to act positively but did not. So did she. Instead, they led the country of one billion people into backwardness and suffering. They did not actually help China to become a better society.

From this reality of history, you can see that a nation that was thousands of years old had a deeper problem than that of the newer societies like Japan and the United States.

You might agree that the Empress Dowager had a short and narrow vision. She was narrow minded and did not correctly respond to the international situation to bring happiness and prosperity back to society. How about the young leaders who engaged in the new revolution under the banner of communism? They were the same. They did not even know the world or themselves. It was their ambition to engage in leadership and divide the booty from the political struggle. That was in their minds. This is not my personal viewpoint; it is historical reality.

The imaginary model of communism failed in Russia after 75 years. It will come to the same end in China. In Russia, now the leaders are facing the nightmare that they have taken society nowhere. Because human nature cannot be transgressed, the communist system did not work and the Russians have finally decided to end the old system of impractical communist idea. However, as long as the communist party uses its army as the party army, the real hope of the people for democracy and free life still faces a journey down a muddy road. This is true of both Russia and China.

My mother and father lived during the time that Empress Dowager was in power, and also when her son, Emperor Kuan Hsu was arrested and permanently confined for trying to implement a program of modernization. My parents also saw the arrival of communism. I was fortunate never to experience living under communism because I had gone abroad.

It is ironic that the communist regime intended to protect the Chinese nation against the injustice of dynasty rule under the Empress Dowager, yet it was another woman, the wife of the communist leader Mao Tse Tung, who initiated the bloody cultural revolution. The ten-year cultural revolution was her personal expression of social political ambition. It is valuable to know the story of Mao Tse Tung's wife.

Forty years ago, before the communists achieved their revolution, the army of the communist party was hiding on the west side of China, in Yeng An, the capital of Shiang Shi. The woman, Chung Chiang, was a second level movie star from Shaihai. She went to Mao Tse Tung to join communism. Chung Chiang was smart enough to know that if you wish to engage in political activity, you have to go to the boss. So she made Mao Tse Tung interested in her and wished to be married. The comrades, the close important leaders in the communist party, were against the marriage. Mao Tse Tung refused their opinion. He thought it was his personal matter. Why should all of the party leaders be nervous about it? After disputes, the leaders agreed that Mao Tse Tung marry her, but only after signing a paper saying she would never interfere in political affairs.

After the success of the communist revolution, a power struggle started between the two wings of the party. The extreme left wing's leader was Mao Tse Tung. He began to feel his power slipping. The unhappiness and jealousy of this selfish leader provided a chance for his wife to start the cultural revolution by using the nation's youth to begin a violent attack. Many right wing leaders were killed, including generals, and many innocent people were also killed.

After the ten-year revolution and following the death of Mao Tse Tung, the right wing had an opportunity to reassert its power, and so it arrested and jailed Chung Chiang. At her public trial, her response to the judge was, "I have achieved revenge upon my enemies." Thus, all the bloodshed and persecution of the ten-year revolution was brought about merely for personal revenge.

Do you think the choice of Chinese people to adopt communism is wiser than the choice of women to bind their feet? Both are unnatural. Communism revealed the deep sickness of the Chinese leaders in the past and present. When Mao Tse Tung was alive, the majority of people were taught by the party to sing a song. It went like this: "The sun rises in the east, Mao Tse Tung is our savior." However, all the time Mao Tse Tung was in power, more disaster and destruction was brought to China than if the leaders of the right wing had been in power. There are no grounds to establish the idea that Mao Tse Tung's leadership or his wife's behavior was correct.

We can conclude that both male and female leadership can be disappointing. It is not a matter of man or woman, it is a matter of doing something correctly or incorrectly, well or poorly. What matters is whether your motivation is correct and if the model you adopt is serviceable.

We have not received any light or psychological support from the examples I have given in this chapter because those examples are the negative side of human nature. As an individual who appreciates the high spiritual values of human life, I am looking for something that has a longer value than short personal glory like the actions of those two women. Men and women do not need to look only to live a life of one time, but to live a life of all times.

Among all lives on earth, few creatures of nature have the opportunity to attain spiritual achievement. In the background of other animals on the earth, the first requirement for further evolution is to attain human form. This spiritual reality is truthful knowledge of this prehistoric spiritual tradition. Humans are naturally privileged to directly attain high spiritual evolution. In material life, woman has a better spiritual quality for development, while man's tendency is to run around everywhere, tempted to do so many things or compete for unworthy things by keeping in constant rivalry for something meaningless.

Now I would like to introduce you to Meao Sang, a woman whose spiritual image lived all the time. She lived during the time of Prince Chien. First I will tell you about the Prince. During the Chou dynasty, historical records started to be kept because writing developed. Before that, people recorded events of history by carving words as simple pictures on cow bones. That was done mostly in the time of the Sharng Dynasty (1766 - 1121 B. C.) Records of this time can still be seen. Much earlier records were made by tying knots in rope, but they do not exist any more. Starting with the Chou dynasty (1122-286 B.C.), people found various ways to write books. They understood the use of cloth, and they wrote on it and also on pieces of bamboo.

During ancient times, society was natural; the world was less tempting to people looking for spiritual development. The natural society provided a supportive environment for people looking for individual spiritual development. They did not need to prove their spiritual pursuit to anyone. There were lots of spiritually developed persons. They did not care how you titled or called them, because that is not what they valued.

In the written record, the first young prince who did not pursue a political career but extended himself in spiritual pursuits was Prince Chien, the son of Emperor Ling Wahn (571-544 reign B.C.) of Chou. He lived in Tien Tai San, where our tradition was inspired. He achieved himself. Later, a poem was written that described this:

> "The prince went to the mountain
>   looking for his immortal teacher.
> When he succeeded in accomplishing
>   his golden immortal medicine,
>   he could reach high Heaven.
> He lived in his deep cave for just seven days,
>   but in the world,
>   a thousand years had already passed.

That poem was written in red characters on paper as my first lesson in Chinese calligraphy. I traced over the red letters with black ink. I did this tracing over the characters in this poem for a number of months.

That poem was a communication of the prince's achievement. Over 2,500 years ago in human history, people of spiritual development knew that there was a different time system in another dimension of the world. We know, for example, that the earth time system is different than that of Jupiter, Mars and all the planets, not to mention other solar systems or other star systems. Even the Bible was written according to the earth time system. But this poem and the possibility of spiritual achievement give us a clue that ancient achieved ones truly experienced a place that had a different time system. You know, ancient people did not have much literature, so that description must have come from spiritual experience. Long before Prince Chien, there were many spiritually achieved people. He was a student of ancient spiritual attainment. During his time, many others achieved themselves too, but they were not as popular or well known. We can also find a different time system in our deep meditation. Prince Chien's achievement was different from merely having a spiritual experience.

Tien Tai Mountain became known as a spiritual mountain. It was famous for the achievement of Prince Chien and many other immortals. There are so many beautiful legends about the immortals that they could be collected in a big book. Tien Tai Mountain is also famous for Taoist immortal herbs. Later than Prince Chien, Master Kou Hong, whose Taoist name is Pau Po Tzu, also cultivated his immortal medicine there.

Each generation had someone of achievement. In each generation, there were some individuals who represented the immortal tradition. The immortal tradition is not like a worldly religion. The activity of religions is passed down in a lineage from person to person. In the immortal tradition, the passage is spiritual. The achieved spirits can directly teach or inspire someone who lives several generations later, even a person who is unrelated to the spiritual learning or who had no earlier spiritual experiences and learning.

My mother's teaching had the physical and spiritual lineage from Mother Chern, the lady of Yellow Altar. A male student of Mother Chern, Master Sui Sen, continued Mother Chern and become very influential as a great Taoist. He was exalted as the spiritual source of a later developed school which was called the School of Pure Light, a new promotion starting from Sung Dynasty (960-1279 A. D.). My mother's learning was from woman teachers who directly continued the art of Mother Chern. Each generation chose only one woman as the main teacher.

Now I will tell you about Meao Sang, the woman who was a timeless symbol of spirituality. During that period, the earth was natural, and there were many tribes and many small kingdoms. The Chinese cultural or political center was in the northwest. In the south, there was a small country, led by a royal family that had three daughters. The first daughter was married, the second was engaged and the third daughter was still single. Her name was Meao Sang. The father had decided to marry Meao Sang off to a general, an effective fighter who could help the father defend his throne. It was a mutually beneficial arrangement, but the princess refused. She said, "No, I am not going to be married. It is not that I am against the particular person. It is that I choose spiritual development instead of marriage."

The daughter's wish was against the father's decision. At first, the father used lots of patience and tried to persuade her. The mother also tried, but all failed. Then the father treated her very badly, with all kinds of punishment, trying to convince her to change her mind. But Meao Sang would not give up. She said, "I can live as a ordinary person, but I am not going to be married. I need my own spiritual development. I am not looking for, nor do I enjoy, momentary material fantasy."

With her willful and determined decision, she made enemies out of all the family members. But she did not change her mind. After she achieved herself, she become a spiritually powerful woman. When her father had a serious physical problem, she helped her father.

She also helped her father realize that it is not the highest thing to be a king or a queen in the world. At that time, having the position of king or queen was above all, because physical strength was considered the source of all achievement. In today's commercial world, if you do well in commerce, you can satisfy your material desires just like a king. In ancient times, there was no other way to do it than to be king. You had to have enough military strength to achieve whatever you wanted. Only then did you have a chance to satisfy your personal material desires for social fantasy and momentary external glory.

Meao Sang chose a different way. After her achievement, she started as a healer, going from place to place, offering advice to people who were confused, giving help to people in difficulty, and curing people when they were sick. Most Chinese women wore skirts. Men wore robes. Meao

Sang wore a wide robe to cover her feminine figure, but she was a woman. By abandoning the conventional feminine way of life, she could go anywhere. Many difficult things happened to her; she was still a beautiful woman, so often men and jealous women were obstacles. But she also had loyal followers. Finally she achieved herself because she was dedicated to the problems of the world, and not to her own enjoyment of her father's throne. People remember her great virtuous fulfillment which later made her fill in the blank of a Buddhist teaching that the universal spiritual deliverance can be through the help of a woman.

Later, Chinese religious leaders combined the theory of Quan Yin and the real achieved woman, Meao Sang, together to be the real Quan Yin. The original Buddhist imagination of Avalaknesvara Bodhissatva, who is a man in a Buddhist book, made him became the Goddess of Mercy in China through gradual cultural transformation. Even during the Tang Dynasty, the picture of Quan Yin in some Buddhisms was still a man with a moustache. The Indian Buddhists did not accept the image of a woman. The image of Quan Yin, a kind and motherly spiritual energy, was gradually changed to be a woman and become well accepted by the Chinese, because traditionally, there were so many spiritually achieved women. Thus, how could only the male statues of Buddha present the spiritual reality? The spiritual teachers changed the image to that of a woman to commemorate her as a symbol of all the women who achieved in cultivating Tao. Thus, Quan Yin became a popular figure in China and was accepted as the Goddess of Mercy. She was an image of being supportive to people in trouble or in helping others with general psychological life.

The Chinese religion is based on Taoism, which advocates individual spiritual cultivation. Western religion is different. Western religion is social religion. They organize and group people, then create a kind of social influence. The old Chinese spiritual path is related deeply to personal life. Thus, all the families and individuals could use the image of Quan Yin to help themselves in their personal lives. Therefore, the worship of Quan Yin is psychological and also spiritual from her support. She also serves as a spiritual example to those individuals who do spiritual cultivation. She is a spiritual model of a woman who did not choose to be a mother, wife or princess. Instead, she chose to be spiritually developed so that she could understand more and give useful advice. Living close to the plain people, she could offer help and support.

Sometimes, women, just like men, have ambitions for high position, wealth and the admiration of society. But the model of Quan Yin tells us differently; you do not need to be highly placed in society, have a full money jar or be admired by others. If you choose real service to people, you are helpful, useful and serviceable wherever you are. You can establish your spiritual confidence as a person. You can have spiritual dignity within yourself, and do not need other people to prove it to you. All women can achieve themselves by spiritual practice.

Quan Yin's - Meao Sang's - achievement was to refuse her family's pressure and persecution. She left the family to achieve herself through a bitterly hard life to live on plants and small offerings. Usually she did not accept offerings. Through her great kindness, she willingly gave a helping hand to whomever she could help. This is why I recommend Quan Yin as a model, a concentrated image of all women who have achieved themselves by choosing to nurture their spiritual potential for spiritual achievement. By keeping her image in mind, you might find a better vision of life.

Chapter 6

Moonlight in the Dark Night

Q: Master Ni, you have given us some grandiose examples. We would like to learn some small examples which are closer to our level of ordinary people.

Master Ni: All right. There was a scholar, an indirect friend of our family, who lived in the rural mountains but possessed many valuable books. He had a large private library. I was interested in visiting him to study his collection, and because I knew he would not let anybody take a book out of his home, I wished to stay at his place for several months. My family made arrangements for me to visit.

In the adjoining county, Sui Ang, there is a river called the River of Flying Clouds. It starts far back in the mountains and flows inland. To get to the city where the man lived, one could either walk or ride a ferry boat upriver. The boat trip lasted for a day or a night. When the boat went upriver, it followed a precise schedule that coordinated with the arrival of the high tide. When it went downriver, its departure was coordinated with the withdrawal of the tide.

So I took the boat and went to the gentleman's home. I greatly enjoyed the collection of books in his library. Some of his books were new to me, but some I had seen before. In the old time, people who wished to obtain a governmental position by examination needed to study a type of book called bagowen. They are beautifully compiled books with a rigid style of writing. I was not looking for them, but had an opportunity to see them anyway. Our family did not have some of the books that taught ancient mathematics related to the *I Ching* system, so this gave me an opportunity to look over those interesting books.

One evening, after I had finished reading and studying the books, I bid the owner goodbye and went to catch the boat to return home. The tide was high and the full moon was shining brightly. Its light reflected on the water. We waited in the boat for the tide to start withdrawing. Our voyage began; it was a warm pleasant night and the voyage was smooth and speedy.

A boat usually carries about 30 to 40 people. Sitting close to me were a mother and grown daughter with an interesting piece of luggage, a chest. The chest was big and tall, made out of wood and painted red. It was a special kind of red chest like the opera people used, so I knew they were opera people. I couldn't help but look at the girl, because she was so beautiful under the moonlight. The girl also kept looking back at me, but at that time I was shy and I did not dare look into her eyes and smile at her. But she kept looking back at me. I occasionally looked back because I liked the beautiful gentle face, and our glances met briefly several times.

With the exchange of light between us under the moonlight, a sweet feeling started to sprout. But we dared not greet each other. I do not know whether it was my pride or just shyness. I believe it was mostly shyness, because how do you start a conversation with a girl, especially with her mother sitting there? She was around 16 or 17, I am not sure, but she appeared beautiful to me.

The attraction between us did not go unnoticed by her mother. The mother greeted me, saying, where do you come from, and what does your family do, etc., which was the customary conversation when strangers meet in China. I told them I lived in the land of paulownia trees of Wenchow county. The mother suddenly asked, "Do you know Doctor Ni, Yo-San?"

"He is my father," I replied.

"Oh!" The woman said, "Your mother was my boss. She was younger than all the people in the opera group except me.

"At the beginning we thought that your mother's way of management was hard, but nobody complained because she really took care of us well, differently from your grandfather. Your grandfather sometimes became very excited, sometimes excited in a different way - he was maybe a little too extreme because of financial stress."

She continued, "Your mother did not only do well financially, but she also made other improvements. A troupe of Chinese opera can number as many as a hundred people, more or less, because the big-name performers do not like to take the small roles in an opera. They always wait for the main parts, so your grandfather needed to hire lots of people to accomplish each performance. But your mother laid off the people less skillful in acting and let them find new jobs. Then she required that big-name performers do the small roles when they did not have a big part.

"At the beginning, everybody was unhappy about that, but your mother had a way of convincing us. She said, 'It does not matter whether it is a big role or a small role, whatever comes to you, you must earnestly exercise your talent, according to the demand of the role. That is called being a good performer.'

"At the beginning, most of the big names did not like to do it, but at last they faced the reality. Interestingly, they came to find enjoyment in doing the small characters, because their script was so light, it was fun to do. So they accepted the reality.

"I was especially helped by your mother. My father was a scholar, but he passed away early, so my family had no support. My dream of marrying into an honored scholar's family was shattered. My mother still had young sons, so I was forced by my family's situation to learn how to perform opera. When I participated in the opera company your grandfather sponsored, I did not think it was an honorable job. I thought it was degrading or humiliating for me, a scholar's daughter. This made me unhappy in my career as an actress.

"Anybody with a problem could hardly escape the eye of your mother. Your mother discovered my problem, and she told a fascinating story. I remember it so clearly; I will remember it forever. I have told the story to my daughter, and asked her to remember the great teaching, the great education we could receive from no one else."

Sitting on the boat, I listened to the woman with interest, because my mother was usually not a talker. She was not like my father, who was more communicative.

To her daughter, the mother's story was repetition because she had heard it many times, but to me it was fresh inspiration. I never knew that a performer could have such depth.

The woman continued, "This is the story that all of us in the four opera companies cherished. At that time, the acting business was not highly respected. It is still the same way now. Usually the performers come from poor families and need to struggle in life. They are not strong enough to be farmers, nor do they have special interest in any other profession, so they become performers. It was easy to lose self-respect. That is the biggest problem - once we become performers, we lose self-respect.

"It was your mother who saved us. We not only worshiped the universal mother as our spiritual support, we followed the spiritual practices your mother taught us and listened to the stories she told."

The woman paused. During the silence and later while she was telling her story, we could hear the soft murmur of the water and see the two shores of the river with their beautiful landscape as we were riding under the light of the moon. Because it was a whole night's ride on the boat, we had time to take a break. The woman offered me some of the fruit they had brought along on the journey. I ate a little bit, and she slowly continued.

"This was the story your mother told us. Around the time of the Ming Dynasty, there was a young girl who had a background similar to mine: she was born to a scholar's family. I will call her Plum Flower. Her family suffered poverty and it was necessary for Plum Flower to go stay with her uncle. Unfortunately, her uncle was a gambler who was fond of drinking. After she had lived with her uncle for about six months, he met an old couple who were looking to purchase a daughter. The uncle sold her. He did not even check out what business the couple was in. The money was paid and Plum Flower was taken away to a big city.

"Her new life was different from the old. The old couple hired musicians to teach her to play music, and brought in scholars to teach her how to write poetry. This went on for several years until Plum Flower became proficient. After she was fourteen or fifteen years old, the old couple required her to entertain the visitors who came to the house. They would drink wine and listen to her poems and the music she played. Funny thing, though; the visitors were always well dressed and there were never any women. They were all very friendly.

"One day the couple told Plum Flower that her job would have more responsibility. After she entertained the group of men in the living room, she would have to take one of the men into her room and entertain him privately by playing music. Suddenly Plum Flower understood; she was to become a prostitute, a Chinese old-style prostitute.

"She objected. 'I was born into a scholar's family; I know what personal respect is. I will not do this.' But her stepparents said, 'We paid lots of money to bring you here. All those years you dressed well and ate well. We also hired different tutors to help you. Where do you think the money comes from for your food? Well, the money must now come from you. Even if you are an honorable lady and have good sense, you have to have a conscience about how you repay the money.' Plum Flower started to cry. Finally she found a conclusion: 'Okay, I will do this. If men come to this house, I will accompany them by singing, dancing, playing music and making poems; but I will not sleep with anybody. Sleeping with anyone has to be my own choice.' The two old people were happy about her accepting the terms.

"So she started that career. After one or two years, one man came along who had lots of money and who greatly enjoyed Plum Flower's beauty and her age. Maybe he was a businessman or a retired government official. He came many times and gave lots of money to the old couple. One time, he gave Plum Flower lots of wine; he made her lose the strength of resistance and he raped her.

"The next day, she felt bad about it and decided to kill herself. She never had a chance to do that; the old couple had everything planned. They came to her and said, 'Forgive us. It was not our intention. The person was a man of power; we are only a poor family. We will be out on the street unless we make some money. Do this career; if you do not accept, we can not live here anymore.' Plum Flower could not see any way out, so she no longer resisted. However, it was a wound. It was an external force that changed her to be a real prostitute and make more money for the old couple who, by the way, were professional procurers. You do not need to doubt that they purchased several other young girls and put them through a similar process. They were all living in the same house, but the old couple had kept them separate until now. However, none of the other girls was as intelligent or beautiful as Plum Flower. So she began her career.

"One day a young military officer of minor rank came to visit her. Young officers do not earn a lot, but this one used all his wages to be with her. He was somewhat different than the others, she thought. She enjoyed his youthful, upright and straightforward attitudes. The young man was enchanted with Plum Flower. He told her that he loved her and declared privately that he wished to marry her. 'The only problem is,' he said, 'I do not have money. When I get some money, I shall come to uplift you from this fire pit.' They made a strong vow to each other and said they loved each other. The young officer told her, 'If I sleep with another woman, if I do not marry you, I will die by arrow.' The woman said, 'If I do not see you again, I will kill myself.' The man left with promises to find money and return.

"Unfortunately, the beautiful dream was not fulfilled. Behind a military officer is a high general, and immediately, because of urgent circumstances, the young officer was sent to the border to fight the war.

"She waited, but the promise turned out to be empty. She wrote a lot of poems telling of her melancholy and the misery of her life, but they only made her appear more attractive and become more famous among the clients.

"Now, let me tell you a different part. In ancient times in China, the young scholars passed the government examination level by level. A group of young scholars would pass the first level and continue to receive a governmental education. The young men gathered together to talk about a beautiful angel who lived in their town, who was good at poetry and played such charming music. But the price for her was high. Everybody talked about her.

"One scholar in that group did not have a father or mother. His parents had left him only a small inheritance, and he could barely support himself enough to continue his education. I will call him Plato. He heard the other men talking about the girl. Each of Plato's friends came from a good family and had the financial strength to make merry with different ladies. But in his life, he could never think about making merry anywhere. The description of the talented young woman awoke in him a question. Plato wondered how a girl could write poetry as well as the scholars themselves, who were educated full time by famous teachers. He heard about her a first time, then a second time he heard about her from other people. The third time Plato heard about her, suddenly he had a thought; 'I live my life, studying all year. Never, not once have I seen anything worthy. Is that not a waste of one's life?' This girl sounded special, so he decided: 'In my life, I have to see her.' He made the decision, but he did not have money. However, he owned several good books, and had some old scrolls from his family inheritance. He sold all of them. He took the money and bought himself some new clothes. Then he went to visit the girl.

"To his great astonishment, the girl really was like a woman who came from Heaven. She was beautiful, graceful and intelligent. She was also talented. She became a great consolation or satisfaction in his life. Plum Flower also enjoyed Plato because he had the talent and purity of a young scholar. She had suffered a broken heart from the young officer who never returned for her, so she believed that all men who came to such a place and mentioned love were just using a fancy word to win her favors. All the other women in the house said never to take the men seriously. It had been a deep disappointment to her, but she had started to learn to be numb hearted, and now she did not feel the deep sorrow of her life.

"When she met Plato, Plum Flower's life came back. She felt that among all the visitors, the scholar had a special quality about him. They started to talk and discovered that they had good rapport. They talked about everything. The girl finally said, 'I would like you to visit me again.' The man said, 'No, I cannot visit you again.' When she asked him why, the man told her straightforwardly: 'I only have a little money left for my living for the rest of the year. I gathered this much to see you because I adore you and worship you, and so I have come to you to fulfill my lifetime wish. You are my one fantasy, once and for all.'

"Plum Flower was moved by this, because she had never heard anybody speak so sincerely nor who would make such a sacrifice for her. The men who came to her usually had lots of money and could not be affected by scandal or threatened by poverty. She never experienced such great sincerity and respect from a man. She felt love for him. She told Plato, "I am not here for fun or making money for people. I am here waiting for someone trustworthy for a lifetime. I will serve the person, whatever the life condition is. By your action and your true interest in me, I am moved. I will accept you; I wish to marry you.'

"Plato said, 'Do not talk about that. This is the last fantasy; I do not even know how I will live next month.'

"'However,' Plum Flower said, 'after seeing you, I will never take a man into my room anymore.'

"They had a good evening together, but it was a bitter-sweet time because they had to face the reality of poverty. Although Plum Flower had a small amount of money she had saved secretly to buy her freedom, it was not nearly enough to fill the big hole of the greed of the stepparents. So no decision was made for marriage. But privately, Plum Flower made a decision in her heart: I am going to marry this man.

"When she went back to continue her career, she served wine, played music and wrote poems, but she refused to take any man to her room. At the beginning, her stepmother and stepfather tried to persuade her sweetly. After she did not listen to them, they threatened her. After the threats did not work, they beat her. They did not like to lose a tree whose branches you can shake to make money fall down. Such a tree takes time to nurture. They did not want to give her up. To a weak woman who feels desperate, death seems the only choice, although she proved to be a woman of great spiritual strength and determination later. To choose life · means too many difficulties.

"Just when Plum Flower was without hope, a Taoist came to visit her. Usually we do not associate Taoists with prostitutes; how can a spiritual person visit a prostitute? It was also told that the Taoist was Master Lu, Tung Ping, but I do not think so. Because he is so famous, many good and bad things are attributed to him. However, the Taoist came to visit her. She treated him respectfully, and did whatever she did. The Taoist discovered that there was a deep sorrow in Plum Flower, and that she could not be open-hearted. Taoists do not enjoy a woman who is not open-hearted.

"He said, 'Tell me your story.'

"She replied, 'I love a young man, a scholar, but he does not have money. I am hardly in a position to be able to find a man who could be trustworthy for a lifetime and not have contempt of my past and my present. The scholar wished to change my life, but he could not because he is poor.'

"The Taoist did some service and left. From that night on, Plum Flower's body gave a bad odor. The woman did not refuse to accept anybody who paid the stepfather and stepmother, but no one could stand to pay money to suffer the bad odor. People called her 'bad odor beauty.' Men stopped coming to see her; slowly she was deserted by all her clients. Her stepfather and stepmother took her to all the famous doctors, but no one could help her, no matter what they did. The stepparents did not know what to do, because the tree their money came from was now sick.

"About that time, the Taoist went to visit the young scholar. He said, 'Would you do a service for me? I have a book that I need somebody to copy for me. I will pay this much.' Plato was happy to do it. He copied it quickly. Most scholars would take a week to do it, but he finished in one night and then went right to see Plum Flower.

When she saw him, Plum Flower said, 'You told me that in your lifetime you could see me only once! How did you get the money?'

"'I had a job,' he said, 'Copying a book, so I got some money to come back and see you.' Then they planned. Plato went to the old couple and offered to buy Plum Flower. He had not earned much money, but Plum Flower gave him her savings. The stepmother and stepfather considered it, saying 'She has a bad name; this affects our business, because it affects the name of our house.' Reluctantly, finally they decided, 'In this case, we need to throw her away. If anybody gives a little money, this is a blessing. Let us take the money and let her go.'

"Plum Flower took her simple but practical belongings and went to live with Plato. Now the scholar had a wife, and they lived together happily. She had warned him about the strong smell, but a man with a true, deep love will ignore it. She had said, 'I have developed a bad disease; my body smells so bad. Will you still marry me?' The young man said, 'Doubtlessly I will marry you. It is your body, it is not your soul. Your soul is fragrant.'

After the marriage, Plato wanted both the body and soul of Plum Flower to be fragrant. He looked for a doctor, but the young couple still did not have much money.

"One day, the Taoist visited them. 'I have medicine that can help take away the odor. But I do not have any use for the book your husband copied for me. As a gift, I give it to you.' He gave her the medicine, and the woman had no odor at all. It is a Taoist trick; it is not hard to do that.

"The other scholars could hardly believe Plato's good fortune. Such a poor fellow - how could he marry such a beautiful girl? Everybody admired him.

"The couple lived happily, because Plum Flower was diligent in working and did some embroidery to sell. In this situation, she could live a respectful life. It was less important to live everyday with rich food and pleasurable music than to live without dignity of the soul. The scholar was also busy trying to find work to do. At home, Plum Flower was curious about the book left by the Taoist. She looked at it; the book had lots of words that she did not understand totally. The main thing she understood from the book was, whatever your life situation, whatever you are, you must do your best. Doing your best is the dignity of life. It is the most respectful thing you can learn in the experience of human life on this plane. There were also some suggested disciplines and practices. Because of these things, she gave up reading the book. She was impressed by the writing but she did not understand it deeply.

"Then misfortune struck. Because of working too hard, and from lack of nutrition and too much cold, Plato passed away. The only hope in Plum Flower's life was suddenly taken away. It was a terrible shock. Immediately she had no more support. She thought of killing herself, to die for love, but anytime she thought of doing that, she felt that the Taoist book was a kind of support. It gave a warning, and forbid such behavior. So she exercised her great determination, although she was practically a weak woman. She bore her sadness and buried Plato, who left her nothing except an empty house.

"It is difficult for a single woman to live. What could she live on? Many people knew that her husband died. Many people knew that she no longer had that disease. Her husband had been her protection. Before him, the disease had protected her. But now all the protection, husband and body odor, were gone. The Taoist words rang a bell in her mind. 'Whatever fortune you face, whatever service or walk of life you do, do your best. When you do your best, there is dignity in life.'

"To Plum Flower, there was no respectful quality in a prostitute's life. She thought, 'What type of life is that? Men are attracted to me so they all come around.' Again men began to give her gifts and money; they said it was out of sympathy. But Plum Flower understood their purpose. But she only played music, sold tea, danced for people and used poems as communication with people so they would pay. Nothing else. Before, she had been under misfortune plus under the control of evil force, so she had to become a prostitute. Now, she ran into misfortune, but no evil force. She did not choose to be a prostitute again. The Taoist book inspired a new career. She changed her attitude to offer service and help from where and what she was. As the book said, wherever you are, and whatever you are, spiritual people can always give help to people who come to them. She had never wished to be a prostitute. In the world of men, there was no noble person who would sell tea, sing or dance in exchange for a living. She regretfully faced the reality of her life and clearly understood this was a service she could give. Thus, she eliminated the thought that she came from a dignified family, and also eliminated the thought that she had been in misery as a prostitute with a great deal of self pity. Before, she was only half minded, or had no heart involved; she had served men half-heartedly. Now she was different; whatever she did, she did with great sincerity. As she now understood life, she wanted to give her best service to all people.

A place to serve tea was considered a low place, and people in this business were considered low class. But now, Plum Flower thought differently about people who came to her, "Men need what I offer. They have their own reason, for fun, to escape troubles, relief from an unhappy home, whatever." So she started to open up; she provided whatever she could do. The men who came to her for tea began to see her in a different way. Something about being around her made them change their life attitudes. Many customers slowly recognized her spiritual quality. They changed their attitudes and respected her. They said, 'This is not an ordinary woman; this is a goddess incarnated.'

"During that time, many customers came to the tea house. They would not let her give up her work. Even if they stayed with her for one moment, they would receive some light from her. It was a public service where people could go, during a time when a woman of beauty was usually someone's private possession.

"One day, a group of soldiers lead by a general passed by the town, and the general came to visit Plum Flower. To her astonishment, the general was her old lover. From the low rank of officer, he had become a general. His first order was to send away all the soldiers. 'Now I am going to marry you,' he said. 'I did not fulfill my promise, but now I have come back to marry you.' The woman said, 'It is too late for you to marry me. You are a man of position; you are a general. I have married once. My life is changed. I serve tea to guests who come to my house; I am not qualified to be your wife.'

"The man said, 'If you do not marry me, I also am not going to marry, but give me one promise. Allow me to live next door, to be your neighbor.' The general requested retirement with a big pension. He had lots of money, so he bought the neighbor's house.

"The general had won a great victory on the border, but he did not like to abuse or kill people. Plum Flower still had visitors, but mostly her attitude was to help others. She became an inspiration to the general's soul. He thought that Plum Flower's misery was his punishment, his responsibility, because of his love for her he thought she was in misery in her new life. Then Plum Flower told the general what she had learned from the Taoist book, 'Whatever you are, do your best to reach your spirit, the inner God.' The general said, 'Now I am not a soldier fighting in the war. I am at your side, and I will do my best to help you. That is my life goal.'

"That was the end of the story. A general and a woman experienced the misery of life, but each of them cherished a beautiful soul. In a soldier's life, it is a misery to be defeated; it is also misery when victory happens through the successful killing of many lives. The general had achieved himself from the rough life of a low-ranking soldier which needed to take a lot of hardship, almost like being a slave, which was a misery. Both of them had past mistakes or past miseries, but they recognized that life is not to take; life is to give. Life is not to build one's personal ego or personal self-pity, but life is to cure other people's self-pity."

That was the story my mother told as it was told to me by the opera woman on the boat. But she added something to the story. "Do you know what I am doing now? I am still an actress. My daughter plays the younger roles in the opera. Although I was born to a scholar, and I should marry an honorable scholar, I think that in my life and my position, whatever I do should serve people. I need to show people how to enjoy themselves for a short time, take away their nervousness, take away their tension, help them relax and enjoy a good life. It refreshes their life. It is valuable, and has spiritual value. My attitude was changed by your mother's influence. Not only do I act, but my daughter also acts. She also serves people to relieve their emotional burdens of life."

So I sat in the boat, riding on the withdrawing tide, quickly flying down the river and watching the landscape pass by. That was a beautiful night. I had just received a teaching from someone I would never see again. I wondered, was she not Quan Yin coming down from Heaven to teach me? I do not need to dream of being a general, I do not need to dream of being a politician or of having a high name; I need to be whatever I can be and thus I will be satisfied.

Student A: Her customers, by calling her a "goddess" are over-reacting.

Master Ni: During the time I was in China, a beautiful, pure girl or woman was considered as a goddess by men. It was a sort of spiritual recognition. It was not so serious unless the emperor called them so.

Student B: Such a long story for a simple teaching!

Student C: This story is very beneficial for all people. It shows that you should always do your best no matter what your circumstance. Also, even though the girl was very desirable and could have easily remarried, she chose to remain single to be able to offer her nurturing abilities to all people. To me, this answers many questions people ask about all relationships, being single and friendships. The natural energy of a woman is to be nurturing; if they would extend themselves to others, this would help to develop and strengthen this energy.

In today's society everyone wants to be rewarded for their deeds. I think this is why mothering is so hard. You need to be very clear and strong about your role. You cannot say you are only going to do a good job if you get rewards. If you raise a happy, responsible child who is useful to society, everyone is rewarded subtly. This is a mother's job. If people in general are nurturing to each other, without any expectations, all society benefits.

Chapter 7

Religion Can Stimulate a Young Mind

Q: Master Ni, how did a spiritual person like your mother raise you as a child? Did she teach you about religion? What kind of spiritual training did she give you, if any?

Master Ni: When I was a little boy, my personal feeling was that the discipline of my mother was extraordinarily strict. In other words, I thought she did not give me a break. However, my mother said that it was I who did not give her a break. Perhaps it was because I received so much attention from her that it seems she did not give me a break.

As a young boy, I always disappeared from her sight, so she sent my sisters to look for me. Wherever I was, she knew about it. If she felt I was safe, she said nothing. If she did not feel that I was safe, I was given instruction on what to do or told to come home. She watched me carefully.

My mother chose Chinese calligraphy as the practice of my mentality when I was little. A young boy is restless and calligraphy can quiet him down. Chinese calligraphy is sort of like painting pictures, but the characters are more like symbols. It takes high concentration and discipline. There are several styles. Beginners need to start with the easy ones, and then when some attainment is achieved, they can go on to learn the difficult ones.

You know, Chinese words are pictures. When I was little, my father bought a box with several hundred cards that had Chinese characters on one side and their corresponding picture on the other side. If you do not know the Chinese character, you look on the other side to know what it means. There is some resemblance between a Chinese character and the object it describes, especially after it is explained, so the characters are fairly easy to accept and remember. Every day, I had to recognize ten words for my mother. I could not escape it; my mother did not give me a break. I wanted to go out and be busy at play outside of the house. It was not hard to learn the characters by memory, but once I got out of the house, I forgot them. Next time, I had to do it over again. That was harder.

A child starting to learn calligraphy uses papers with the characters already written in red ink. The child just has to put the black ink over the red ink. By doing that, a youngster learns how to hold the brush correctly. My mother considered this the first step of spiritual training for a young boy.

I had lots of curiosity. One neighbor was an old carpenter who specialized in making buckets and round shaped furniture like basins. I would go to touch his tools, not knowing that it was dangerous to do so. Although I learned sawing by hand from him, the old carpenter did not teach his trade. He taught me his favorite songs and bid me to remember them. They went:

1

All the day, I round up the bucket.
The value exists in the middle emptiness.
I keep polishing it over and over,
Until there is no trace of ax and chisel.

2

The leaky body makes the unleaky basin.
No water can be spilled from the bottom.
It is made in roundness and tightness.
To symbolize the freedom inside and outside.

Years after, I was suddenly enlightened that his songs were about spiritual cultivation. Leak is a metaphor for energy leakage and spiritual scatteredness, which should be channelled. This is symbolized from the way "leaky" is used in the song.

Our house had several doors and windows. I was very active physically and I liked to have some fun by jumping in and out of the window to show how high I could jump. At the beginning, my mother gently scolded me for doing it. When I did it again and again, my mother kept warning me. "Don't do it. This is a bad habit. You need clearly to understand that a door is for walking through and a window is for air and light." I did not understand that much and continued jumping, and my mother severely spanked me for disobeying. Then I understood that my mother was teaching me more than not to jump from a window for fun. She also wished me to become an upright person. An upright person makes a road a road, and does not take a shortcut and ignore the main road or main path of life.

Whatever interesting thing I could find, I would stand there looking for a while. I also used to go to watch another neighbor who was a tailor and had a sewing machine. I would try to do something when people were not watching. It was my personal interest to play in vegetable or flower gardens. My mother did not encourage me to play with the other children, because she thought that the things they did were not beneficial. But I liked to stand watching them. They played a game taking turns rolling a big Chinese coin on the ground to see which one could roll it the longest distance. It was kind of like gambling. I really did not find it interesting, so I went to play by myself. The girls played hopscotch. They also played a game like hackey sack using a ball with a coin for weight and a feather. The girls liked that game a lot, but I was not interested in those things.

My interest, which to me was a great adventure, was not what most children are interested in. I would go to one neighbor's house for a while to see what the people were doing, and then disappear to go to another neighbor's yard to see what they were doing. Although I was always welcomed, my mother worried about me making trouble for people. All the childish behavior and wandering in the field pushed my mother to guide me with strict discipline. She became one of the important educators in my life.

When I was about seven years old, I observed a young scholar with a modern education reading novels aloud in a temple. People would go to listen to him and pay pennies for his reading. In our neighborhood, there was an opium house. People would go there to smoke opium, including the young scholar. This young man was from a good family in the city, but because of his opium habit, he had failed in life. He had to do the low paying jobs, and he always borrowed money for his habit. A person who smokes opium loses all his energy and become terribly addicted to opium. Almost all clear-minded Chinese recognize that opium is the worst enemy of the Chinese people, because it caused the corruption of Chinese society. Many useful people do it, then become useless.

My father used to take me to the temple to listen to the scholar read. He read the novel about master Dtao Gi, the Mad Chi. I described Dtao Gi in another book. The young man was a talented reader; he gave a performance which amused his audience. Each time he had money, he went to use opium, passing by my father's clinic on his way. So my father knew about his trouble. One day, my father stopped him and said, "You are a useful young man, you can correct this habit." The young man felt ashamed and said, "I do not know how." My father said, "I will help you," and he helped him out with herb formulas. The young man wished to give something back to my family, but he had nothing to offer. My father found out that the scholar had learned something that we did not know; he had learned English. So my father said, "You can teach English to my seven-year-old son."

By that age, I had already learned close to a hundred Chinese characters from flash cards. I did not have any problem with that because each word is a picture. Because I did not have an English book, the scholar wrote out a notebook for me with English in it. When I first looked at it, my impression was that English was just like soybean sprouts. It was hard for me to recognize one English character from another. Each of them had a different sound, but no picture to tell the meaning. I did not do well, although the scholar was patient.

My mother helped me understand that I did not need to become achieved but only to be familiar with the learning; then, in the future I could learn it easier. In only a few lessons, I learned, "Ball, cat, dog, boy and girl, and one, two, three." That was all I learned from the teacher. Many decades later, I used that foundation of vague impressions and a Chinese-English dictionary to give me some language skills to use in the United States. This is why I still use a kind of simple English and I usually write instead of speaking to be able to convey more to all of you.

From the scholar, I learned another thing: when I grow up, I will not do opium. As I remember, with my father's help, that scholar restored his good personality and returned to society. Years later, he became an editor of the local newspaper.

My father made suggestions to my mother about my education. Reading, speaking, writing and calculating are basic tools for a child's development. Adding some basic spiritual practice and disciplined physical training of Taoist art forms a child's good personality for the benefit of all life beings.

My mother became a teacher to help me in the early stages of life. She never gave me any formal classes or formal speeches. She liked to take me out in real life to see things and arouse my curiosity. If I was interested, I would ask her questions. Then she had a chance to instruct me with her answers. That is how she taught me.

My hometown was quite rich and admired as the country of rice and fish. If people had a few acres of land, they usually turned it into a productive rice paddy. They always had an ox, cow or buffalo to help them till the land. Everything was produced from the land for their good life. Lots of fish were in the canal and the lake. People raised chickens and ducks. So the life in our hometown could be considered easy. We had a mild climate and some scenic spots, so it was a pleasant place to live.

My hometown was not too big, but it had many surrounding small villages and lots of farm land. Even in my small town, there were five big temples. Two of the temples worshipped male deities. One temple worshipped a female deity. There were also two Buddhist temples, one for monks and the other for nuns.

There was also one special deity that did not like to live in a temple, but wished to live in an ordinary house. It lived in a statue clothed with beautiful satin. Communication between the deity and people was accomplished by two pieces of bamboo root, cut in the middle. Usually a person raised and lowered the bamboo root in front of the deity three times, then threw the bamboo root up like tossing a coin to see how it falls. If the pieces of bamboo were one face up and one face down, it was understood that the person had the deity's agreement. If all the pieces of bamboo were face down, it meant no good. If all were face up, it meant the deity was laughing. This was the system of communication with this deity. Each year, three days after harvest moon, on the eighteenth day of the eighth month, people carried the satin covered statue all around the villages and then moved it to a new village for the next year.

The village and the house were chosen by using the bamboo root to communicate with the deity. In many villages, people wished to receive his protection, so they made him their personal guardian angel. Thus, most of the villagers were god-children of this deity.

The parade was gorgeous; our town even rented horses for the occasion. Some people rode on horseback, and others walked in the costume parade. On this festival day, some people dressed up as sinners. In ancient times, guilty people awaiting punishment by the government were dressed in a certain clothing. These religious people in my hometown wore that garb and then they walked in a parade. I asked my mother why so many sinners were walking on the street during the parade.

My mother explained that they were practicing humility. Those people did not consider they were perfect. They thought they were guilty. They thought they were not strong enough and that they needed support from the spiritual level, so they dressed in that way.

However," my mother added, "now it is time for you to learn something about different religions. All different religions are different customs. It would be helpful for you to learn all of them equally."

Thus, when I was around eight years old, my mother took me to the city, which was about ten Chinese li (approximately three miles) from my hometown. We took a boat to the south gate of the city and walked inside, down the beautiful, stone paved streets and past stores filled with marvelous things. Sometimes my mother took me shopping for special clothing or other things we needed for the house.

My hometown was one of the five Chinese harbors open to the western world under the treaty made between the

Ching dynasty and the British. Thus, my hometown contacted the world culture earlier than the other places. In the town was a protestant church. I think it was Baptist. One day, my mother took me to see that foreign church. Many Chinese people who were followers of Christianity were there. In the church, there was a big pool with water inside. Normally the pool was empty and covered up with chairs, but that day the chairs were moved and the pool was filled with water. People dressed in robes were standing around it, and a priest stood in the water. He read something from a book, then dipped the people's heads into the water, one by one.

I asked, "Why do they do that?" My mother said, "This custom started with the Indian people of the Ganges River. People who think they have sinned use the water to help them cleanse their soul. The Christians adopted that custom as part of their religion. The foreign teacher here says they are cleansing the original sin."

I asked, "Can the original sin of a person be washed away?"

My mother guided me deeper. "No. If anything is original, it cannot be removed. For example, when you buy a piece of clothing that is red, green or blue, or if it has flowers of any color, and you wash it, does the color wash away? It does not. However, if you wear that piece of clothing and make it dirty, you can wash away the dirt. Similarly, the sense of sin comes after life starts. People are born pure and clean, but because they play outside, they get muddy and need to be cleansed, just like you do after you go chasing frogs."

Later, when I was in my teens and had more knowledge, I discussed baptism again with my mother, and she gave me further instruction. By that time I was inquisitive and asked lots of questions. "The Christian church thinks the birth of humans into the world began with the ancestors Adam and Eve. Adam and Eve came too close to each other and gave birth to children: that is what they called original sin. In other words, if Adam and Even had not come too close to each other, they would not have angered god, and would have stayed in the Garden of Eden."

I asked, "What does that metaphor mean?" She told me about the tradition of Wu Wei. Wu Wei means to have no need to do anything extra in order to glorify life. Life is naturally respectable. Wu wei compares with Adam and Eve being together.

Adam and Even did nothing extra to their life nature. Thus, the conception of original sin could be established. In spiritual purity, wu wei means that anything a person does makes trouble or disturbs that person's spiritual purity. Any single action taken does not maintain the wholeness of the soul any more. In depth, this means that anyone who can act and still maintain original wholeness is doing a high spiritual practice. If you project any thoughts, desire or action other than what is necessary, they are all considered a downfall. So spiritually, not doing anything extra, or not overdoing anything, is considered the highest principle. Otherwise, any action taken is a sin. That is the definition of Wu Wei.

My mother explained further to me, "All people have original spiritual purity. People contaminate their spirit by bending when receiving pressure in the world. Nobody can avoid experiencing pressure, but you must do your best to keep yourself upright. Spiritually, do not be entangled in worldly affairs because they cause emotions and deep bondage.

"In Western religion, the birth of children or establishment of the human world is considered original sin. Because the thought of having children was original sin, Adam and Eve were driven out from Eden. However, this is all a metaphor."

I would like to take my mother's teaching deeper for you. Once people have children, the pressures of life increase for the parents. They may be pushed to do something to harm their spirit to provide the things their children need. Thus, they have the crisis of spiritual downfall. Also, when the population greatly increased on earth, the quality of life declined. Their descendants made lots of trouble. They lost the quality of life of Eden. The idea of returning to the quality of an Eden-like life later established the religious teaching of salvation.

It is important to restore personal innocence and avoid worldly life entanglements. By doing so, you return to a spiritual Eden. This is not complicated to do, but you must do it by yourself. Because it can be done anywhere at any time, any place can be a spiritual Eden. Nobody can do it for you. The idea that the church could redeem your original sin is not real. It was a psychological manipulation by the church of those who could not see the truth for themselves. Real spiritual growth depends on each individual's personal spiritual development.

Once I see something, if I have a question, I will keep the question in mind or talk about it until I totally understand it or have a satisfactory answer. This was true when I was young and it is still true today. When I was eight or nine years old, my mother took me twice to a Catholic church. In a Catholic church, people are more serious than in a Buddhist temple. On my first visit, I saw the people sitting in pews. Then, one person lifted up a partially naked Jesus nailed on the cross. The person held the cross and walked down the aisle with it. A group of people followed in a row and kneeled down on the ground, imitating the suffering of the captured Jesus. Then on the way, station by station, they reenacted the events that occurred when Jesus was going to be crucified in the wilderness. The followers prayed to have a strong emotional expression from the beginning of the ceremony until Jesus was crucified. This was the spiritual process of the followers in the church.

I asked my mother, "What are they doing?"

My mother said, "They are re-experiencing what happened to Jesus."

I asked her, "Who is Jesus?"

My mother said, "The western church teaches that Jesus was the only son of God."

I asked, "If Jesus was the only son of God, how could Jesus be crucified?"

My mother answered that according to the Christians, because humans had become corrupt and lost, God became angry and decided to destroy the entire world. But God still had some love for them, so he sent his own son to save the world. Thus, it was God's plan to let Jesus be crucified, and his blood become ransom to save people from the wrath of God. My mother said that was what the church taught.

My impression was, "It seems God makes a lot of trouble for himself."

That was the time I thought over original sin and how it must have related to the story of Jesus. Later, I wondered: if original sin existed, was the sin installed or built into human nature in the first place? If the sin was built into the nature of the human ancestors, Adam and Eve, it was God's fault because God created them. Why should something that was not good enough be installed in human ancestor nature in the first place?

Then, it did not make sense that God became angry, because people were just expressing what was installed within them in the first place. If that made God mad, and he decided to destroy the world, then why did God send his only son to become savior of the world? He was only sending his son to be killed.

It was told that Jesus' death was a ransom for the people's sin to quiet down God's anger. But it was also told that Jesus' death was God's plan. None of this seemed logical to me at the time.

Because I was childish, and I did not know about it, I brought my questions to my mother again and again about this topic of Christianity. My mother wished me to learn by myself. "This is what the church explained. Keep thinking about the information you have in this moment until you have your own good answer. Then I can help to verify your answer."

So I continued to think about the matter. This was my reflection before I presented it to my mother. "It is not that somebody died for somebody else. It is not that somebody was angry about people's sins. God, the conception of God or the real being of God, and his son, the real being of son or Jesus, are all the internal spiritual being of an individual. If you know the individuality and independence of spirituality and spiritual responsibility of each individual, it can possibly be accepted as a good metaphor. In spiritual learning, one should not be confused by the name used.

"'Jesus' is a term for the internal spiritual reality of each individual self. All religions serve as metaphor. If you trust it is something literal, it is your own immaturity. You fool yourself and receive no spiritual benefit. Usually this is where people are trapped. All spiritual teachings are valid; they provide different service to you if you understand them and are not confused by them.'"

When I told my mother my ideas, I also added, "Sometimes we do wrong. After we do wrong, we feel unhappy or become angry, so we send a new energy to correct the problem. For example, when we apologize, the whole wrongdoing becomes externalized because we are expressing our emotions outwardly. Individual internal spiritual process makes more sense than external religion. Internal spiritual reality is provable, while external religion is not." This was what I understood about Christianity.

This was my mother's response or verification of my understanding. This kind of teaching establishes an external image. The image can cause a real response of spiritual energy within a person and this response can be used by the person to serve his or her own life. However, in the learning of Tao, we believe that before a person acts externally, it is important to be in harmony internally. That means that your own high spirituality consents to the action performed. The harmony of the duality must be attained.

"This means that if you wish to do something, and your high spirits do not agree, then do not do that thing, otherwise your spirits will be disturbed. For example, when you face temptation, if your conscience tells you not to do it, but you do it anyway, you cause internal disharmony for yourself. At that moment, you do not see the anger or the self-destructive fire that you are creating. Your impulse may be strong enough to ignore your internal disharmony, and if you follow it, real internal damage or destruction will happen in a practical or real way."

My mother helped me understand the difference between the spiritual structure and belief of the foreign churches. My mother's understanding was much deeper than mine.

After the city wall of Wenchow was torn down, a new Buddhist temple was built not far from where the gate had been. One day they were having an open house and my mother wanted to take me there. I had seen so many Buddhist temples, I was not interested. However, my mother intended that I see it. Her feet had been bound to be very small according to old Chinese custom, but because she was naturally healthy and frugal, she hardly ever hired a rickshaw. She walked everywhere. She was still strong and full of energy even after a big day of shopping. Although I was young and had no foot problems, I was tired and protested. We went to the Buddhist temple anyway.

It was a new temple, but full of people. Inside, I saw many new gold-colored statues and smelled the fragrance of strong incense burning both inside and outside. At the beginning, my attention was attracted to the smiling big bellied Buddha in the first hall. I said to my mother, "Buddha must have been a vegetarian, but how can a vegetarian be so fat?" Many people heard my question, and laughed at it.

My mother pointed out that he was not actually fat; the fatness was just a metaphor for having tolerance while living in the world. Tolerance is like a container which is deep enough to contain all the bad emotion, people's aggressive approaches, or whatever. This is what the big belly stands for. We seldom saw people with big bellies among the Chinese people in the street, except our old carpenter neighbor, who specialized in making buckets of all sizes and basins. He was fat.

On each side of the entrance hall to the temple, there was a big, colorful, fierce looking giant. Each of the giants acted as guardians of the temple. Behind the big bellied, smiling Buddha was a statue of Quan Yin. Then, in the center of the main hall were three statues of Buddha in gold. At the side were many other golden statues, all men. There was no other woman statue except Quan Yin. Quan Yin in Buddhist scriptures was a man, but Chinese spiritual leaders changed him into a woman. Mostly at the open house, nothing happened; we just saw the inside of the temple. Like most Buddhist temples, it was elaborate and richly decorated. My visit there was valuable to my learning because their teaching in books or preaching denies the value of worldly life. It promotes the abandonment of worldly life to live like a monk. A contradiction was also seen: All statues were colored in gold. They highly value the color gold. Does it not express a kind of spiritual fantasy?

Some Islamic people lived in my hometown. They opened beef stores where you could also enjoy a beef dinner. My mother never let me eat beef, because in a farming society, most oxen were part of the work force. They should not be killed and eaten after all the labor they did. But because she wanted me to experience something about the Islamic culture, she lifted the restriction. So I went to have a beef dinner and chatted with the Islamic people. They said that their god was the true god or true lord. My feeling was that the Islamic religion is masculine dominated. I thought the beef tasted good, but the most interesting part of the dinner was meeting the people. Their customs were different from those of our family. My visit there was valuable because different customs express religious variety. Variety is what tells the unity. Unity should not be expressed by monotony. People who are beneath customs are controlled by customs. People who are above customs enjoy variety. This is the spiritual position I chose. It takes a long time. Since then, I keep adding to the variety. I like to try different things, one thing at a time.

After I returned home from the Islamic restaurant, my mother explained, "All those religions - Christianity, Buddhism and Islam - are masculine religions, religions of manly energy. They have a natural tendency to compete, fight, expand or extend to one side of the imperfect, imbalanced human nature. It is a cultural or spiritual mistake. This spiritual mistake can be corrected. Without that correction, a balanced, peaceful world can hardly be obtained. In spiritual nature, the feminine is fully recognized."

My mother also warned me, if you are going to teach people, never guide them in a wrong direction. Mohammed created Islam. Islam was inspired by Moses' Judaism. The male spiritual religions will compete with each other without end. That will become the worst side effect of such masculine energy worship.

In nature, you can see that in the after-Heaven stage, man represents forward energy. It is the energy of expansion. Woman expresses withdrawing and contracting. Only when the two energies cooperate can a good world be brought about. If any one side is overextended, it brings only disaster, and people lose the connection and cooperation of the other side. Thus, religions must exalt both manifestations of energy, not just one.

"Human leadership is almost totally dominated by men. However, they only know to move forward, they do not know the benefits of withdrawing. They only know expansion, they do not know collecting back. Therefore, when they face a crisis, they go to an extreme; they totally destroy without immediately stopping the mistake in the middle."

Many of you have experienced World War II. You witnessed Japan, Germany and Italy united together as a center to conquer the entire world. If those leaders knew to stop, they would immediately have made an adjustment before something went to an extreme. All people make mistakes.   I think the destruction in Japan, Italy and Germany would have been less if they knew not to be so aggressive. In their personalities, those leaders lacked the opposite of expansion, which is feminine energy.

If a man is a good leader, he has feminine energy as well as masculine energy. If a woman is put in leadership, she must have initiating, creative energy. No single element can be a perfect model. During the last three thousand years, masculine worship has dominated the world. It is not a good education, and it should end.

Taoism honors the feminine principle of peace and cooperation. When the *I Ching* developed, the ancient achieved ones did not put "Chyan," universal or natural impetus, as the first hexagram. It was "K'un," receptive or feminine energy, that took first place.

If we examine the sixty-four hexagrams, any time yang energy is on the top and yin energy is below, disorder results. That particular type of construction means disaster because both energies move in opposite directions and go to extremes. That is exemplified by the hexagram Pi, which means disaster.

On the other hand, when the feminine energy is on the top as leader, the masculine energy is below in a position to accomplish. This expresses a beautiful picture of energy organization. When the yin feminine energy spirits are on top and the masculine spirits are below, they meet each other in the middle. Then you find accomplishment and something brought about as a good, new prosperity. That is exemplified by the hexagram Tai, which means peace.

The religious promotion from the middle east was the psychological response of the troubled minds of a defeated and humiliated people. They needed an aggressive image of conquering force. Thus, the forceful image of God was brought forth. This is a one-sided spiritual projection. In India, religious creation moved towards the opposite extreme. It expressed withdrawing in life. It accepted the defeat in life. It recognized that worldly life is trouble, sometimes hopeless. It exalted totally giving up. In reality, India does not do this, in culture especially, but Buddhism holds this attitude.

Taoist teaching is not the male worship or the negative trend of female worship. Its teaching is the balanced and centered way. It teaches the everlasting truth of life that we call Tao. Tao is the right course of life. Not the life of today, not the life of yesterday, it is a life of everlasting truth. It poises itself in the center among any one-sided trend of a time and its thoughts. Balance is important as personal cultivation. A woman needs to learn to be creative and have initiating spirits, and a man needs to learn how to organize, compromise and harmonize. It does not matter who, a man or a woman, is in leadership; what is needed is the good combination of the two kinds of energy.

It was a mistake to let the creation of masculine images become over exalted as the spiritual leadership of the world. Spiritual leadership is not masculine only; it must be as the *I Ching* instructs us, with the feminine spirit above, and the masculine spirit below. Then a new, good picture of a well-ordered world will be presented.

Worldly things can never be stopped. Step by step, any time man takes leadership and gives up the other important part of energy, the other part of his spirit, it will bring only trouble. This is natural or spiritual disorder. When feminine energy is above, and masculine energy is below, they present a positive picture of cooperation and harmonization in making a new, good step. Being above or being below means the type of energy position. It does not mean the physical differences of a man or a woman.

Women need to exercise themselves more to correct the spiritual mistake of the past three thousand years. They can do this by dedicating themselves to balanced worldly and spiritual learning and spiritual work. Masculine energy belongs to action; feminine energy belongs to the spiritual level. It is not a woman's characteristic to compete or conquer, but feminine energy can be a good guide with motherliness and sisterliness to help the world. This will bring about new world harmony and world peace.

Student A: How should women proceed in doing this?

Student B: Many women today are in management positions, could you give some advice on how they can be good leaders without becoming overbearing and aggressive?

Master Ni: Individuals have gender differences. Management is work. It can be done with appropriateness and correctly balanced energy, and without overextending one type of energy of a single gender. The teaching of reaching balance can be found in most places in my books.

Chapter 8

Using the External to Learn the Internal

Q: Master Ni, as a young boy, how did you respond to the religious experience with your pure, free mind?

Master Ni: This question is related to the last one. Some discussion will be heard again in order to show how new points were brought forth from a young free mind. However, my mother gave her help to deepen my vision later (which is given in the next chapter).

As a small boy, my mother often took me with her when she went shopping and sightseeing in the city. We walked together in the city streets, and went to see many different kinds of temples and churches so I could learn about them. She showed me the baptism in a Baptist church. She took me to see the practice of the stations of the cross in a Catholic church. She showed me the open house of a new Buddhist temple. I had many opportunities to see other religious practices and customs. She also let me freely observe the religious festivals of folk Taoism in my hometown. When I was young, I was emotionally involved in the excitement of the colorful festival parades on the streets.

After I was ten years old, I was capable of reading novels. I also had some understanding of human emotional patterns from watching Chinese operas. At that time, I considered that I understood life very well. When I demonstrated some pride about my understanding of life, my mother thought it was time for me to begin to learn spiritually. Here, I describe how she instructed me to understand human religious behavior.

My mother showed me that the church holds the image of a man as God. However, she guided me to learn that no man is a god unless the man is achieved. Also, no woman is a goddess unless the woman is achieved. Although the male-dominated society makes man a god, it is a spiritual goal for each man to achieve godliness. Sometimes, a man's world makes a beautiful girl into a goddess. That is man's fantasy and is not necessary truthful, just beautiful.

In spiritual learning, one needs first to learn what spiritual reality is. Because spiritual reality has no form, people usually need something like a conception, idea or image to achieve an understanding of it. So what western culture calls God is just an idea to help people understand spiritual reality. The image of God as a powerful king or father is also just a conception or idea to promote understanding, but it is not the reality itself. Truthfully speaking, God is the spiritual nature of each individual.

Each individual's spiritual nature comes from universal spiritual nature. The idolization or personification of spiritual nature is the religious skill that attempts to shape the inexpressible universal spiritual nature for people's understanding. It is out of a reluctant situation that the wise one teaches the subtle truth to undeveloped people, because he knows that the concepts and images can be misleading. However, words or pictures must be used to help people understand. This is called "Using the false to teach the truth." In different countries and regions of the world, different terms, conceptions and images are all metaphors used to demonstrate the one subtle truth. The idolization of a teacher, etc., is also the application of the same skill. The teacher serves as an example in awakening each individual's own internal spiritual nature.

In western religion, people mention God. They pray to God and worship God. Those practices are designed to wake up an individual's internal spiritual nature. However, it is unwise to turn these practices into fixed rituals and to hold firmly onto any description of God. By being bound to ritual and description, people become unwise. Doing something as a ritual is unwise because life is flowing, not rigid. Each day is new, and the purpose of doing a practice may not meet the situation of a new day.

Before spiritual development, people are attached to rituals. They believe in the exact descriptions of spiritual nature. This makes them unable to reach the truth that the wise one wishes to teach them. The real help that rituals and descriptions offer comes from understanding the meaning behind them.

The church tells of original sin and the need for baptism. Original sin was when the human ancestors Adam and Eve did not follow God's commandment, but ate the fruit of wisdom. This made God angry and he chased them out of Eden. In truth, Eden presents the metaphor of this beautiful world. The ritual of baptism is to teach people to wash away the original sin from the human ancestors. Unless it is deeply understood by people, it does not actually help them much.

All religions, from all races and regions, have a similar conception of God and creation and so forth. Each religion has its own set of concepts, images and names. God, Brahman, universal spirits, Buddha, Allah, etc. are some of the names. Although there are many names, the reality is one. It is the natural spiritual reality within each individual. Even though it is inside people, it is also universal. When it comes to universal spiritual nature, nobody has more and nobody has less. No race has more and no race has less.

In teaching, communicating or transmitting the existence of universal spiritual nature through concepts, some do better and are more skillful. However, that is the painting on the surface; most religious teachings and rituals are irrelevant to the deep reality.

Most important, whenever you enter a society, a community or a special region where people gather for worship, you respond appropriately with your spiritual nature. This means that you observe the customs of the people around you whether you agree with them or not. When you understand the true meaning is at the reversed direction of these ornamental displays, look inside yourself.

God is within. God is not outside yourself. God is not a ritual. God is not the ornamental layout. The ornamental layout creates an atmosphere. People earnestly wish to reach the deepest, innermost spiritual energy within themselves, and some turn to ritual to try to find it. However, ritual is useless unless you understand the meaning behind the ritual. If you reach this point, all religion can be of service. If not directly to yourself, at least it is of some help to some people on some level.

The first thing you need to understand is what is Godly or what is your own spiritual nature. The second thing you need to understand is that Eden was the human world before it was twisted to today's mixed place of happiness and unhappiness. Eden is a conception of the world being a beautiful garden. From this, you can understand what the book says: After the humans' downfall, they could not live in Eden, which means they could not maintain their life and the world as beautiful and happy any more. So they were chased into the world; this means they created a bad environment for themselves. Their beautiful and peaceful world became an ocean of troubled water.

Please do not be confused by the terms Eden, Heavenly kingdom, spiritual paradise, nirvana or the clear stage of mind. They are all the same place. They are the peacefulness and pure natural spirit within yourself. That is also one of the goals of spiritual cultivation.

Christians wish to cleanse all the guilt, or the original sin, which caused a person to leave the Heavenly place or Eden.   Baptism is supposed to fulfill that function.   A person who is clean can enter 'the Heavenly kingdom.' Basically, baptism is the hope of restoring one's happy life in a beautiful world. That is a psychological fantasy of the human mind.

Judaism's conception of Eden is the same as Christianity's conception of the kingdom of God or Heavenly kingdom. The concept of Eden and the Heavenly kingdom of the Christian world is not different than the spiritual paradise of Amitabha Buddhism. In it, there is no death, there is only eternal life. More truthfully, there is a better world.

The metaphor of Eden always tells one thing: the original spiritual reality of humans was pure and clean.   It was not like that of later human people.   The downfall meant that people could not maintain their spiritual purity to live a spiritual life. To return to a life that is spiritually pure is why people need delivery, salvation or restoration. The words "delivery," "salvation," or "restoration" are all descriptions of the change that takes place when a person returns to original spiritual purity.

Religious leaders whose teaching becomes rote or fossilized do not lead people to understand the beauty of their own spirit. Mindless repetition cannot serve the goal of being able to understand the true spiritual meaning of life and to live a spiritual life.

The western religions first declare that you have sin, then you need salvation. Buddhism first establishes the bitterness of life, and then tells of the need for delivery. No matter where people live, it is after they experience life in the world, and the pressure for survival and to obtain material goods, that they distort their own natures. They build up thick, dark layers of self protection and extend their greed. Thus, they change their original spiritual nature. They begin to compete or engage in violent reaction to gain what they like or think they need. They suffer an internal kind of pressure that comes from unnecessary desire, vanity and ambition. Sooner or later, they become slaves to that unnecessary desire and it runs their lives. All of that causes trouble.

Without using religious rituals, how can you change yourself to return to spiritual purity? It is a process of seeing what is unnecessary in your life. This includes such things as possessions, habits, people, emotions, ways of speaking, desires, attitudes or beliefs, etc. When a person awakens to see what is real, true and necessary in life, and give up what is false, troubling and unnecessary, you can restore purity to yourself. You reach a different place. Some people use external teachings of religion to arrive there. Either way, through religion or by self effort, you arrive at a better life. One of the pitfalls or dangers of religion is to become entrapped by the external teachings and become separated from your own internal truth.

There are two kinds of fruit that can be achieved as a result of living a life. One kind of fruit is evil, and one kind of fruit is wisdom. If you eat the fruit of evil, then you have a downfall. If you eat the fruit of wisdom, then you receive eternal life. The disillusion of Adam and Eve was not because human ancestors ate the fruit from the wisdom tree, it was because they ate the other fruit.

The human body is a tree. The unripe, evil fruit is in the lower branches; this means too much sexual expansion. The fruit of wisdom is on the high branches; you need to grow high to reach it. This means spiritual development.

The vines and lower branches of evil climb on the ground where it is easy to pick the fruit. However, the fruit is not good. If you eat a little bit, it is okay, but if you eat too much, you become sick or die. The fruit on the high branch of the tree receives more sun, moisture and good air. It is the fruit of wisdom, which is a good life.

Eating the fruit of evil is self-destructive. Eating the fruit of wisdom is nutritious for the essence of your life. Learning to be wise is not hard, it just means a change in habit from staying on the level of the fruit of evil. I have described the two life trees in one of my other books, the *Story of Two Kingdoms*.

My mother explained the meaning of baptism to me. She said that it is good for us to be aware of the mistakes we have made that have caused us to be greedy or unkind. Humility comes when you truly see the origin of your mistake and learn how to keep it from happening again. This does not negatively affect your confidence, because you know that you have the potential for change and improvement. Thus it becomes a positive expression of yourself, a kind of confidence. People who live in the world need confidence, but true confidence is different from being overconfident or arrogant.

True confidence comes from knowing your spiritual nature and brings humility in its positive sense. It leads to acceptance and openness. On the other hand, people who are overconfident hardly ever accept good advice from other people because they cannot hear anything except their own mind. That type of confidence is fundamentally sick fruit.

People who have not learned true confidence in spiritual nature are often commanded or pushed around by the people of overconfidence. In other words, people without confidence are pushed around by the people who are overconfident. Neither one of them has attained their own true growth. Both lack of confidence and overconfidence builds the strength of evil groups which conduct people's behavior wrongly and creates trouble. This has happened often in history on both large and small scales. The people of weak confidence follow the people of overconfidence. Neither of them have attained the goal of a healthy life.

As a spiritual student, you need to have confidence in the spiritual nature of the universe. The positive way to have spiritual confidence is to recognize the inadequate wisdom of your small, limited self. You need to learn to be open to what the universe offers, and evaluate it so that you can follow good advice, especially good spiritual advice.

When you begin to awaken spiritually and see your mistakes, you sometimes feel guilt. This happens because you become aware of wrongdoings which were previously kept hidden from yourself. It is okay to see the guilt, but after you become aware of it, see what improvements can be made and let it pass. Do not let the guilt stay with you and become twisted.

Usually people think of wrongdoing as something done to other people. This is true, but wrongdoing is also something you do to yourself. For example, when you are sick, like when you have a cold, it is a wrongdoing because you did not take care of yourself. When your body is damaged for whatever reason, it is a wrongdoing because you did not take care of yourself. Once you accept the awareness of what you are doing incorrectly, then your feeling of guilt will guide you to the correction. Guilt can serve as a warning of your own conscience. Thus, do not block yourself from feeling humility when you make a mistake. By this I mean, once you understand the spiritual depth and inner power of humility, you will not be afraid to admit that it is your own mistake or guilt, but will always use it as a guide to help keep you on the right track of humility. The guilt will show you that you need to learn more and be more careful in the next opportunity.

Once you have humility, it means you are growing in your relationship with the universal spiritual nature, and you will never be overconfident. You shall gain a healthy confidence in life.

The feeling of guilt or inadequacy brings about your growth when you are humble. First you have guilt, then you extend yourself to correct it: I need to wash away all the trouble and mistakes, I need to change myself. It is when you wash away the sense of guilt that you can see clearly and correct the mistake. The initiating teachers of religions knew this, and symbolized it through the ritual of baptism. However, baptism itself is not the cleansing of guilt. The cleansing of guilt happens internally within yourself.

The washing ritual is different in different religions. Baptism started from the Indian people who lived near the Ganges river. Once a year, the people would go down to the river to internally give up their guilt and wash themselves as the symbol for their new purity of spirit. The Catholic church performs the same ritual. It is usually done by a priest sprinkling water on a baby or a believer. A few churches buy big receptacles and fill them with water so the people can immerse their whole bodies. The most serious ritual in esoteric Buddhism or Tibetan Buddhism is similar. It is done by sprinkling or pouring water on a student's head, and is termed obhisecana or murdhahistitka. It is symbolic. Each time the student learns a new thing, the ceremony of sprinkling water is performed. The water is called guan ding.

All these religions perform the ritual of baptism differently, but it is the same ritual. Whether you do an external ritual or not, internally it is valuable for you to recognize or admit a mistake that you have made or some negligence you have committed. We need to be aware there is no way to correct the past, then we need to remind ourselves not to repeat the same mistake.

In learning Tao, you do not have to have the sense of guilt. You also do not have to cleanse the guilt if you live on the normal track of life. Everything is nature. You do not need to do anything to prove yourself or to become holy. You are holy anywhere.

So it is not necessary to participate in a public ritual. A wise student who sees the words used for spiritual purification ceremonies can cleanse his own guilt. He can think about it in his morning meditation. "I need to wash my own soul from the possible contamination from all the past." These thoughts, this decision is the highest cleansing, highest purification, and highest baptism.

One practical way to get help or prevent your life from going beyond the natural life track of normalcy is to read "Tai Shan Kan Yin Pien" in my book, *The Heavenly Way*, which will now be reprinted with the new title, *The Key to Good Fortune is Spiritual Improvement*. If you keep reading it, you shall receive your own spiritual cleansing or baptism. I was guided to read that article when I was a young man. I do not know how many mistakes I made, but during my childhood, I was sometimes disobedient to good advice. That does not mean that I disobeyed, it means I did not take good advice seriously from whoever gave it to me, even my mother and father. I always tested the advice; I tried things myself. I often proved myself wrong, caused mistakes, made trouble, and was negligent and forgetful. Sometime I refused to wear enough clothing or dress correctly and became sick. Or I would overeat, or oversleep and become sluggish. That was all my wrongdoing. But I always thought I was all right and more than perfect. But after making a mistake, it is important to extend your better knowledge not to experience the trouble again.

When I read the "Tai Shan Kan Yin Pien," I started to have some reflection of my own trouble. It took some time before I received the actual benefit. I was awakened to not do the same things as in the past. The article gives practical help. I wish you would refer to that article for your own soul cleansing and purification. Then you will discover that you are a new person, and you will open yourself deeper and develop more space inside your spiritual Heaven within. That is important.

I have seen many people receive help from external religion. Some rascals, irresponsible fellows, nasty individuals and criminals cannot be taught in regular ways. They would find it difficult to learn the spiritual truth directly. Thus, it is easier to help them by means of external religion in whatever form is most fit for their level and stage of internal spiritual evolution. I have seen some rascals become monks or serious followers of religion. For some of them, their behavior or attitude towards life is changed.

Although they are moving from one extreme to another extreme, it is of some help. We cannot say that external religion is totally useless, but people can only go so far with it. You know now that delivery or salvation is internal, but the original sin of spiritual darkness can be performed externally. Churches establish redemption, salvation or delivery because of original sin. Churches teach people that original sin was caused by our human ancestors. They made love, so they established sin, which made God angry. In truth, that is not a correct message. The real message is that original sin is not human ancestors having sex; original sin is each individual's **own ignorance**. It is ignorance or lack of awareness of spiritual reality.

How do we correct our original sin? That is our spiritual undevelopment. We have to open up to search for spiritual truth by listening to all good and truthful spiritual advice. To get rid of original sin means to eliminate spiritual ignorance. Small growing children do not know spiritual reality; they only know they like to eat and play within their capability. Adults lose the connection with their own spiritual nature by living with the limitation of only basically eating and having sex. This is why people need salvation or delivery. This is why you need to do your cultivation as your redemption from the original sin of spiritual ignorance.

The stories presented by the old religions had not reached their maturity. By this I mean, the teachers who taught them were still immature and did not completely understand them, thus, immaturity was reflected in the version of the story. We do not need to condemn them, because the earlier stage of spiritual teachers did their best.

We need to do our best to reach our own truthful spiritual goal. Growing spiritually is not to establish an argument. It is taking a step forward to examine yourself and see what has been reached and what has not.

I would like to repeat a line I have mentioned before. *In learning Tao, you do not have to have the sense of guilt. You also do not have to cleanse the guilt, if you live on the normal track of life. Everything is nature. You do not need to do anything to prove yourself or to reach holiness. You are holy anywhere.*

Chapter 9

Using the False to Learn the True

Q: It is interesting that as a child you learned about many religions. I am sure you were glad that your mother gave you this great depth in learning.

Master Ni: My mother sowed the seeds of further growth for me. But she said it was my natural tendency, and parents or teachers should know the potential of a child or pupil and help the child's own interest. I continued my learning and deepened my understanding as I got older. I would like to share some of it with you now and also more of what I learned from my mother.

My mother guided me to learn that when people are born into the world, everywhere is Eden to them. This is because their minds have not developed yet. The human ancestors were the same as a big nude worm and knew only eating and sex. This does not mean that people did not have human bodies, but in that spiritual stage, they were not much more developed than snakes that wriggled on the ground. Even though they were limited to that kind of behavior, at least they did not have the self brewed poison that human society later developed. Today, people play with thoughts of destroying the world. At least this type of insanity did not exist in ancient human society.

Spiritual awareness is a new growth that also came about in later times. Original sin is the ignorance of knowing only eating and sex; it is physical enjoyment. Through millions of years of evolution, the main performance of human life was still in that direction, because few people attained enough spiritual awareness to be able to arrange their lives in a balanced way. Therefore, there was much war and competition for material opportunity.

Most humans have not yet attained spiritual awareness, so they have not been able to arrange their lives correctly for spiritual development. They do not look for boundless spiritual opportunity, but only look for limited material opportunity. The limitation of materialism is not only outside; the limitation is also inside. For example, someone can eat ten slices of bread when they are very hungry, but if they eat ten loaves, that is spiritual ignorance.

We do not think humans can live on air only. Material provisions are of course important to all. At least not every person can learn to live only on air, because most individuals need different forms of energy. That is the reality of human life. Most people need to eat some meat; spiritual truth does not mean everybody has to become a vegetarian or an ascetic and give everything up. However, most people make their own troubles, or do not achieve happiness, because of their emotional desires. Emotional desire is called spiritual ignorance.

The original sin of Eden was actually people's spiritual ignorance. It can be understood that Eden was no more than a protected place in which neither happiness nor pain existed; there was only ignorance. After the fall from Eden, people themselves rejected being like crawling or wriggling worms. Spiritual growth began when they stood up to receive sky energy. Then they developed to become human. When they understood spirituality, their hearts lit up.

We do have ignorance. We cannot deny the original 'happiness' in Eden as the religious leaders imagined was original sin. In spiritual reality, there was no happiness, but there was the sin of spiritual undevelopment. If people remain in ignorance and want to be protected, that is practically the same as spiritual original sin, because those people do not receive their spiritual growth.

People of spiritual development do not have to repent the original sin. Because the original sin is non-existent, people need not be afraid to experience a life that is full of trouble. It is the opposite or better reality to live in the world rather than to live in the world like Eden. By living in the real world, not the imagined Eden, your spiritual reflection begins, and this leads you to receive spiritual growth. It is not the conception of original sin, but the mistakes we make in everyday life that cause us to become troubled and suffer.

A person with correct spiritual vision will honor the writings in "Tai Shan Kan Yin Pien." It is helpful for those interested in internal salvation, redemption or delivery.

Do not laugh at the inferior spiritual stage of most people, the clumsy pseudo-spiritual books of immature religions or the spiritual conventions that provide only childish stories. People do their best. Now it is your turn to do your best. If you wish to teach and help others, the most important thing is to help yourself first.

When my mother took me to the Catholic church, I saw people crawling on their hands and knees, moving from station to station, praying and yelling with strong emotion for the suffering of Jesus as he went through crucifixion. This made an impression on me. I thought that those people had trouble. Then my mother guided me to know the reasons why the people acted that way, and I thought it was irrational. How could it be of any use?

The church conventionally teaches that Jesus was the only son of God and that because God was angry, he decided to destroy the world. However, after he made his decision to destroy the world; then he sent his only son there. This seemed contradictory to me. He made a plan for Jesus to be crucified and used Jesus' blood as a ransom or redemption for the worldly people's sin. Then the worldly people received salvation. It is such a clumsy story.

Actually, it is a clumsy rendition of a story that does have some spiritual meaning. It is a metaphor for the internal spiritual reality of an individual. It is not God who will destroy the earthly world, it is people who will destroy the world. The world, for each person, is one's body. Also, you have the only son of God within yourself; it is your own spiritual essence or inner spiritual being. It is within yourself. You need to respect it and not neglect it. Learn to keep it from falling into a worldly spiritual state.

The Bible says that each of us is God's child; nobody is not a child of god. But if everybody is a child of God, then how can Jesus be the only child of God? Jesus can still be the only one because he is a metaphor for the spiritual energy within each individual. He is the only one because only one spiritual nature in the universe simultaneously exists inside of each person. Jesus carried the mission of awakening each individual's internal spiritual nature. Awakening the individual spiritual energy within each individual self is the mission of any spiritual teacher. The function of spiritual teaching is to awaken the inner god or spiritual nature. If universal spiritual energy is God, then the spiritual energy living in the individual is the only son of the father god or the mother goddess.

A teaching is awakening energy. Jesus' work presents spiritual awakening energy. All spiritual teachers work in the same direction as Jesus; there is no difference. Surely in different regions, there are varied religious customs and different names, but their purpose is still one. Any bona fide spiritual teacher presents the awakening energy of God. Thus if you are a true spiritual teacher, you are the manifestation of individual spirituality to awaken each individual spirit. That is called the universal spiritual echo.

When East Indian people say Om, they say it is God's name or it is God. You do not trust it as a mature explanation of God or of the divine spirit. However, the word Om can be a spiritual echo of the person if used correctly. Spiritual echo is individual internal response. What other words besides the word Om is a spiritual echo? There are many. Except for noise made by machines, all voices and sounds are spiritual echoes. The hum of wind passing through the trees, the crash of the ocean waves breaking on the shore and the melodious trickle of the rivers and streams, are all spiritual echoes. Not only chanting, humming, mantras, prayers etc., are spiritual echoes; all sounds are echoes. However, God is reachable without an echo. God is your own internal spiritual source.

The church says that Jesus was crucified for you. In truth, it is not the external Jesus who was crucified. The wrongdoing of your past is crucified. A spiritually awakened teaching awakens your spiritual nature. At that moment of the crucifixion, you are spiritually awakened. The metaphor or meaning of the crucifixion is not that somebody shed blood to pay for the wrongdoing of somebody else. It is a spiritual metaphor to show the division between the two stages of spiritual undevelopment and development. Before the internal crucifixion of your wrongdoing, you were a guilty person because of your ignorance. Now you are awakened to your own spiritual nature.

The crucifixion and baptism are both metaphors for spiritual cleansing or purification. The crucifixion happened to your evil doing and the old bad habits of your past. Any type of spiritual practice as internal cleansing done in an intensified way could be presented by the image of the crucifixion of old evil habits of the past. The old Jesus dies, and new spiritual energy is growing new life within you.

Spiritual symbols can be useful. For example, the sign of the cross can be a reminder to constantly bury your ignorance and spiritual confusion. It can be a reminder to constantly purify yourself. It can also be a symbol or reminder of your new spiritual life, which was born at the moment of your spiritual awakening. In ancient times the sign of the cross did not mean crucifixion; it symbolized the shining sun. To awakened people, the sign of the cross has two meanings: first, it means the old past has died, and second, it means the spiritual life is newly born. It does not worship death, which is what happens when people worship the crucifixion. You receive no protection from the cross. It may carry the abstract image of the sun; but you receive protection from the sun as the real energy. Your new life has more opportunities for higher spiritual attainment.

We need to cultivate to achieve ourselves. We need to get rid of the old to attain the new. Our new life depends on spiritual cultivation.

The above knowledge is the instruction my mother gave to me about western religion. On various occasions, she took me to different Taoist folk festivals, Buddhist temples and churches. She give me instruction about customs of oriental or Chinese Buddhism, and customs of the temples.

Once I asked my mother, "Does god get angry? Does god build hell fire to burn the people who disobey him?"

My mother gave me some most valuable instruction. She guided me to learn that "In depth, hell fire means the disharmony between your internal spiritual nature and external life. Most people's behavior is the result of impulse. Impulsive behavior brings hell fire.

"Both God and the desire of the mind live within the same individual. When there is disharmony between the mind and the body, God becomes angry. Many people end their lives by their own hand or some other way, slowly or rapidly, but always unnaturally. It is due to internal disharmony of the person's thoughts or ignorance that made the spiritual energy or God withdraw. Then they die.

"So the spiritual practice to do every day is to remind your mind of internal harmony of the three spheres of your being: body, mind and spirit. Spiritual energy is the most important partner. Without developing your spiritual energy, you only have your mind and body, and each will go in a different direction. That brings inner disharmony.

"Spiritual cultivation is a lifetime enterprise. Not for one day or one minute should you stop cultivating. Spiritual cultivation is always to look for harmony and the balance of the three spheres. Spirits are not an external existence. Your spirit is the essence at the top value of everything in your life. You do not need to treat your spirit separately as a different being. You only need to be sure that with each projection of your mind and each of your behaviors, your spiritual energy is contained or present. You need to watch for your harmony. Look for obedience of your spiritual nature, not by overextending your desire for mind or emotion, or overextending your physical energy for physical fun. Those will cause disharmony within your life being.

"The religious concept of the big God in the sky is the same as the god or essence of your life being. In reality, God is the god of your life being. Spiritual disharmony or disorder is the same reality of incorrect life. It is the same bad reality that destroys the world. God will not destroy the world. If your world is destroyed, you are the one who does it because your unbalanced mind makes it happen. Your mind is the dictator; when it loses its clarity and balance, trouble happens. Each individual who learns spiritually does not need the superficial help of church or temple. They give only external teaching.

"Most individuals need to have time for self inspection and to do spiritual practice. Most people need to look for the internal harmony of their life being. That is the secret of success and a healthy life."

Some people live a successful life. A successful life happens when a person attains internal harmony. First we need to define success. Most people think that success is owning a big house, driving a big car and having many servants and much enjoyment. However, personal success is individual. It can be spiritual attainment, physical health, good relationships with your family, harmonious relationships with the world, no misbehavior and so forth.

If you are looking for the standard of success, you need to read the *Stepping Stones for Spiritual Success*. Once you study that book, then you will know what you would like to reach. An individual who reaches success must earn internal harmony or harmony with God.

People argue with other people because people argue within themselves all the time. In a family, congress, the nation, and the international world, everywhere you hear arguments and confrontations. It is because people have lost harmony. If any big thing, small thing, big being or small being loses harmony, they will not attain success. The secret of success is internal or spiritual harmony. Success can be defined as something that you enjoy for a long period of time. Success is not temporary which you enjoy for a short while and is soon gone like the wind.

When people are disharmonious with their inner gods, they are also disharmonious with the external world. This can be seen anywhere in the world: in the east, west, middle east or anywhere.

The most important achievement for each individual or a big society is to attain harmony with God. Thus, the building of external religious expansion is purposeless. Unfortunately, different churches, temples and religions, all acting in their individual interest, look for individual expansion without keeping in harmony with universal God.

If my spiritual advice has any value, it is to directly promote two things. The first goal of spiritual attainment is that each individual have clear spiritual vision so as not to be confused by different religions. The person who has clear spiritual vision can never become entrapped by the small practice of a religion. This person uses these religions only to borrow and use their metaphors and establishment to nurture and cultivate the inner truth. In other words, in our genuine spiritual practice, we use external things such as statues, pictures, rituals, etc., but we do not need to extend ourselves to accepting or becoming involved in the religion itself. Borrowing the religious practice to nurture our internal spiritual energy is enough. That is the first understanding to teach the spiritual student.

The second goal is to attain harmony with the inner gods, individually and in a worldly sense. Today, God is angry. God yells and says he is going to punish you in hell's fire. Do you know what? Hell's fire is only anger. Anger is the fire of hell. There is no difference between anger and hell; they are the same.

For people who have not yet truthfully attained their spiritual growth, God is the human ego. After you are truthfully reunited with your own spiritual nature, God is your own spiritual nature. Only egotistical gods get upset by people who do not follow or obey them. Until they reach for spiritual development, each person establishes a big ego. This big ego wishes to give life to the one who obeys and to destroy whoever disobeys. Each person is like that when they are still undeveloped. I have seen wives and husbands be like that. Then if they do not get along, the more power- ful one says, "Get out, I will not give you support any more." It is the same pattern in society and in the international world where development has not yet occurred. Find out how not to be disharmonious with your inner god or disharmonious with the universal god.

The people of swollen ego who have not attained inner clarity and balance live in the fire of hell. Those people are mad; they are crazy. Hitler and the warlords of Japan during WWII were crazy to look for personal expansion without looking for internal harmony with God.

I borrow the language of various religions to teach the truth. People may still need to borrow the different forms and different languages of religion to awaken to the un- formed spiritual truth within. Such a person could be a wise person or an achieved Taoist. A Taoist does not create anything to fool people. Lincoln said, "You can fool some of the people some of the time, and you can fool all of the people some of the time, but you cannot fool all of the people all of the time." But religions are the exception, because they have caused negativity and brought disharmony among people. This is maybe not necessarily true because not all people are involved with churches and religions.

Careful spiritual self cultivation will restore harmony between an individual and his or her inner god. I mean, harmony brings clear vision, thus a person of self awakening with high spiritual attainment has clear spiritual vision. He or she must have harmony with the personal individual god. The individual god is also the universal god. I borrowed these words, but the truth is yours.

Chapter 10

Love Can Be Fulfilled Rationally

Q: When you were a spiritual student, were you allowed to have emotionally enjoyable moments?

Master Ni: Many of them. Except I was not allowed to be crazy and barbaric when I was a young, active boy.

In China, there are many kinds of opera. Some operas are related to historical events, so if you have some historical knowledge, then you understand and enjoy the opera greatly. Other operas are folk tales. In any kind of Chinese opera, all the action is portrayed symbolically. It is not like western opera where a door is a door, a room is a room and a garden is a garden. In Chinese opera, there is nothing on the stage.   The postures or motions of the actors and actresses tell the entire story. For example, when someone is riding a horse, there is no horse on the stage; you see only a riding whip in the hand of the rider.

In ancient time, young girls were protected and lived upstairs; thus in the opera performance, a maidservant must go up and down the stairs symbolically. She must take the same number of steps to go up and to come back down. It is all symbolic; it takes a certain cultivation to learn to enjoy it. Is it not interesting?

All children, myself included when I was young, mostly enjoyed only the symbolic martial arts part, with warring, fighting, somersaults and acrobatics. We understood that type of symbolism perfectly.

One opera company consisting only of women started a few counties away in the same province of Chekiang. Women played the men's roles. There was no man except in the band. Other than this opera company, all the troupes of opera performers consisted of men.

There was one opera that was popular almost nationwide. It was a love story of a man and a woman, Liang and Ju. It was a favorite play of the Chinese people. I would like to relate the story to you.

During the Jing Dynasty, from around 205-419 A.D., most Chinese people were still simple. They enjoyed a life of farming with nature's support, peace, beautiful scenery and people's kindness. People really enjoyed their lives. In the educational system, there were schools for boys, but beginning in their childhood, girls helped their mothers and learned housework. They learned cooking, sewing, making shoes, and weaving. Women who could do such things and care for all members of a family were of great help and were respected.

There was a rich family who lived in the countryside with many children. Ju was the ninth daughter of the family; she was lovely and smart. She heard that there was a school about two day's journey away. She was ambitious to attend the school and learn as the boys did. But in the conventional society of her time, women were over-protected and did not go to school. Even coeducation in the United States has a short history. Ju had ambitions to receive a literary education with the boys. Her family definitely refused.

This did not discourage her. She had a plan to convince her father that her ambition was not unreasonable. She became sick and lay in bed. The father and mother became anxious and sent for a doctor. The young doctor who came said, "I am good at taking care of women's problems." The father and mother let him see the daughter.

He examined Ju. When he returned to the parents, he said, "Here is a prescription for your daughter's recovery," but the prescription contained something too hard to obtain. In his conversation with the father, an argument was almost started. The father insisted, "My daughter is not really sick, it is just a small illness, and she does not need such a serious prescription."

The doctor said, "Even with my good herb formula, your daughter will not get well unless her wish is fulfilled; then everything will be all right."

The father said, "That is ridiculous. My daughter's wish is to study with the boys. How can that be fulfilled?"

The doctor said, "It can be fulfilled if she dresses like a boy. Nobody will know."

The father refused the idea. "If she were to dress like a boy, I and everyone else would know. If I thought she could do it, I would agree and let her go, but I do not think she is smart enough."

The doctor then took off his hat and said, "I am your daughter."

This made the father angry, but on the other hand, he really understood his daughter's wish. Finally, the father agreed to let Ju go to school. "When you finish your education, just come home." He bid her to be careful. He said, "You are a girl. Even if you do well in school, nobody can know you are a woman. Be careful, do not fall in love with any boy." She had promised the father, "I will never do that, please let me go. I will be safe, I will not make trouble. I will not disgrace the family name." Both sides were correct. "Whatever you do," her father cautioned, "Consider how you might make your parents worry."

Ju was happy. She packed her luggage, dressed in her boys clothes and started on her way with her maidservant. On the road, she met a boy named Liang who was about her age and who was also going to attend school. They made acquaintance and went to school together. They arranged to share living quarters at the dorm, and they began a friendship which would become very close.

Liang and Ju stayed together in school for three years. Their relationship was limited to friendship; although sometimes they slept in one room, nothing happened between them. That was because during the whole time that they lived and studied together, Liang never thought his companion was a girl. Ju did nothing to reveal her secret, and neither Liang nor anybody else knew. Liang was a real gentleman; he earned respect and a strong love from the disguised girl student.

Ju always felt happy around him. It was a great friendship, pure as white paper. It was nothing more than an innocent, friendly love.

After three happy years had passed, the girl's father sent a servant to the school with a message that she was to come home. Ju was obedient to her parents and she prepared to leave. Just before leaving, the girl visited the wife of a teacher and gave her a letter and some personal belongings. She said, "After I leave, please give these to my roommate."

On the day she left, Liang went with her part of the way. At that time, almost all travel was walking, so they walked together on the beautiful country road. Ju found it hard to tell Liang that she was a woman and that she loved him and wished to marry him. She kept trying, subtly and indirectly, to tell him the truth. However, no matter what she said, he always smiled and rebuked her, saying, you are being silly.

They walked eighteen li (about 6 miles) together, then they reluctantly said goodbye to each other. Finally Liang turned back to return to school and Ju went on her way home. When he arrived back at school, someone told Liang that their teacher's wife wanted to see him, so he went to see her right away.

The teacher's wife gave him Ju's letter and personal belongings, saying, "In the whole world, who is closest to you?" He replied, "Besides my mother, my roommate was my closest friend. I am going to miss him, now that he has left." The woman said, "If your roommate was a girl, would you marry her?" Liang replied, "Now you are being silly too. You know, all the way I walked with my friend today, he kept asking me similar foolish questions. I began to get annoyed about that. How can he be a girl? If it were true, surely we will marry each other." The teacher's wife said, "Your roommate is not silly; you are. Open the letter."

The letter said, "During the three years we studied together, I came to love your personality. I deeply appreciate each moment of your life and the presence of your life being. I almost cannot live without you. If you have the same feeling about me, please come to my family and propose to my father. With my father's agreement, we shall be happily married. Under Heaven, nothing could be happier than you and I together. Here are my earrings. I had to take them off so you would not know I am a girl. The earrings that I did not wear for many years now belong to you. Please come as quickly as possible."

This startled Liang. It made him, on the one hand, very excited. On the other hand, he thought, "How stupid I was!"

He decided to go immediately to her home and propose marriage.

Unfortunately, at that time, Liang's family also sent a servant bearing a message. His mother was sick. Naturally he would first take care of his sick mother, then visit Ju's family. So he packed and went home to take care of his mother. He was happy. "After my mother is well, I am going to meet my friend and marry her."

Waiting for him to arrive made each day as long as a thousand years for Ju. However, because she was the age to be married, her father began to look for a suitable marriage opportunity for her. Ju tried to refuse and postpone the situation in many ways, but the father and mother said, "This time, we do not agree with what you say. It is time for you to be married."

Ju did not dare tell her father about Liang, because before she left to go to school, her father had made her promise not to become interested in any boy.

Anything can be forbidden, but one thing that cannot be stopped even if forbidden is the love between a young man and a young woman. Ju hesitated to tell her father the truth. She expected that when Liang came for courtship, everything would be clear when her parents saw what a good person he was. She knew that they would be satisfied with her choice.

Unfortunately, the news had spread that her father was looking for a suitor for her. When a powerful duke with a good family and social position asked her father for Ju's hand in marriage, her father agreed. "This is a good family and the son is well educated. He would be a good choice for my daughter."

Marriage agreements were serious at that time. Once made, they could not be changed. He told his daughter, "Your marriage is decided. It will be the first son of Ma's family. They are a reputable family, have a strong social background and a well educated son. You should be happy about your father's choice for you; this is how much your father can do for you."

This was a shock to Ju. She objected strongly, but it was of no use. She did not know why Liang did not come.

She was not sure whether the friendship was false, or whether the man could love her only as a friend, as a boy. She had all kinds of thoughts. She did not know what happened. At that time, correspondence was difficult. Letters were sent only by special messenger.

The next day, Liang arrived. Ju greeted him in the family room, and then brought him to the living room of her living quarters. He was happy, but she was as stiff as a stone. He did not understand what had happened to her. He said, "I rushed over here to see you and propose marriage. You are my woman; we will live together forever and love each other forever."

Ju shook her head. "It is too late," she said. "Why didn't you come immediately?"

"What's too late?" he asked. "My mother was sick, so I had to go take care of her. After she was well, I did not delay one second. I came immediately. What is too late?"

She replied, "I could not tell my father about you because he is so strict. My parents started looking for a suitor for me. A powerful, influential family forced my father to accept the marriage proposal, and so my marriage has been decided. Now you come, but there is no way to change the promise. I wish I were two persons, then I could meet my obligation to my parents and also be with you."

"This is misfortune!" Liang responded with great frustration and disappointment. With all the beautiful, sweet thoughts in his mind, he suddenly understood that this was bad news. It was like raising a man up to the clouds, then letting go so he falls down to the rocks at the foot of the mountain.

Ju said, "Please accept this new reality. Do not feel disappointed. My heart belongs to you. My soul belongs to you. My love will never be withdrawn from you. Even if someone forces me to marry, they will marry a heartless woman, because my heart always is at your side."

Liang told her, "I wished to come here to enjoy the sweet dew from Heaven. Now this is my bitter blood." He was angry, sad and disappointed. She forced herself to help him to drink all the best wine, because there was nothing that could be done. Then he left.

She stayed at home to face the situation of misery and the approaching of the wedding. However, her heart followed Liang. Every day, tears dropped from her eyes. The marriage day was fast approaching.

One day, a messenger came from Liang's family with news that Liang was dead. He could not tolerate the grief; he had vomited lots of blood and died. So a servant was sent to tell Ju the bad news with Liang's last words. The message read: "In this life, we have no hope to be paired like the swallows, flying together over the lake and sitting in the willow trees. Maybe in my next life, if we come back again to live, I can marry you. I feel deep sorrow. I could pay the three years of deep love as friends with my immeasurable deep love back to you now."

The marriage arrangement had been a shock to Liang, and now his death shocked Ju. With great sadness, the girl decided in her heart what should be done. Although they could not be together in this life, they would not be separated forever. She held fast to her wish to be joined with him. No matter what was in front of her, she would do what she had secretly decided.

On the day of her marriage, she went to talk with her father. She said, "Liang was my best friend in the world. Now you ask me to marry a different person. It was my fault that I did not tell you immediately; it was too difficult to tell you I had a lover."

Ju's parents said, "If we had known we would not have made the arrangements; but now, we could not help. We have already accepted the gift and betrothal to Ma's family. Now you have got to be married."

Ju continued, "But now Liang has died for me. At least I need to visit him to worship in his tomb before I can be married."

Her father said, "Nonsense, how can that be? You are going to your husband's house."

She said, "You will carry my corpse over there unless you let me fulfill this wish to make my personal offering to his tomb."

He had to yield because Ju's emotion was so strong. He loved his daughter, and helped her prepare the offering to the dead person. It is Chinese custom to make a white lantern and some paper items as symbol of clothes, money, or whatever. So the bride won the last battle with the family. She got into the marriage sedan and they took her to the tomb.

She saw freshly dug dirt gathered over the tomb covering her lover's coffin. She could never see him again. The great sadness cut her like a sharp knife. At the tomb of her lover, she made a solemn offering and read a mourning song she had written.

> *We saw each other last at my home.*
> *Now we cannot see each other again.*
> *We cannot be together or grow old together.*
> *I thought Heaven would grant my wish*
>   *for marriage to you.*
> *But our names were not in the Heavenly Marriage Book.*
> *Instead of the happy magpie singing good news,*
>   *the black crow sings of misfortune.*
> *I hoped to reach the shore of happiness,*
>   *but the bridge over the river has been broken.*
> *My marriage sedan does not take me to marry you;*
>   *instead I wear white to mourn you.*

After finishing the mourning song, she called his name. "Liang, now I cannot see you. I can see only a heap of dirt over your body. I called Heaven, I called earth, but I could not call you back to life. My decision cannot be changed. I cannot marry any other person. My love, we could not be together in life, but we can be together in death." At that time, the sky started to darken; a storm appeared with strong winds and loud thunder. The people around Ju were wet by rain and saddened for her weeping, but in that moment, the girl gathered all her strength and hit her head on the tombstone, killing herself on the spot. All the people were stunned as though hit by thunder. As they watched, the soul of the young girl joined with another soul, and they both transformed into butterflies. One was green, the other was more flowery. They flew high in the sky until they disappeared.

In another version of this same story, at the moment she mourned him and extended her wish, the tomb suddenly broke open and she went right into it. Many people tried to save her and pulled on her skirt, but pieces of her skirt changed into butterflies with green and red spots on the wings and flew all over the sky. You can imagine the souls of the lovers forever existing between Heaven and earth.

My mother took us to see that opera. I saw sisters, neighbors, friends and daughters all crying there. Many middle-aged people's memories were refreshed and they missed their past lovers. Even if they did not have a real experience in love, they still had an imaginary one when they were young. All shed tears for that story.

Almost every year, the story of Liang and Ju was brought back to the stage to make all women tearful. This love story was a tragedy. If all the tears were accumulated, it would turn a piece of desert into an oasis. However, no immortal has tried to do that.

Q: Master Ni, what was your reaction to seeing the opera?

Master Ni: I made trouble for my sisters and the neighbor girls who watched the opera with us. They insisted that it was Liang's fault. I said, it was mostly Ju's fault. I gave the reason why: Ju was a tomboy. When she decided to go to school, she was so determined that her parents could not stop her. After her parents arranged the marriage, she was still determined and before the marriage went to make an offering at Liang's tomb. She was also determined at the last moment to hit her head on the tombstone. But she was not determined to marry Liang. She was determined in the less important matters. If she had been determined to marry Liang, there would have been no tragedy of his death and no broken heart of her father and mother. All would have been avoided. Her weakness had a reason: her father's word had been given to other people. It was a small reason for her being weak. If she had been determined again, then trouble would have been avoided.

In argument, all the girls insisted that Liang was a weakling, so it was the man's fault. I lost the argument because my mother had told me that men should give only understanding to what women say. A man should learn not to argue with people. People need to be understood rather than argued with and won over. That was a rule in ancient Chinese society. Also, argument is not my nature.

So every year, we repeated my comment on Ju, but I always lost to a group of girls in a tongue fight. However, there was a true story that I thought supported my view.

About 3 or 4 miles away from my hometown, there was a businessman in the lumber business who was quite prosperous. Each time I went to the city with my father, we walked past the businessman's house on our way home. He and his wife always came out to greet my father. My father stood there and chatted a little while, then we continued on our way. They usually invited us to go into their house, but my father did not like to do so. He always declined, saying, "It is late, we need to go home now." Once, when we arrived home, my mother asked me where we had been and what I had seen and learned that was new. I told her about the people who greeted us warmly, and invited us to their house to receive a special treat.

My mother suddenly laughed. "Oh, your father has a special relationship with them," she said. "When the man was young, he was smart and capable, but he did not know what to do with his life. He just kept wandering around. Once, he fell in love with a girl who is now his wife. Her family was well off, and she was already betrothed to another rich family. But when the girl and this young man met each other, they fell in love.

"The parents strongly objected to the couple's union, for two reasons: first, the arrangements were already made for her to marry somebody else's son. Second, the man was no good because he could not do anything, and not only that, he was also poor. Thus, they told their daughter, 'What happiness can you have with him?'

"They arranged the wedding date with the rich man. The wedding was to be several months later, because it would take some time to make the necessary jewelry and special new clothes for the marriage. Although the two true lovers wished to see each other, the father and mother did not allow it. Several days before the wedding, they simply locked the daughter upstairs, and did not allow her to come down for any reason. The man knew about her marriage, but he felt love so deeply within him, he was even in pain.

"Finally, he discussed the situation with his friends, and made a plan. He wrote a note and put it on a stone. He went to the back alley at the girl's house and threw the stone through the upstairs window where she was staying. The girl read the simple message. 'If you love me, tonight I will wait for you below your window. You jump and I will catch you on the ground. If you do not love me, forget me. I wish you to be happy.'

"The struggle in the girl's heart had been going on for some time. She was just in the pain of not being able to find a way to marry the true lover. Now, this was the last decision she needed to make. She was decisive and responsible in love, so she prepared herself to go with him.

"The man went there during the night with four friends. Each friend held one corner of a strong blanket for her to jump into. She started by throwing down some luggage, but after she had sent down several bags, the man said, "We don't need any more luggage; just you!" The girl jumped down into the blanket, and the man carried her away. He left the things she had thrown down, thinking that they did not need them. But his friends picked some of them up and brought them along.

"The couple stayed together and declared that they were married. However, the man still had no job, and he did not know what he was going to do to support his wife. He happened to see my father and described his problem. My father laughed, and said, 'You were determined to marry your wife and your wife was determined to marry you. Determination is the first important foundation for a successful life. So let us discuss what you would like to do.'

"My father continued, 'First of all, you are not scholarly, but you are strong. Second, you need to gather some money as capital to do whatever business you are going to undertake.' Finally my father had an idea and continued, 'You know that the city is next to a "cup" river with a deep ravine. The mountains along both shores of the river are so full of trees, they are home to the logging industry. The river carries the logs down from the mountains to the buyers. If you would like to do that, I know someone in the logging business. My name can be used as a guarantee for the first purchase. Usually if you buy some lumber, you need to pay cash, now if you use my guarantee, you do not need to pay cash immediately.'

"The man followed my father's instruction and went over to see the mountain. He met with the friends of my father who were in the logging business. On one side of the mountain, his group cut the trees and used a branding iron like a cattle brand to mark the ones that were his. Then they put them into the river and let the logs flow downriver next to our city. Then the man caught the branded logs and put them up for sale. He was an active, cheerful person, and the business was not hard for him. People bought goods from him, so he sold them, and paid the money back. He did this again and again."

When I saw them, they were middle-aged people. They had five children and were quite rich. It was determination that made his life achieved. I use this story to support my view that it was Ju's fault. But I was still a loser in the argument, because the girls said Liang should have been determined like the lumber man and taken action to do what was necessary.

I would like to tell you the truth and the spiritual learning that can come from the story of Liang and Ju. Is the story true? The story is not true. A real man named Liang lived and died in that county. He was a good magistrate and was greatly loved by the people. It also happened that a good family had a daughter who died in the same county, maybe even in the same year. But the two individuals did know not each other. People put their names together and made up the story after their deaths. Their tombs may still exist. The story is pure literature, but most young Chinese believe it is true.

I requested the spiritual meaning of the story of Liang and Ju from my mother. Later I understood that it really does not matter how the lovers became butterflies. In my hometown, there was a special kind of butterfly that would always be seen in pairs. People fanatically nicknamed those butterflies Liang and Ju.

In my spiritual teaching, I use this story to tell about the important company of mind and soul in one's life. They cannot be separated. If one dies, the other would die too.

Most people's mind and soul are close together but do not know each other. When people cultivate themselves spiritually, union of mind and soul will be fortified. This was my mother's instruction when I asked the spiritual meaning of the touching opera. She made sure that I understood. "This you need to learn: during all emotions, real or unreal, you need to keep calm. Emotional transfer can make people mad, sad, cry or feel happy. Drama writers use this skill. Religious leaders also use this skill. Politicians know to use this skill to get what they want, too." People of spiritual cultivation live above this level. You can correctly guide people's emotion in a constructive direction. Never fool people or conduct them to a negative end.

Chapter 11

The Attainment of Inner Clarity

Q: Could you tell us about your mother's essential practice and her personal spiritual achievement?

Master Ni: The last time I visited my parents, I had attained some life experience that I could combine with my spiritual learning. I produced a formula for myself to minimize my mistakes, as my own instruction to myself. I wished to know if my parents thought my plan was good. Thus, I presented the following to my mother:

Spiritual Practice of Reaching Success

Ordinary uncertain behavior

Need -> Action -> Either positive or negative result

Successful behavior:

Need -> Examination of the need -> Do not choose anything that has less than 55% certainty for success -> As the action proceeds, retain the flexibility to change it or to stop it -> By following the above steps, the result will be positive.

Effective action means to control good, useful and proper action, to keep your mind objective and not to expect too high a result.

The Practice of the Successful Life:

1. Decrease to the least all kinds of combat in your life.
2. Break off the trouble and obstacle of physical illness, evil spirits, or long-related resentment from personal or business relationships and social life.
3. The Inner Light is nurtured by the centered and unshakable vision that can overcome all possible mistakes.

134 The Mystical Universal Mother

My mother nodded her head to express approval, but she asked, "You pointed out not to risk something that was not 55% sure. How do you avoid miscalculation?"

My answer was, "Attain inner clarity."

She only smiled. Although I could talk about inner clarity as easy as picking up an orange on the table, I discovered that I could not attain inner clarity unless I had an objective understanding of a situation.

The goal of my mother's spiritual cultivation was internal intuitive knowledge. External knowledge is what somebody teaches you. Internal knowledge is what you know from inside without the need of anyone to teach it to you or tell you. This was my mother's number one spiritual goal. She believed that you can really learn nothing from outside to equip yourself for always living an effective life. Unless you develop your internal knowledge, external knowledge can mean only some help or assistance in certain circumstances.

The second spiritual goal of my mother's cultivation was the freedom to come and the freedom to go. This means for her soul to be able to enter and exit from her body at will.

Most people look for blessing or immortality to be their spiritual goal. In general Taoist cultivation, people look to live long and happy lives and to enjoy their health. My mother believed that blessings and longevity are only a side effect of spiritual health. If you attain spiritual health, or the health of the mind, physical health can also be attained.

So the second goal of my mother's spiritual cultivation was the freedom to come and go. In general, people cannot decide that life is freedom. We come to live in the world, and we have a body form. The freedom to go means your spiritual achievement knows when to go, and you can decide when to leave the world. It is simple as leaving a house.

This goal, the spiritual freedom to come and go, is based on developing your internal knowledge. There are a few lines in the *Tao Teh Ching* about internal knowledge from the ancient culture. Lao Tzu says,

"You do not need to go outdoors,
you can know things under Heaven.

You do not need to look out the window,
   you can know the situation of the world.
The one who goes out very far,
   attains very little knowledge.
What is valued is to know without learning,
   to understand without seeing,
   to accomplish without needing to do.

This is what we can study from Lao Tzu. When you reach the depth of your own personal spirits, you shall have this knowledge and capability. In another chapter, usually designated as the 52nd chapter, Lao Tzu says,

Everything under Heaven has a common source;
   that common source is subtle.
It is the mother of everything under Heaven.
Once you spiritually reach this subtle source,
   or have the same vibration as the subtle origin,
   you reach everything.
You know everything,
   but you still keep your spirits together
   with the subtle root, the subtle source.
Then your life energy can never be exhausted.

Practically, this guidance is to stop all the holes, all the leakage that lets external disturbance come in. To close the door means do not let yourself be tempted, because if you are, then your energy will go out. And do not be bothered and drained for any external things. Once you open the hole to allow things to come in, then you become attached to small things or big annoyance in your mind. Once your mind is jammed with emotion and unclear thought, there is no room to grow the Inner Light. Then you will be exhausted. In this case, you can never really achieve or allow your spirit to reach the nutritious source.

These two chapters come from Lao Tzu and describe the way you can possibly attain internal knowledge.

Still more specific guidance comes from the ancient ones. It is worthy to learn the guidance to prepare yourself for pursuit of internal knowledge. Internal knowledge does not require book learning; it comes from inside.   It is something that you just know. It does not suggest you need to learn through the detour way of religious practice.

My mother's instruction guided me to know: "A person's practical goal is to look for the full development of mind. If you can fully develop your mind, then there is no need to bother looking separately for internal knowledge. You do not need to worry about either internal knowledge or a fully developed mind any more. All are there within what you have reached. You do not need to pursue anything else. Inner clarity or internal knowledge comes around by itself. What you need to do is learn or achieve full growth or the full development of your mind.

"Here are some important specifications from the ancient achieved ones.   If you remember them and keep practicing them, you shall achieve.

"Your achievement still depends on you and how you meet the requirement of maintaining your calm mind and letting your mind grow naturally without external intervention of emotional reaction."

This was the guidance she gave:

1.   Our formed body receives birth from the unformed truth. All formed things come from the subtle sphere to the apparent sphere.   But what is formed is not what you should be attached to. If you think or worry only about your attachment to what is formed, then you cut your connection with the unformed truth.   Not only does formed life comes from unformed truth, all thought, all conscience, and all emotion comes from the nothingness of the unformed source. Therefore, feelings of either guilt or blessing have no reality. Do not attach your mind to them.

2.   Your mind can be motivated by good thoughts and good behaviors; that is your desire or intention. All these good thoughts and good behaviors are within you originally.   They had no form but were only latent energy. From this, you might be able to see the original truth and also what is untruth or unimportant.

There are two ends upon which you can perch your spirit; on one end there is the unformed truth, and on the other end there is the formed untruth or variable stuff. If you live on the end of thought and behavior of the formed untruth, then you live in a world of untruth. That world is full of variable, momentary, passing thoughts, emotions and behaviors which are far from the deep reality of life. Not only good thoughts and behavior, but also unbeneficial thoughts and behavior, are all seen in the sphere of untruth.

Into all your creations, you put lots of energy, stress and struggle. Your creations could be good or they could be bad. Even the good ones are illusive. Illusion has no reality; mostly, illusions, good or bad, just keep you busy. Anyone in the stage of liking to materialize life energy in thoughts, ideas and emotion is only playing with bubbles, just like bubbles produced by water, soap and air. I consider thoughts and emotion as illusion, because they are not the important truth of life. They do not connect with the unformed, deep root of life.

3. We pay much attention to the body, but the body is borrowed. It is the raw material gathered by spirit. So we have a body. If you do not care for the unformed being, and care only for the formed being or body, you lose the root of your life. When I mention the unformed being, you think it is your thoughts. No, your thoughts are not unformed. They are formed, concrete or knowable because of circumstance. If no circumstance is presented internally or externally, from where can your thoughts and emotion arise? Because you have thoughts, you have motivation, you have emotion, and then you have thought again. Those emotions, thoughts and ideas are judged according to whether they are good ones or bad ones. What is good and bad about them? All mental constructions are illusive, so it is vain to put too much stress upon them.

People put too much strength into what is illusive. They fight, suffer or even die for illusions. They do not know to respect the unformed truth of life.

4. When you live inside the body, you see that you have a body. By seeing the body, the wise one reaches the subtle body. It is the substance of your life. It is your spiritual energy. It needs further development. You need to understand the attitudes that you established from your childhood or the early part of your life because your attitudes can block your realization of the subtle body. Some attitudes were established even before your life was formed. Attitudes or habits are the untrue mind. Any attitude or habit is dissolvable. It is possible to dissolve the untrue form of mind.

This mind you now have was developed from your constant responses to worldly events. The reactions of the mind take form as responses or behavior patterns. Because they come from the mind, they are not the spiritual substance of life. The mind is composed of response or reaction to the world; thus, the mind is formed or untrue. Only that which has no form is true.

Most people live on the level of their bodily or physical life. That means that they respond to what they see and hear; they think about it and have desires. But there is something which is different; it is the level of spirit. The substance of life is a subtle level. The level of spirit is above the level of the body and the level of the mind. The difference between an ordinary life and a spiritual life is joining your spirit and life together with the mystical mother, which always lives and always gives birth to life. The possibility of eternal life exists for one who lives on the level of spirit.

5. All people's original spiritual nature is pure. That original spiritual nature has no birth or death. But your mind and body have birth and death. The body and the mind are illusive nature; they are untrue because they are impermanent. If you hold the untrue

to be true and neglect what is really true - the subtle source, then you could be called the lost one.

6. If you set up your mind to look for spiritual support from an externally established God, this is because you do not see that the subtle source of your being is God. If you attain the truthful knowledge that there is no other god besides the subtle truth - the subtle source of your life - you also know that the pain, trouble, agony, good and bad of your life experience is totally irrelevant. At least, it will not forever be your problem. Then you will live happily without fear of so-called life and death or anything. Life, death and other variable things exist at the end of the life tree that is far from the subtle source of eternity, the subtle life of immortality.

The above six guidelines are for the full development of your mind. Make yourself ready to grow your internal knowledge and the freedom to come and to go.

There is some guidance for the spiritual practice of attaining internal knowledge and the freedom of the soul. When humans come to this stage of cultural development, there are many teachings, religions and practices. Usually people only become confused by them and do not know which can help them attain their goal. Knowing what to do in life is the effective life of spiritual attainment. When some people learn some of the practices, their minds are only blocked more. Even a person who learns all the practices may feel more insufficient than before.

In other words, if you go around learning many religions, you may still be in a stage where you react to external spiritual situations or attractions. On the other hand, you may subtly know that there is still something truthful and you can learn to be able to grow your mind fully and attain internal knowledge. It is not suggested that you jump from one external learning to another when the learning is somebody's immature creation. They might be like a psychological program or a religious practice that does not allow your mind and your soul to receive help for growth but leaves them barren like a desert with only dry sand.

Thus, learning from a variety of religions can either be a negative search, if you are trapped by any of them, or a positive search, if you take the essence to supplement your psychological life.

The ancient achieved ones kindly gave us guidance, which also was given through my mother's teaching, to guard our minds from wild wandering, so we can focus on attaining the inner clarity that nature endowed within each of us. This guidance can be known by you.

1. All spiritual teaching was originally not anywhere. To know that is to embrace the original spiritual purity. That is important practice to be with, that is also to serve your physical life as well. This practice helps you to reconnect your physical life with the non-physical truth. Any practice that helps you unite with the non-physical essence is helpful. No other practice has more truth and is more direct. Many practices in my books have the purpose of keeping your concentration upon the inside of the body as a means of linking your mind with the essence of life.

2. In spiritual learning, for beginners or others in a different stage, if you feel you have not caught some higher thing, or that you have not experienced reaching any authority in the spiritual realm, this does not necessarily reflect an internal spiritual insufficiency. It means you are still looking in the wrong place. The mistake is known by the intense desire to search and look for something outside of yourself.

    All teaching and all spiritual guidance, if truthful, comes from the subtle source that everybody has. No higher wonderfulness or excellence can be born from any source other than your spiritual nature. All people's spiritual nature is the same. If you keep looking for and accumulating the many small practices, you will never reach the goal. The true practice is to guide yourself from the small practices directly to embrace the unformed subtle source from which you attain your life and capability.

3. There is a search in your mind, and there is a response outside your mind. Once you eliminate the desire, then the response is also eliminated. Once the desire is eliminated, you restore the full brightness of the subtle source.

4. The desire to search, the need to learn, comes from you. Once you dissolve the internal longing, you are where you are. Achievement is still external measurement. True achievement is immeasurable. When you have achieved the immeasurable achievement, this is true achievement.

5. It is important to thoroughly understand your mind. If you are bewildered by external religions, or confused by external small practices, that confusion originally existed in your unachieved mind. Once you understand this, you will stop making trouble for yourself. You understand it is emotion looking for a new expression or a new substitute. This brings about more obstacles which directly come between you and the truth.

6. You need to destroy the seeds of hell held in your mind. What are the seeds of hell? They are something that makes you feel good, so you do that thing, usually a self-indulgence, being egotistical and giving in to self-aggrandizement. If you keep doing this, you dig yourself deeper and deeper and make your own personal hell. The problem is that you are holding onto a dream of your immature mind. You developed a dream during your childhood or from your external cultural environment, and it presses your soul. Dreaming is a habitual tendency of mind, but it is not helpful in spiritual cultivation. When you can eliminate your dreams, then you restore the brightness of the subtle truth.

7. Your mind should have no doubt about nurturing the pure light and attaining full growth. Full development can be yours when your mind is not full of impulses or desire. If your mind is full of extra impulses or desires,

it means that you envy or admire other people for doing better than you. This expresses that you have not attained truthful spiritual growth. In order to work on yourself, there is no other direct practice connected with inner clarity and freedom of soul than cultivating a calm mind. You only need to check that the practice you are learning is a truthful way.

Keep the above instructions in your mind, and every day, hold to a regular time for doing meditation. This will help you achieve your purpose of higher attainment. Select one of the following practices. Do it consistently until you achieve the purpose of improving your inner clarity before you start to do another. This is the guidance of my mother's tradition.

1. Visualize yourself as a clear sky, nothing but a sky.
2. Visualize yourself as a big clear lake, nothing but a lake.
3. Visualize yourself as a big mirror, nothing but a mirror.

In order to attain inner clarity, you need to do a number of things. The following list is a good beginning.

A. Avoidance
1) Avoid using drugs, alcohol, coffee or strong tea if not for medicinal purposes.
2) Avoid emotional disturbances.
3) Avoid holding preference in making judgement. This means, when making decisions which involve others, base your decision upon the objective situation rather than on what you want for yourself.

B. When you meditate, pay attention to quality rather than quantity, such as how well you sit with perfect concentration and a calm mind instead of how long you are able to sit.

C. A good meditation relies on good preparation internally and externally. That means cleansing your emotion and making arrangements not to be disturbed or interrupted.

Cleansing your emotion means to wait until your strong emotion is no longer active or engaged.

D. Never be wild emotionally or psychologically. If you are, then it will be hard to come back to a still mind.

E. Meditation is a tool to help you to attain good concentration and a calm, quiet mind. It is a greater help to remain composed and quiet on all occasions, and to supervise your own mind so that you do not let it wander. This supervising energy is the mind joining the spiritual energy, and it creates a beneficial reality. Inner clairvoyance and spiritual inspiration happen unnoticeably in most circumstances when this is practiced. You may not even know how you have attained your goal, although you may experience some strong clairvoyance.

1
Spiritual growth has a different speed
than physical growth.
People may grow to become a hundred years old.
But they may not attain one bit of spiritual growth,
by being busy-minded for external pursuits.

2
Within the body is the mind.
Within the mind, there is the sen (spirit)
as the core of life.
The growth of mind differs from the growth of body.
The growth of sen (spirit) differs from the growth of mind.

3
It is the principle of spiritual cultivation
-to let the sen (spirit) grow naturally
with the peace of the mind.
-to let the mind grow naturally
with the peace of the body.
-to let the body grow naturally
without interference from the ungrowing mind.

4

In one's spiritual unification,
  bring the mind to unite with the body.
By doing so, one can attain the highest performance
  of the body.
Let the sen (spirit) unite with the life,
  Thus, one is able to make the life last a long time.

5

One's physical being and spiritual being
  should be always united.
When union happens,
  it is like a shining silver bowl
  filled with white snow.
It is also like the egret standing
  in the moon shadow.

6

When one's spirit and body are absorbed in each other,
  complete integration is achieved.
Any particular thought of mind will separate them.
But the harder one tries to hold them together,
  the distance between them widens greatly.

7

One side hides in the dark,
  the other is seen in the light.
Just as dawn is the union of light and dark,
  twilight also brings unity.

8

When you look in a mirror,
  you and your image stare at each other.
Do not mistake yourself as the reflection.
Yet, it is your actual life that produces reflection.

9

One's sen (spirit) is like a baby
  unknowing of its own form.
It is there.

There is nothing special to talk about
When the spirit and the body are in total harmony
   with each other.

10

If you look for your sen (spirit),
   it disappears.
If you practice being yourself,
   it unites with you!
It is such a simple reality,
but it takes a fool
   a million years to be enlightened.

Chapter 12

Encouragement from Examples

Q: Please tell us about your mother's teacher, Mother of Yellow Altar (Mother Chern). Did your mother learn directly from her, her writings or a student of her spiritual background?

Master Ni: My family and most Chinese families are directly or indirectly descended from the Yellow Emperor. The Yellow Emperor was the ancient spiritual leader. He searched for teaching from many different spiritual teachers and learned their practices. Not all his descendants were interested in the practices, so some practices were lost. In each new generation, people are all new students, and most of them need to start all over again and search for the new experience. They are not always able to take the benefit of the traditional heritage of original Taoist culture.

Now I would like to start by telling about the Yellow Emperor. I like talking about him because he made special discoveries with the help of several spiritually achieved women who helped him achieve himself.

In ancient times, a woman's spiritual or social position was not like it has been in the past two to three thousand years. In these years, in some regions, women can talk in public; such a thing did not happen in earlier times.

The mother of the Yellow Emperor was Fu Bao. Legend tells that one night Fu Bao, who was the wife of a tribal chieftain, saw a light circling one of the stars of the Big Dipper. She felt the energy dropping down from that star; she felt touched, and she became pregnant. Later, she gave birth to a baby boy. This boy become the Yellow Emperor. When he was born, he was the son of a tribal chieftain.

The title of Emperor was given later to the boy. His spiritual qualities of wisdom, kindness and bravery, and his continuing spiritual cultivation, earned him respect and his title. Yellow refers to centeredness.

During the Yellow Emperor's reign, which was 2698-2598 B.C., there were 18 brotherly tribes who declared themselves to be the children of God. Their leader was Chih

Yueh. Actually those 18 tribes were not totally evolved like other human people; they had beast-like bodies and human heads. They were strong and fearless. They did not eat vegetation or grains; they ate only meat, including human flesh. Obviously, they did not get along well with other tribes.

The aggression of the 18 cannibalistic tribes became the trouble and challenge of people who had attained higher development and wished to safeguard their own tribes. Those tribes were the Han people and the descendants of Shen Nung. Shen Nung's heir took leadership and tried to stop the invaders, but failed. Something needed to be done. The Yellow Emperor, at age 16, was elected to be the new leader. He wished to end the suffering of his people and defeat the ferocious Chih Yueh. So he gathered the strong young men of the tribes and went into battle.

After 150 days of fighting, they still could not defeat Chih Yueh. They began to believe that defeat was inevitable, and almost gave up. The young Yellow Emperor felt bad that he could not lead his men to victory. He began to pray to ask for help. One night, he stayed up late praying. He became drowsy and in his half-sleep state, saw a great wind blowing and carrying a lot of dust. From the dust came a huge flock of sheep followed by a man with a heavy bow and arrow. After the young Yellow Emperor woke up from his dream, he asked for an interpretation from the wise elders who served as his advisors. They told him that in a vision or dream, wind means a command or order, because the wind causes all vegetation to bow low. Dust means trouble, but the clearing of the dust meant that clarity or order was restored. This suggested that the normalcy of a peaceful society was going to return.

The Yellow Emperor also had an intuitive understanding of some parts of the dream; he wondered if some help was going to come to him from the wind. He also knew that the heavy bow the man held meant great strength. Also, it seemed obvious that a person following sheep would be a shepherd. All together, he wondered if there was a strong shepherd named Wind or someone who might be related to those symbols who existed in real life that could help him. He sent people to search for such a person.

The young leader finally found not one, but two people who were related to his description. One was a woman, a tribal leader called the Queen of Wind. The other was a man who was called the Powerful Shepherd. Yellow Emperor invited them to join his effort against Chih Yueh and the 18 tribes. They were helpful, and he discovered that they had a kind of special energy. They became his generals. At that time the word "general" was not used, so they were perhaps more appropriately called his helpers in the fight against Chih Yueh.

The last battle between the Yellow Emperor and Chih Yueh occurred in the wilds of Chu Lu. Both armies were there, waiting for battle. Chih Yueh had the ability to affect the weather. To keep his army hidden from Yellow Emperor, he caused 100 miles of thick fog to occur in Chu Lu. For three days and three nights, nobody could see in any direction.

So the Yellow Emperor prayed to the Big Dipper. He received a response from the Mystical Female, who gave instruction to the Queen of Wind to create a tool with which they could navigate and find the opposing army. Thus, a big compass was invented by the Queen of Wind. It was put in a cart and pushed everywhere. At this time, the Queen of West Pond also sent the Blue Lady from her spiritual domain to teach the Yellow Emperor how to use the five tones of music of a musical instrument to guide soldiers in the fog so they would not get lost. She also taught him the spiritual way to know the movement of the enemy army.

This was a war between the two ways of life: barbaric and civilized. However, the young emperor received teaching and inspiration from the spiritual realm, and this time, with the help of spiritual beings, new equipment, learning and strategy, the young Yellow Emperor finally won his victory and drove most of the half-evolved people from the land.

This was the early life of the young leader who became the emperor. After he was throned, he spent at least 19 years pursuing the study of medicine and Taoist practices. He reigned from 2698-2598 B.C. He left this world by riding a yellow dragon and flying away. That yellow dragon could have been a UFO, but I trust it was his own energy transformed. It can also be viewed as the energy transformation of his spiritual baby. During the sky journey, the physical being of the Yellow Emperor vaporized and he disappeared. The essence of mind and the spirits of the Yellow Dragon, the spiritual baby of the Yellow Emperor, joined together to accomplish the spiritual union.

But the important thing is, that on Earth, he left men and women who worked together to bring about the progress of worldly life.

I cannot forget to tell you about one practical woman. Luo Tzuu, the wife of the Yellow Emperor, discovered the silkworm, and how to make silk. She made the first silk clothes. The Ni family can be traced back to their grandson, Emperor Chuan Shu, who was a spiritual leader (1514-1436 B.C.). However, it is valuable to see that in ancient times, women were involved in social activity. Also in ancient times, the deities were women.

From the influence of Luo Tzuu, cooking and making clothing became the main function of women in a family while the men hunted, farmed and made war. Because women naturally did not have time for other things besides raising children, that became one of the woman's duties. There was no other great task for the women except helping the family and raising the children. All that tedious work belonged to women. Once this custom became rigid in practice, women were recognized as being suitable only for working inside the household. Now that human life has changed, the activity of women has widened again.

My mother's spiritual study and spiritual tradition correlated with my father's tradition. It started with a woman teacher who was called Mother Chern. She had a powerful student, Master Shu Shen. He could be considered as one of the most upright and pure spiritual models. He learned the ancient guidance of spiritual practice. Then he used what he had achieved to protect people from harm due to natural disaster. He lived around 373. A. D. His school was established later to commemorate his spiritual merit by having helped people and is called the School of Pure Light (or Jing Ming School).

I would like to tell you a little bit about Mother Chern. She lived in Danyan county. She cultivated herself at a small place called the Yellow Altar. It was named that because of her practice in centeredness. Nobody knew how old she was, but they could see that her hair did not turn gray and her teeth did not fall out. She always looked young. People came to know that she had a lot to teach, so they made her a teacher and called her Mother Chern.

She cultivated herself during the time of the three kingdoms at the end of the Han Dynasty (220-264 A.D.). One day, before she was known as Mother of Yellow Altar, a young man around 15 years old came to her and respectfully expressed that he wished to be her son and offered to take care of her. This means he wished to be like a stepson or godson. Mother Chern responded by saying, "You are grown-up. It is time for you to take care of your own father and mother. Why leave your own mother to take care of me as your mother?" So the young man went away.

Some time later, at the same place, a boy appeared who was around 3 years old. He kept crying. Nobody knew whose son he was. When the boy saw Mother Chern, he held her skirt and would not let her go. "Please Mother," he said, "Have pity on me." Out of sympathy, Mother Chern took him home, raised him and taught him. The boy was smart. He learned quickly from books on all topics and possessed knowledge such as astronomy, geography and medicine.

When he had grown up, Mother Chern told him, "I am a person who cultivates Tao. I have raised you, but I do not know who is your source. So how do I help you?"

He said, "My source is one of the bright suns in the sky. Before I came, I was given the name Prince of Sun. You do not need to help me, because I know all the important books containing knowledge of natural energy of herbs and other things."

Mother Chern said, "You are older now and have become a man, an adult. Will you look for a wife now?"

The man immediately said, "I am not a worldly being and so I cannot be married in the worldly way. I came from the sky to fulfill my spiritual duty. My spiritual duty up to now has been to practice the love between mother and son. It has confirmed my virtue. By the way, I previously transformed myself into the 15-year-old boy who came wishing to take care of you. Because you refused, I transformed myself into a small child. Now I can be with you and transmit the secret and the art of eternal life to you. After that, I will have accomplished my spiritual mission here and I will return to the spiritual origin.

"After I teach you the special practice, Mother, you can become a spiritual teacher and call yourself Mother of Yellow Altar. (This presents the sun as the Yellow Altar.) You will give the secret of spiritual achievement only to the right people."

Mother Chern originally wished only to cultivate herself; she had no interest in worldly teaching. However, at the being's direction, she became a teacher of the public. Her teaching concentrated on the four virtues. By fulfilling or embodying all four virtues, a person will make oneself immortal. These four virtues are jing (spiritual purity), ming (inner clarity), chung (spiritual centeredness) and hsiao (devotion to fulfill the spiritual duty of helping all people.)

Then the Prince of Sun gave Mother Chern the important practice of how to achieve oneself. He also gave her the knowledge of how to use herbs. Afterwards, he said farewell to her and flew away. Mother Chern followed what the Prince of Sun taught her and learned to cultivate herself. She also ascended after she accomplished her cultivation and achieved spiritual completion as a pure spiritual being.

When Mother Chern was fulfilling her spiritual duty as a teacher, Shu Shen and Wu Mong heard that she was teaching. They traveled a long distance to express their wish to learn from her. Mother Chern knew that these two men were able to achieve themselves and have their names in the immortal book. Therefore, she taught them the art of the Prince of Sun and the spiritual practices which could help and serve people. The two men were grateful to her.

When they left, Shu Seng told Mother Chern that every year he would return to visit and take care of her. Mother Chern said, "You do not need to come back. I will soon return to the country of one great God." Then she picked up a piece of spear grass, which is a kind of grass with a pointed tip, and threw it in the direction of the south. The piece of grass was caught on an air current and traveled far. Mother Chern told Shu Seng, "Go home now. On the way southward, there is a place about twenty miles from here. If you find the piece of grass I threw, just build a symbolic altar there and, if you like, visit it every autumn. That is enough." Soon afterwards, a dragon came down from the clouds. Mother Chern got on it and flew away.

Shu Seng did as she instructed. In the border of the county of Fong Chern, the temple of Yellow Altar that he built existed until the Yuan Dynasty (1280-1367 A.D.). It was told that the altar Shu Seng built for his teacher Mother Chern served as a monumental building for his teaching.

The story of Mother Chern was kept in the Taoist books. However, I would like to tell you the esoteric truth about Mother Chern's achievement that was not written in the books. In ancient times, many people flew down from the stars and planets. They came to the earth directly or incarnated in human bodies and fulfilled their purpose of teaching. So the story that the Prince of Sun came from the stars is acceptable by the Taoist tradition.

My mother helped me understand that the Prince of Sun was Mother Chern's own spiritual energy convergence. He was the fruit of her spiritual cultivation. In Taoist terms, such an occurrence is the sublimation of personal Yang energy as Yang Seng or yang spirit. This means a person practices spiritual cultivation of internal spiritual intercourse of yin and yang, and gives birth to a spiritual baby. The spiritual baby can sometimes transform to be a human being. Mother Chern achieved that; her spirit could transform, but at the beginning she herself did not recognize it. The second time she accepted it, although she still may not have understood. My own experience is that once spiritual energy is produced by the union of your mind and body, it can transform into anything. It follows the suggestion of your mind. If you learn the Taoist immortal way, it transforms to be exactly like your own self, but younger and more perfect, because it is your own essence. It can also transform to be a child.

That was the spiritual achievement of Mother Chern. Her achievement was similar to that of some women advisers of the Yellow Emperor. The secret part of Mother Chern's teaching was the pre-historic spiritual practice as the original Taoist practice. She taught that in addition to what the Prince of Sun had proved to her. She taught spiritual women to make the sun as father, husband or son in the sense of having male energy in their lives.

Without understanding the reality of spiritual achievement by having achieved it himself, a general scholar could only write about the level which he imagined. That is the case with the version in the Taoist Canon and why it was inaccurate or incomplete.

Master Shu Shen had served as a magistrate of the town of Jing Yang at the age of 42 during the east Jing dynasty (317-419 A.D.). After Master Shu Sen experienced the limitations to the amount of help a government can give to its people, he began to learn spiritual arts. First he learned from a teacher named Wu Mong. He and his teacher heard about Mother Chern in Giang Do of Jiang Su province, which is now called Yangchow. Shu Seng was a humble young person who was ambitious spiritually. He went to learn the practices and art of Mother Chern, who was also called the Mother of Yellow Altar. His teacher, Wu Mong, then learned the art from him. Originally, Wu Mong was the teacher of Master Shu Seng; Shu Seng now become the teacher of Wu Mong and taught him what Mother Chern taught to him. You can see that ancient people are more humble than the people of today. In learning, age is not important. Most important is a person's development and the value of what he or she teaches.

Mother Chern also taught some women students. In the Taoist Canon, many of her teachings have been recorded through Master Shu Sen. But they are mixed with religious expressions of later generations. This makes them different from the pure teaching that my mother received.

The School of Pure Light (or Jing Ming School) was developed late during the Sung Dynasty (960-1279 A.D.) with the purpose of continuing the art of Master Shu Seng. The name of the school could also be called the School of Purity, Cleanness, Clarity or Brightness, depending on how it is translated. In Chinese, it is called the Jing Ming school. The direct teaching of Mother Chern became the teaching and the practice of the School of the Mother of Yellow Altar. It should not be mixed up with the later developed teaching of the Jing Ming School. It was established much later under the name of Master Shu Sen, judging by the book of the Jing Ming School which was collected in the *Taoist Canon*.

The last master of the Jing Ming school of Master Shu Sen was Master Wuan Yuan Gi, whose active time was during the Yuan Dynasty (1280-1367 A.D.). He taught in Szechuan province and had a big and deep spiritual influence on the people of that mountainous region. Szechuan province is renowned for its achieved Taoist teachers. People who live there enjoy spiritual practice. After Master Yuan Wan Gi ascended in Tzu Liu Jing, a temple was built in his memory. The temple was in the county of the Well of Self-Flowing Water in Szechuan province.

About two or three hundred years after the ascension of Master Yuan Wan Gi, a group of Confucian scholars gathered in this temple to hold a discussion about their future and the situation of the society. The students were Confucian scholars, and accordingly pursued government positions as their means to improve society. They first made an offering and prayed to Master Yuan Wang Gi. This was around the end of the Ching Dynasty (1644-1911 A. D.), when Kuan Hsu was Emperor. This was around the end of the Dynasty. At this time, China was already in deep trouble, because the western powers had extended their colonialism to China. The two strong neighbors, Russia in the north and Japan to the east, were encroaching on Chinese territory. It was the Russian Tzar's dream to have an unfrozen harbor in the south, which would be in the north of China. The newly modernized nation of Japan was interested in China's vast and rich soil. The Japanese responded early to western power by adopting the western system in their society. They began to run their political system structure like the British. The new Japanese government kept the king, but added a premier and a congress. The premier and congress were both elected and cooperatively decided policy. This is similar to the British system in which there is a king or queen, a prime minister and a house of commons. Basically the king or queen has no power to influence the country's political decisions both in Japan and England. This is different from the United States system in which there is a president as the executive branch, congress as the legislative branch and courts as the judicial branch. In the United States, the distribution of power is balanced between the three branches.

The Japanese adopted the western system in all areas. This enabled them to move to industrialize society and enhance their strength with new weapons. As her power and efficiency increased, Japan became more and more ambitious to acquire the wealth of China. At that time, anything that came from China was valued and admired. Pupils in Japanese schools were taught aggressive attitudes towards China. The teachers would point to some tasty fruit and ask the pupils, "Do you like this sweet fruit?" The students would say, "We like it." Then the teacher would respond, "If you like it, go to China to get it." That is how Japanese students were educated at that time.

At the end of the Ching Dynasty, political power was in the hands of Empress Dowager. The colonial encroachment was a problem but she was too ineffective as a ruler to do anything about it. The emperor Kuan Hsu (reigned 1875-1908) was a young boy under the regency of the Empress Dowager. He started real political involvement. In 1898, the Empress confined him because he had an interest in using a formula similar to the one the Japanese applied in China. He wished to apply a model reformation to save China from the deep water of colonialism. The hardliners of the old political system of the Ching Dynasty refused, because with the implementation of a system similar to that of Japan, sovereignty would shift from the hands of the Manchurians to the Han people. Free elections would have made that change, because the population consisted of more Han people. It was not agreeable to give up sovereignty to the Han people, because the ancestors of the Manchurians conquered the Han people many years previously. Unfortunately, the Empress Dowager short vision and selfish motives. All the scholars and ministers who supported emperor Kuan Hsu's reformation were openly executed by her order. She executed the supporters of her son. Emperor Kuan Hsu himself was forced to give up political power and was kept under close guard. He was held in one of the buildings of Beijing's Manchurian palace. His favorite wife who supported the reformation was forced to drown herself in a well. Both the palace and the well still exist.

The demand of political reformation stimulated and stirred up the minds of Chinese scholars. The emotion of the young scholars became more involved in looking for a solution. With disturbed minds, these young scholars wished to find a way to help the country. One group of students used the public temple as a gathering place. First they worshipped Master Yuan Wuan Gi, then they started to discuss the future and what they should do. Nobody could give a definite vision or guideline that was acceptable to all. The discussion became very hot. Somebody said that China needed a revolution. Somebody else said that China did not need a revolution, but just adopting the western system would improve the country. Then they talked about the many dark spots in their own future as scholars if such a western system were to be adopted and used. So people became very hot in discussion and nobody found a solution.

An older person with very light energy was discovered to be present in the meeting. They did not know where he came from or who he was. The older person told them, "You know, the Chinese problem cannot be helped in this time, because the majority of Chinese are still asleep. They expect somebody else to be responsible for their lives. So if you wish to do anything, you will only sacrifice your life engaging in revolutionary action against the Ching Dynasty. Life is valuable; if you sacrifice yourselves, it will bring no help to China. Some of you here have better potential. Why not think about cultivating Tao? As you develop yourselves in this way, you can help yourselves and help other people."

Some scholars in the group burst out in strong response. "What is cultivating Tao? That is an old superstition. This is a new time. We are new scholars."

Then the elder asked them, "If you think it is superstition, then why did you gather here and pray to Master Wuan Yuan Gi?" Some of the scholars replied, "We prayed here as a social custom. We do not really trust that there are immortals. We do not really trust that there is God."

The elder said, "People who believe in immortality cannot necessarily even reach it. For the people who do not believe in immorality, their belief does not mean that it does not exist."

Then the scholars started to argue among themselves. The older person gave some spiritual suggestions. Some students commented, "We have already heard this from the book about Master Wuan Yuan Gi. To know about this is one thing, but to ask us to invest our lives in this pursuit is another. Especially now, when such an important political crisis exists. There is not even any proof that immortality is real, anyway."

The elder asked, "What proof do you need?"

One scholar replied, "Our ancestors said that people could fly up or ascend to the sky, but we have never personally seen such a thing."

The elder said, "Immortals do not necessarily fly to the sky. They enjoy the freedom of life. Their life being can be many ways. An immortal is somebody who lives in the zero dimension. You know, in ordinary earthly life, there are dimensions, divisions and all limitations. Once you achieve immortality, all dimensions are dissolved, and you can have freedom." He told them that governmental service is small service, and spiritual service is bigger or greater. In saying this, Master Wuan Yuan Gi was not referring to serving oneself by taking all for oneself. He was referring to serving oneself by developing oneself, and then using one's development to serve the world. He also gave some special spiritual guidance at the meeting. However, it seems that the group of young people did not receive his message because they were too focused on worldly glory as Confucian scholars.

The scholars told the old man about the western achievement and the new sciences that they were interested in learning from the west in order to save the country. The discussion again became very hot. Some of them said, only if we witness somebody fly up to the sky will we be convinced. They kept talking, and at last the elder said, "I believe that you are sincere to achieve yourselves in your own way. So I withdraw from the argument. I will go now." He finished talking, then suddenly his face transformed into the face of Master Wuan Yuan Gi, he flew up into the sky and then totally disappeared. Everybody suddenly woke up: this was Master Wuan Yuan Gi himself, who appeared just to help them. Afterwards, many of those students regretted missing the opportunity to directly receive more teachings from him.

Chapter 13

Self-Delivery

Q: Master Ni, it seems that all the conventional spiritual teachings are one big mess. It seems that the techniques used in politics and religion are mixed together. How can we deliver ourselves from the confusion?

Master Ni: As I understand it, your question is about whether religion or politics are really going to help you. Their promises are sometimes too good to be true. The fantasy of religions and unrealistic economic projections such as communism all create pulls in people's lives. Many people offer their lives trying to realize unrealizable objects.

This question has already been discussed in many places. Rather than continue to talk about the never-ending mess of religion and politics, I would rather tell you about something that might more directly help your life. I would rather tell you about self-discovery and self-delivery. I would rather help you understand that it is not necessary to be bewitched by politics or religion. To help your own life, it is necessary to work to improve your own life rather than wait for someone else to do it. To help you do so, I will tell you some helpful things I remember about my parents and how they shaped me, brought me up, when I was young.

I always felt my mother was my disciplinarian. My father also disciplined me, but his punishment was often escapable. If my mother decided to discipline me, punishment was inescapable; usually I would be caught. She had various ways of correcting me. Sometimes as a lad, I wished I could run away from her.

My mother sometimes talked about her experience as a mother: even a baby of a few months old knows to bargain. The mother needs to learn to be reasonable with the child; she cannot be too firm or too easy. She can yield to a child's reasonable bargains, but be firm with unreasonable bargains. She should never be managed by the baby. An indecisive or disorganized mother does not help a child grow emotionally and reasonably. As my mother said, to be a mother is a big task. She needs to learn to be reasonable all the time towards her children. She must learn to be unemotional and always in control to be a model of good life for her children.

My mother's understanding of the nature of slightly older children was distinctive. She thought children were just like uncarved, unrefined pieces of precious stone like jade. If when carving a piece of jade, the sculptor does not remove the surrounding coarse rock, the jade cannot express itself as good jade. A piece of good jade needs to be correctly shaped; then it can show its greatness. She believed that similar to a piece of jade, all young children have a natural potential within themselves for greatness. Each child has a different potential. The parents, especially the mother, must learn to understand and help the child bring out the potential which will become one's personal direction in life.

Chinese society has been troubled with disastrous leadership, internal power struggles and the wrong direction. The leaders who are in power were once the children of their fathers and mothers. It is often a question in people's minds how children can turn out to be a certain way. Most fathers and mothers do not know that having a peaceful mind and mood is the best nutrition you can offer your children. Rather, they wish that their children would become rich, powerful and leaders in society, so they impose this desire upon them. The children pick up their desire and make it their own.

In China, there are two ways to become rich and attain authority: 1) either become a big bandit or 2) become a monarch or share the power of the monarch. Becoming wealthy through diligent and intelligent management of life and working for the government can change one's social stature. That is more agreeable to all people than becoming a bandit, obviously. A typical Chinese father and mother wished this for their children because they knew that the children's good fortune would also affect them as parents. The children often spent their whole lifetime trying to meet that wish, but would sometimes bring great disaster to society by adopting evil means to achieve that desire. What both the parents and the children did not realize is that people in authority still cannot do and enjoy whatever wish, because of the demands of circumstances. Thus, whether a person is in a high position or not, wisdom and a balanced mind is the most important element of life.

In the west, it is said that behind a great man there is a great woman, and people think it must mean a good wife. It is more likely the mother. A wife can be a great assistant, but the real foundation of personality comes from the mother. A wife cannot discipline her husband. She may be able to provide some good advice, but a mother can provide discipline and education before he adopts bad habits.

If a mother does not discipline her children, in the future she will suffer pain or shame because of her sense of spiritual responsibility. The spiritual responsibility of a mother should be fulfilled when her children are young by providing constant good suggestions, firm but gentle correction, and clear and useful guidance. All of this can help a child greatly, long before adulthood. Usually a man cannot be controlled by his mother any more after he reaches a certain age. However, a mother's hard work always pays off when she helps her young children.

Once your children go to school, the teachers act as salespeople of intellectual knowledge. The teachers do not help them find a good direction in life or help shape them with a firm and upright personality. The personality is formed in the home.

Children pass through the stage of being a dear child of the mother to being the student of the school system. Developing a child is a cultural process, and in some ways in modern society, it is like an industrial process. So, the greatest responsibility for building a good individual and good member of society falls upon the shoulders of the mother and the school teachers. In a situation where parents and teachers do not meet their responsibilities, society worsens. The key point is the position of the mother; it is a spiritual position. The position of school teachers is a spiritual one too. By spiritual position, I mean that what is most important as a mother or teacher is not to make a name for yourself, nor is it making a lot of money at a job;

it is meeting the hard work required to help someone have a successful future.

Whether they earn great or small success, those who can accept some credit are the parents, teachers and policy makers of society. The responsibility of today's education seems to have shifted from the family center to the society center. But, the society has no sense of a total responsibility to build a youngster, therefore, there is no help in building character derived from public education.

My mother knew how to raise a child, like most mothers do. My mother attained internal knowledge or internal clarity instead of attaining intellectual academic diplomas or degrees. She learned and developed totally from spiritual practices. She did not attend any schools.

She applied discipline to me, my brother and sisters in different ways. I think she was more strict with me. However, I still believe I was helped by the spankings she gave me. I know that these firmly administered spankings were mixed with her tears in private. When a mother punishes her child, she does not enjoy doing it. She feels pain when she punishes the child, but she does not show her own emotion in front of the child when giving the punishment. By punishing a child, a mother wishes to shape a firm and upright personality to benefit the child.

Q: The better part of our society is trying to influence the rest of society in giving up "spanking". It seems you are condoning it - but it is a terrible experience for many children.

Master Ni: It was my personal experience in childhood. I understood the many sacrifices my mother made in raising me. I learned to obey her kind heart in helping me form good habits. She influenced my life being and prevented me from having the need to submit myself to armed policemen.

It is possible for any child to escape spankings or other punishment if the parents communicate well with the child, telling him or her what is acceptable and what is not. Thus, the child knows in advance what will upset the parents, such as drinking, smoking, doing drugs, doing things that are disagreeable to society, and fighting, regardless of whether the child is right or wrong. A parent can tell a child: if you start fighting, when you come home, you will be punished. Vandalism will damage your own personality and shame your parents and siblings. A parent can also tell a child: "Rather than do those things, be diligent in your studies, whatever you learn in school, especially a trade. When you stop doing the unacceptable behavior and do the acceptable behavior, other people will notice and begin to trust you. But if you do not, you will find as you get older that your life is uninteresting, because you have not learned and grown. You will wonder why other people do so much better and enjoy life and you do not. Therefore it is important not to make trouble for anyone or for yourself."

This is all easy to do for a child except the difficulty of quarreling with others; at home he will be punished. Also, make the family living schedule become sacred to your children. They have to be home before dark and cannot go out any more. Around sunrise they have to get up and participate in the family activities or work. Good habits are easily formed when children are young and small. With such habits, when your children grow up, they will have nothing to do with policemen or criminal court. They will always enjoy personal dignity and live happily, enjoying the condition where they are, and what they are. And, do what you do respectfully. True, not irrational, punishment shows the concern, good intentions, love and dedication of the parents. The parents express that they expect the young life to have a firm, respectable character.

When I was small, I was punished by spanking. But that kind of punishment did not bother me as much as a greater threat given by my parents. If I did something really wrong, until I corrected my behavior, my mother would not eat. She would fast until I recognized that this was a serious matter. Children are not considerate about dignity. Thus, I could easily ignore the punishment of spanking but I could not stand it when my mother started to fast. It was not hard for me to take the punishment, it was really hard for me to take it when my parents started to punish themselves. They will think that because they are so unvirtuous, the children do not listen to them.

I heard many fathers in my home town shout and yell and mothers scream at their children. The effect was not as good as my mother beginning a fast. Those children became communist leaders and tried to revenge and persecute their own parents. My mother's way, however, would never let me forget the good lessons she taught me. On many occasions, when my friends had a special plan, they would invite me to join, but later they would give me up because they thought I was good for nothing. I never could become a communist-type of person. In my thirties, some people offered me some cigarettes. I accepted and tried, but I gave it up. I could not do anything to hurt myself or others. It would hurt my beloved mother.

In old China, there were many big families who general-ly lived together or close to each other. It was customary that each generation take responsibility to shape the decency of personality in the next generation. Once, however, an over-ambitious grandfather disciplined his young grandson by beating him. His son saw this with the feeling of suffering, but he could not disrespectfully stop his father. So he picked up a stick and began to beat himself. His father looked at him with disbelief and asked, "Are you mad? Why do you beat yourself?" The son answered, "You are beating my son, so I can also beat your son."

Communism arose among the Chinese people because of their strong slogan, theory, belief or faith. It goes some-thing like this: There are two classes in the world. One is those who suppress other people, and the other is those who are suppressed. People are suppressed by government, society and parents. Thus, the communists believed that the way for the suppressed to improve their lives was to unite and attack the suppressors. The communists hold a dualistic point of view: if you are not my friend, you are my enemy. And because the communists cannot learn to make friends and live together harmoniously with the "enemy", they hold that the enemy must be defeated, avenged and ransomed for whatever wrongs were done. This kind of propaganda penetrated all corners of Chinese society as the communists looked for comrades. The ones who joined them were those who did not do well in society or in their own families or those who had psychological resentment for anything. Those people became the source of soldiers who would fight for the purposes of the ambitious, evil, intellectually educated leaders. There is nothing wrong with an intellectual education unless it is partial or if it is not balanced by being able to see the wholeness of life. Those leaders themselves came from the class who caused suppression, but the soldiers did not see that. There was no other religious faith allowed, but only communism. They preached: No parents, relatives or friends are precious in your life. Only communism is your future. So this is how they find the mob; by selecting individuals who do not have independent judgement.

These people grew up differently from myself. My parents always let me have my own judgement first, then they discussed their view.

Before communism succeeded, their guns were pointed at conventional society. I mean, the communist revolution was a success by uniting forces against the conventional society. It was basically using guns, destructive weapons, pointed against a common enemy. After the success of the revolution with the downfall of conventional society, however, the instigators of the revolution pointed guns at each other. The so-called ten year cultural revolution, although it appeared to be a further cleaning out of conventional society, was actually a political maneuver of some party members against other party members. Any politics based on violence and force is nothing more than a group of gangsters; this type of movement cannot last.

I grew up in an agricultural society, in which success in life was not achieved by suppressing others. Success was quite simply a result of being diligent in work, careful in expense and maintaining good management of life. The basic foundation of achievement is harmony and cooperation within the family and with society. I do not think that any other way to achieve can be more trustworthy than those three basic things. I am not a fighter. My parents taught me that the one who deliberately seizes power or wealth shall have that power or wealth deliberately taken away by someone else. This is not high spiritual doctrine.

I think perhaps an English equivalent to this saying is, Easy come, easy go. There is no exception; it is one's own work, no matter how humble, that brings good fruit to life. Being able to work itself is part of that fruit. Chinese communism uses people who do not have independent judgement as a tool to suppress the majority of the people. We shall see how long it will last. This is Heavenly forbidden; by this I mean, because it does not follow the subtle law, it must fail.

Q: I have heard spanking described as being as gentle as a pat on the hand, but I have experienced it as violence. Parents who are not civilized enough to distinguish the difference between a gentle pat and violence should not be encouraged.

Master Ni: It is wrong if a father or mother transfers their emotion by releasing it on helpless children. That is different from spanking children rationally for their own learning. I believe children should be disciplined from a parent's love, because children have more impulse than reason. In ancient times, when children were disciplined, they first had to kneel down in front of their father or mother. The parent would then give them the reason why they needed to be punished. If there was no reason, no punishment would be given. Usually the punishment would happen, not the first or second time the mistake was made, but the third time the child repeated the mistake. The child thus knows that the behavior is wrong, but has still done it anyway.

When a child is a teenager, the most important discipline is not to engage in early sex and have no conflict and fight with other people. Like most parents, my father and mother were nervous about it, with good reason. Parents do not want the young root of a child's vitality to be hurt.

About punishment, I would like to give you an example. When I was in Taiwan, I had a friend who was an evangelist. His son was 17 or 18 years old, just about to graduate from high school and take the entrance exam for college. That is an important time for a young man, because in Taiwan, entrance into a university can determine the outcome of your life. The pressure and competition to pass the exam is strong in Taiwan and Japan. At that time, the young man fell in love with a woman student. It began to affect his grades. His father saw the situation and warned him. But because temptation is much stronger than schoolwork to a young person, his son did not listen. One day when his son took off his clothes and went to take a shower, the father went to the shower room, closed the door, and beat his son. He told him simply: "I have been working so hard to raise the family. I was young when I left my father and mother to come to Taiwan. I could not do anything but become an evangelist. I hope you can be more useful to society than I have been. Now, at your age, you try to fall in love. What do you think love is? Do you think it is important in your life? You have your whole future to love any woman or play emotions. Why do you need to choose this time? I warned you several times, but you did not listen to me." The father beat him. He told me about it. He did that only one time, and his son got the message and did well on the exam.

Children's impulse is much stronger than their rational mind, so sometimes discipline is needed. I surely do not insist on spanking. In today's society, many parents cannot discipline their children because they cannot discipline themselves. Setting a good example for your children is most important. Only when you become a good example can you become a disciplinarian; otherwise your children will not trust you, because you do what you tell them not to do. Thus, I do not insist upon spanking, but I do appreciate my father and mother who occasionally disciplined me when my impulse was stronger than my reason. I accepted it, I was happy. I still feel sweetness for my father and mother who had such deep love for me and did not wish me to go in the wrong direction or damage myself. It was an expression of love. I was not psychologically sick nor needed somebody's beating, but when you are young, you do not control yourself well, you do whatever you like. You do not like your father and mother to always be scolding you too much. But I appreciate it now. However, your case may be different, so I cannot comment.

Q: So Chinese people, or spiritual people, use spanking as a means of discipline?

Master Ni: Before the communist revolution, China was a conventional society which emphasized the moral attitudes of individual life. In order to maintain harmony within a family, each individual had to make a certain sacrifice. So it becomes a spiritual practice to live within a family. It is natural for a father and mother to be dutiful to their children. Also the children learn to be dutiful towards their father and mother. Youngsters must be shaped correctly by the good example of their parents. Family discipline to the children is considered a duty.

Most boys learn to obey the elders of the family. They must listen to the good advice of their father and mother. They will be disciplined or punished if they do wrong. Even after some children are adults, if they make a mistake, they will kneel down in front of their parents, ask forgiveness or offer a stick for the parents to punish them with.

Once an adult son did something wrong, something that was disagreeable to the society, so he was beaten by his mother. Before, when small, he had no difficulty taking a beating from the stick in his mother's hands. But this time, he cried deeply and bitterly. His mother wondered why and asked him, "All those years when you were beaten, you accepted it. Why this time are you crying?" Her son answered, "Before when you beat me, your strokes were hard and firm, so I was relaxed and happy about your good condition of well-being. Now I discover you have less strength and are not in good health. This is why I am crying."

In ancient China, and also just 50 years ago, it was not disgraceful for children, even adults, to receive punishment from parents. We consider the ability to receive punishment as a good spiritual attitude when done from respect and trust. You receive the punishment from your parents. Behind them there is no loaded firearm or handcuffing and jailing you, but love. If one does not discipline one's youngsters, then the policeman or criminal court will do it for you. Is that being kind or loving? However, things have changed. The devotion and mutual dedication of family members does not exist much any more. Now it seems this essence of spiritual practice has changed to be a different type of attitude.

The mother of the wise Yellow Emperor (2698-2598 B.C. reign) was a woman of spirituality. She taught her son that three spiritual qualities need to be attained in each individual. They are wisdom, kindness and bravery. This has become the goal of complete spiritual development for all spiritual students. Whether a person is a man or woman, one should attain these spiritual qualities in order to be a person of spiritual completeness.

My mother once pointed this out to me. "Remember the practice of Yi, Shi and Vi. Yi means inaudible, Shi means invisible and Vi means untouchable. This is an important practice which helps you link yourself with the subtle source. The subtle source issues the energy. The subtle source is not far; it is within each individual. Each individual, if correctly and directly connected with the subtle source within, produces three spiritual qualities: wisdom, kindness and bravery. Yi, Shi and Vi, the subtle source, is productive. Thus, if you correctly follow this traditional guidance, you will grow good fruit for your personality."

The wise Niao's mother suggested that Emperor Niao (reign 2357-2258 B. C.) have five spiritual qualities. They are kindness, faithfulness, respectfulness, wisdom and dutifulness. These five virtues or spiritual qualities were not an external requirement; they are internal growth. She also told Niao that each person is composed of five subtle elementary forces within. If the five elementary forces within are in correct order, usually they will produce a good personality with all five spiritual qualities or virtues. You do not need to look externally for something to obey or something to align yourself with. Align yourself with your own spiritual virtue to know that you are acting correctly.

My mother brought up an important point which I appreciate. She talked about the teaching or practice of spiritual self-delivery. She said that all religions were organized as sort of delivery for other people. However, it made many generations become dependent upon something outside themselves. The people did not learn anything, because they were always waiting for somebody else to save them. That is the problem with externally established delivery. None of those spiritual dependents have ever been truthfully delivered. True delivery must come from the individual self.

The opera performers were typical gamblers, and debtors, and drinkers, living in sexual confusion and being irresponsible with their personal lives. When my mother decided to help them, she used some of the techniques of religious delivery. They worked, but she did not make them dependent upon it. Each performer had an individual spiritual system; that is, the energy of self-delivery. She guided them to reach their own internal spiritual reality. Knowing their own internal spiritual reality helped them wish to learn to improve their lives. That inner desire for self-improvement and improvement of your life is the only force that can affect change within you. With self-motivation, a person can become useful again. Superficial work is of no use in helping individuals improve themselves.

No one could train the actors and actresses like a general training of soldiers. No one could stop their gambling, drinking, opium habits or sexual confusion other than themselves. My mother also could not declare that they could not perform unless their personal lives were clean. That would not have had a good effect. Instead, she helped them awaken their own spiritual energy so that they themselves would come to realize self-delivery. Otherwise they would have sunk like a leaky boat in water and pulled down the whole opera company, too.

All people, in some way, love their lives. All lives have the deep wish for self-delivery. All people wish to do something right, but need only that energy of awakening to do so. My mother's practice was called self-delivery. I use the term, "self-spiritual cultivation" about people who improve their own life. Practically, that is the same concept as what my mother taught as self-delivery. You need to rely on yourself to save yourself. Surely there are some useful practices which were passed down to us, but a full and enriched life still depends upon your own personal intention of self-delivery. Without it, external help is useless.

I totally understood the importance of spiritual self-delivery from the teaching of my mother. After I left China, my mother openly commented, "China can be helped only when the Chinese people find their self-delivery. No other nation can help. Any ideology for improvement of society, if it comes from someone else and is a ready formula to rigidly apply on a new time and in a different society, cannot bring delivery, but only disaster."

Confucius taught loyalty, dutifulness and faithfulness. Confucius' teaching was used by the Chinese monarchy as a tool for earning the people's support. This made everybody serve the emperor, government or political leader as they would a god. That also effectively blocked any improvements that could happen to Chinese society. Chinese literature and history is full of stories of people who died for the misused ideology of Confucius, needlessly sacrificing themselves for an emperor, government or political leader who they could not disobey.

If an emperor's leadership is wise, and you apply absolute obedience, faithfulness and loyalty, you will greatly help accomplish a big task and further the good of society. But if the emperor is unwise or is like a child or managed by people on the side, absolute loyalty or absolute obedience only brings sacrifice to the individual. No real help is given to society.

So the use of Confucius' teachings was too rigid an application of an ideology which caused a lot of trouble. Now study of the so-called materially oriented dialectic method of the communist party is required by the government for many people. The ideology of material dialectic was established by a German philosopher, Georg Wilhelm Friedrich Hegel. Karl Marx and Friedrich Engels took the foundation of his writings and developed materialistic dialectic. They took Hegel's dialectic and intellectually applied it to the theoretical sphere to support what they believed. Such intellectual work is not only idealistic, but it also has nothing to do with natural reality which is complete and impartial to materialistic or idealistic doctrines. This ideology only formed a rigid way of thought: communism. It blocks people from growing flexible minds. It is not a balanced view, but a new ideology that teaches extremes.

Dialectic is the art of arriving at truth by disclosing the contradictions in an opponent's argument and overcoming them. As defined by Hegel, a thesis is transformed into its opposite (antithesis) and preserved and fulfilled by it, the combination of the two being resolved in a higher form of truth (synthesis). As defined by Marx, through the conflict of opposing forces, any given contradiction is characterized by a primary and a secondary aspect, the secondary succumbing to the primary, which is then transformed into an aspect of new contradiction. Basically, dialectic is any method of argument or exposition that systematically weighs contradictory facts or ideas with a view to the resolution of their real or apparent contradictions. The contradiction between two conflicting forces is viewed as the determining factor in their continuing interaction.

Dialectical materialism is the Marxian interpretation of reality. It views matter as the sole subject of change and sees all change as the product of constant conflict between opposites arising from internal contradictions inherent in all things.

My mother believed that this type of ideology would not benefit human society. She thought that the most useful dialectic had been taught in the *I Ching* and *Tao Teh Ching*. Ancient Taoist work is full of natural dialectic. Even Chinese medicine was developed using the Taoist dialectic method.

The dialectic pattern is that first you have a thesis, then an antithesis, then the third step is an anti-antithesis. The anti-antithesis is not the same point as the thesis, but a new point. This can be exemplified by a mathematical equation. In mathematics, one negative number times another negative number equals a positive number, such as $-3 \times -3 = 9$.

In history, the Renaissance was the self-delivery of western people from religious darkness. At that time, religion had developed its dominant force and controlled all aspects of life. The Renaissance was the awakening of the western ancestors themselves: they found self-delivery during the Renaissance. The Renaissance expressed itself mostly in the areas of literature and arts.

Modern science is also the self-delivery of the western knowledge system from the dominance of the religions. But that did not happen before the Renaissance. From this you can see that all ideology can become bondage, and it is not healthy for a nation or a race to stay with any ideology. This is because circumstances can change, but if ideology does not also change, chronic or short-term trouble is caused. For example, if India wishes to be a modern country, there is no way it can happen unless the Indian people find self-delivery by deprogramming the bondage of ideology created by their ancestors' religious ideology. Similarly, Jewish people need to find self-delivery by making a supplement or new elucidation of their ancestors' creations.

Intellectual frames are not permanent truth. The permanent truth is change.

If people in the Chinese western region or abroad who adopted Islam wish to find improvement or progress in their lives, no external force can do it. They must find their own self-delivery. It is the same for the Chinese people and their society. All religious ideologies, and certain political ideologies, were established in a given time and place under a certain set of circumstances; the circumstances no longer exist. What is needed is the mental flexibility to adapt the old religious or political teachings or methods to the new situation of the modern world.

So self-delivery is energy from inside moving outside. Self-delivery is also the truth of an individual. Drug users cannot be helped unless they themselves decide to look for help. With the motivation of self-delivery or desire for self-help, they can find the way to help themselves. To improve a bad marriage, bad business relationship or bad company, help does not come from outside. People may use therapy groups or psychologists, but unless the people truly want to improve the relationship themselves, no therapy will help. Outside help produces an effect only when the people themselves have found the need for self-delivery. Above all, the desire for self-delivery is important for us in achieving our inner clarity. Fastening onto intellectual and religious frames is not practical.

All religions have a self-delivery ideology. Some versions are more complicated than others. However, ideologies are not important; the important thing is your own desire to be clear and know things for yourself, combined with experience in the world. After achieving inner clarity, you know what should and what should not be done.

The basis of my mother's teaching is the attainment of inner clarity. From inner clarity, it is easy to achieve self-knowledge. Self-knowledge grows from inside. It leads you to decide where you need to extend your personal energy and where you need to restrain it. There is no other achievement that is more beneficial or useful. It is practical. For example, some ambition is beneficial and some is harmful. Without inner clarity, ambition becomes an obstacle because you do not know how to apply it correctly. Then, you become the slave of that ambition or desire and are not the master of your desires.

The Integral Way was my father's spiritual principle to carry the essence of the ancient achievement, particularly original Taoism. It was never organized. In the broad Taoist tradition, each generation had some representative teachers or achieved Taoists. They were models, but among them there was hardly any connection, either horizontally or vertically. On my father's side, some representatives in each generation became highly achieved. This was understood by all Taoist followers. However, no formal record was kept to describe exactly who passed the practice to whom. Some records are clearer than others. I think it is important that the teachings and practices are not lost and are kept well.

My mother's teaching was initiated by Mother Chern. The direct passage from Mother Chern has been 73 generations. This is what I was told. Practically, few people even know the names and lives of their great-grandparents. The school of Jing Ming exalted Master Shu Seng to be the initiated teacher. Practically, it became known only after the Sung Dynasty (960-1279 A. D.). The records state that when Master Shu Seng ascended, he and his 42 direct students levitated in the sky. Then his soul exuviated from his vaporizing body, and ascended to the sky in the bright daytime. He was 116 years old (374 A. D.) and this event was witnessed by all the neighbors in the village. This is the only example of group ascension after the Yellow Emperor.

My mother's teaching was a secret passage from Mother Chern. The spiritual direction of my mother is distinctive. She suggested that if you wish your spiritual learning to bring real achievement, you have to first attain inner clarity. With inner clarity, it is easier for you to decide what kind of spiritual discipline or spiritual advice can serve you. She does not suggest that you depend upon secondary religions if you are looking for realistic achievement.

Generally, for the achieved Taoists whose souls are light, spiritual sky travel is possible even during the lifetime. There is no need to wait for the last day. However, it is a separation of body and soul, and is not recommended. Spiritual cultivation is to nurture spiritual energy from the physical foundation of life. A general soul has too much contamination; the soul loses some freedom by obstacles such as bad thought and bad behavior. The soul with contamination is heavy, so it sinks deeply into the ground. Their spirits and soul have no further chance to meet their folks and relatives again. Although some of those souls can be channelled or found by a medium, it is the power of the medium's brain capability of communication. It does not need the real soul to have any freedom to come to him. I mean that by having that function of brain to give the information of the soul in a reading. It is not the soul in person who comes to talk in the medium. It is a brain function rather than objective reality.

When you achieve inner clarity, you will come to know that you are unique in the universe, not the same as anyone in ancient or present times. Nor will there be anyone exactly the same as you in the future. You are a unique person; you have to grow your self-knowledge to know your own uniqueness. With self-knowledge, you can apply your healthy ambition and restrain detrimental ambition. You can work things out to bring only good, positive fruit to your life because you have attained self-knowledge.

There is no limitation to self-development on the spiritual level, but there is limitation in the world, especially on the physical level. Most people trust the systems of fortune telling such as tarot cards, astrology, palm reading, physiognomy, etc. My mother believed that the systems of fortune telling only classify people into categories of personality characteristics and cannot really tell anything specific about an individual.

People born in the same time and place have the same type of energy or tendency, but how much will each individual develop? How different will the people's lifestyles be? This cannot be determined by any fortune telling system.

Each individual is a unique being. You have many personal assets inside and out. Thus, you can organize your energy and external life however you wish and live higher than all other people, if you so choose.

Many people accept the concept of a predetermined destiny. Believing in destiny is a little bit like believing in an ideology. Many people think their lives are predecided. They are bound by the ideology of destiny, so little fruit comes to their lives. They never make an effort to improve themselves, but they only live passively.

When I was a lad, my mother mentioned three things to me. She told me that she was going to pass over before my father, because she knew the drawbacks of being too old. She also said that she would pass over at age 66. And her wish was that nobody mourn her; thus, she prepared her clothing and tomb in advance.

Things happened just as she told me many years previously. She also attained the freedom of the soul. That means she had the capability to come and go from her body at will. When she was 66, several years before the nationwide riot of the red guards and five years earlier than my father departed from the world, she began to make preparations. Society had begun to have much trouble, but it was not as bad as it was going to be. My mother sent for my elder sister to come home. She told my elder sister the purpose of the visit and asked her to help make the necessary preparations. My mother's health was still perfect. She repeatedly told my sister that life and death is totally a personal business. During both life and death, do not make a big deal out of anything to bother other people, to make them serve you or pay attention to you. She did not want lots of people to come to mourn her or to have a big funeral. To her, it was all unnecessary. She had accomplished her duty to all of us and that was enough.

One day my mother said it was time for her to leave before the world became worse and she would have to see all the suffering. She did not want to take the stupidity of the forthcoming political struggle. She did not want to exchange her spiritual dignity for longevity and the necessity of being humiliated by politicians. She went to her room and washed herself. My sister kneeled outside the door of the room. Incense was burned. My mother then lay on her bed and withdrew quietly from her body.

At that time, I was overseas and had to stop all correspondence to spare my parents political persecution. The communists knew I was in Taiwan. Because the communist party considered Gu Min Tang, the national party, to be a political rival or enemy, no correspondence was received without suspicion. They tried to disturb my mother by telling her that Taiwan was such a small island, and because so many people had retreated there, that there was not enough food to eat. They told her that most people had to eat banana peels to survive. That caused some concern from my family, but when the communists told this to them over and over again, my mother clearly knew that it was a trick. One day when they told it to her again, my mother calmly answered, "If my son stays in Taiwan eating banana peels as his main food, at least he has the whole peel for himself. If he lived under communism, he would probably have to divide it and share one peel with several people."

At this time, because she could not correspond with me, my mother gave my sister some information about me and some special instructions for me. My mother talked a lot about me with my sister, mostly to keep my sister from worrying both about me and about my mother's passing.

After my mother passed away, my younger brother stopped talking to my elder sister for one reason. He suspected that at the time of her passing, my mother had given my sister a special gift from the family fortune for me, and that she did not let him know about it. Perhaps he only wanted to have the whole family fortune and the thought that I might receive something caused him to feel insecure or jealous. Whatever his feeling, there was nothing for me from my mother but spiritual advice. The relationship between my sister and younger brother is still strained to this day.

My mother's achievement was not much different from what my father achieved. Yet, the expressions of their lives were different. They both learned important ancient practices. The ancient practices were connected more to natural energy and were less like ideology. From the attainment of Tao, you can become more positive minded. It can inspire you to bring a good result in your work and in your life. The ancient Taoist practices are not a formality that tie you down.

It is important to attain freedom of spirit and freedom of mind. If you have been following a religion, it might create a conflict with religious ideology. Religious ideology tends to set a mold for your thought, emotion and life attitudes. However, the benefit of switching over from religion to spiritual cultivation is great.

Fortunately, there is a good benefit to religious ideology: it helps guide people whose minds are not as developed or who cannot be creative. But it is helpful for all who are ready to leave behind the specific structure of what is right, wrong, good and bad to develop themselves and learn to see truth independently.

All of my parent's teachings serve the same direction as the ancient achieved ones. The purpose is self-delivery. To go along with the practices of self-cultivation or self-delivery, which are given in the book called *Eternal Light,* there are many instructive or informative diagrams. They are shown in the book: *Taoist Mysticism - God and Humankind United As One.* You can view the diagrams and then you will find the clue to reversing the process to receive spiritual immortality. The diagrams are given in the book together with the instruction. With the practice of pure light, you are not dyed, programmed or tied down to a certain type of thought, but you can find personal balance, internally and externally. That is the minimum contribution of these diagrams.

When most people feel troubled, the source of their trouble is the attitudes established in their minds. The mind consists of many different thoughts. Thoughts are based on habit and what we have learned from other people, television, books, education, etc. Thus, your mind depends on your environment. If your environment tells you that this is good and this is bad, this is joy and this is pain, you will believe it and follow it until you develop your spiritual clarity. Things are not as fixed as people suggest to you. You can live above the level of accepting the limited ideas of people. To do so, you need to break or deprogram the way your mind was programmed by people, yourself, and the culture you live in. A good way to do this is the Wu Tao or Taoist Enlightenment Intensive. This is one step toward attaining inner clarity.

My parents taught some simple practices you can use to protect and to correctly nurture your mind and spirit in daily life at any time or location. Some disciplines do not only protect your mind, they also protect your spirit from the internal disturbance of mind. They help you develop your mind further. If you do them, these practices will strengthen your mind and spirit. You can use them to help you attain power over your own mind. The power of mind is what helps you find a good way to move or act in different circumstances.

Mother Chern was quite powerful in spiritual service. Master Shu Seng was especially renowned by the service he rendered with his great spiritual power. He was a healer. Magic power is dramatic, but not ultimately important. Spiritual power is what you gather for your complete virtuous fulfillment. The spiritual power valued by this tradition is self-delivery. If you do not learn self-delivery, any magic power you develop is of no use. The more important practices of the ancient spiritual heritage are to teach us as individuals, societies and the entirety of the human world, to find our own self-delivery.

Mostly, the deep passage of original Taoism was done with diagrams. They are not oral teaching. The essential one is the Tai Chi Diagram Let us discuss their use in a general way. The first chapter of the *Tao Teh Ching* instructs us to view those diagrams in two ways. First, view them without intention, and see how they inspire you and what thoughts they bring to your mind. Just by looking at them, usually you are guided to peace of mind, or balanced mind, centered mind. No words are given.

The second way to view the diagrams is with intention, such as if you are looking for specific guidance to apply to a situation in your life. For example, when you are troubled, you look for a solution by quietly observing those diagrams. They often give you a clue for finding a solution. But never think that the clue is the solution itself. The clue is an inspiration; it will inspire you differently at different times. For example, when a circumstance changes, the clue may still be valid, but its meaning may have totally changed.

In the Tai Chi Diagram, the sages find movement of flow, cycle and balance. People can become sages by lifting themselves above their imbalances. The sages designed the Tai Chi diagram to demonstrate balance as the goal. Much later in modern civilization, the discovery of the atom and the development of the computer were both associated with the hidden clue from the Tai Chi diagram. Binary numbers or binary mathematics were developed from the *I Ching*. A modern Chinese scholar discovered the new tenth planet and received a doctorate degree from France by viewing the ancient diagrams. These are all small uses of the diagrams. The greater spiritual achievement is the individual who can find self-delivery and can thereby use this personal achievement to bring peace, safety and prosperity to all people.

People receive different inspirations because people have different personal, spiritual and mental natures. There is not only one way to teach people, therefore spiritual cultivation to attain self-delivery is highly valuable. Self-delivery does not establish ideology, it helps you develop your own mental and spiritual power. I recommend this reality for you.

Q: As a strong-willed child of parents with little self-control, I had many serious beatings. Because too many parents lose self-control in these situations, many parents today are against spanking. I chose not to spank because of this, but recently have started to use a single "spank" if bad behavior is repeated.

You told the story of repeatedly using the window as a door and finally receiving a spanking for this. Your mother had warned you and you were given an explanation with your spanking. I know many parents would like more guidance on this. Also were you given restrictions as punishment or just a spanking and all was over?

At the beginning of Chapter 10 you say, "I was not allowed to be crazy and barbaric." Did your mother allow you to run around and scream playfully outdoors? It is hard to know where to draw the line between "being a child" and "wild scatteredness."

Master Ni: The only restrictions I was given were short term, just long enough to make me cool down and see the problem by myself.

I was given disciplines and I accepted, but I forgot or neglected them when I was with other boys. Whatever the other boys did, I did also. My mother encouraged me to do serious sports. I liked to play wildly and have adventures.

Chapter 14

The Spirit of Neu Wu

On the spiritual level, this book is dedicated to the Universal Mother. Her spirit lives in all the people of the world. This is a story from old Chinese society about the first woman, whose name was Neu Wu. It has some value for its antiquity. I am reading it from a Chinese children's book and translating it directly.

"Long ago the earth and sky were mixed and the universe looked just like a huge egg. In the egg slept a giant named Pang Gu. Pang Gu slept there for more than 18,000 years or for a length of time that could not be measured. When he awoke, he felt extremely uncomfortable inside the dark and stuffy egg. He swung a big axe at the eggshell and with a deafening rumble, the shell was split in two. The soft and pure white pieces of the shell rose slowly and turned into the sky. The turbid and pitch black remains sank gradually and became the earth.

Afraid that the sky and earth would join together once more, Pang Gu stood there on the earth like a pillar that propped up the sky. He stood there for more than 18,000 years, or for a length of time that cannot be measured. He finally fell to the ground, exhausted. After his death, his limbs turned into mountains, his blood into rivers, his eyes into the sun and moon, and his skin and hair into trees, flowers, grass, birds, animals, fish and insects. His spirit became the god of nature.

One day, a beautiful and kind goddess called Neu Wu came down to this vast land. She was delighted and dazzled by this world where birds sang and flowers gave their fragrance. However, she felt that this beautiful world still lacked something. It needed mankind or other beings like herself. She kept thinking while she walked. Squatting beside a pond to drink some water, she saw her own plump reflection. She grabbed a handful of earth and using her own figure as a model, she molded a little doll. When she put the little doll on the earth, it came to life and called her Mama. Neu Wu was overjoyed. She kept on molding little dolls with the dirt. She molded day and night until her fingers ached.

The dolls she created were still too few for the vast land. A bright idea hit her. She snatched a length of green vine, dipped it in the mire and then splashed mud on the ground. The mud splashes all became small people. Wild with joy, Neu Wu was eager to create more humans. Splashing the mud, she ran across mountains, rivers and plains. Soon humankind appeared all over the world, with all kinds of appearances, but all the same being made from mud and water. From then on, people existed in this wonderful world. They worked with their hands and led a peaceful life.

One day, unexpectedly, winds rose and clouds whirled, thunder and lightening filled the sky. A flame swept across the forest and birds and beasts fled in panic. Shortly afterward, with a deafening sound, half the sky collapsed, and heavy rains pelted down. The god of water, called Gong Kung, and the god of fire, called Zu Yong, were raging in battle for control of the earth. Gong Kung drove the water from the Heavenly river and Zu Yong was chasing after him. Immediately the waters of the Heavenly river poured down with Gong Kung. The earth was split open by the collapse of the sky. Water gushed out endlessly from the crevices. The land would soon be flooded.

When Neu Wu saw her children about to be drowned, she wept bitterly. To save humankind, she lifted a stone and jumped into the hole where the flood was entering. The flood would not be stopped. Both Neu Wu and the stone were carried down by the torrent. Carrying the stone, Neu Wu jumped up again. She threw the stone into the hole. However, the stone was once more washed away. Neu Wu was not discouraged. She gathered many colorful stones from the seas, rivers and lakes and made a shining rainbow heap out of them. Then she put all the reeds she could find around the heap. She started a fire with the reeds. The fire burned for nine days and nine nights. Finally the heap of stones melted. She held the scalding liquid in her hands and jumped up to the sky. She patched and painted the sky for seven days and seven nights and at last it was mended. The rain ceased and the sun shone again.

Colorful clouds floated in the air, but Neu Wu was completely covered with burns. Water was still splashing from the crevices down to the ground. Despite her great pain, she picked up the ash of the reeds and handful by handful filled up the crevices. The water was stopped. Neu Wu had defeated disaster and saved humankind.

Besides this, Neu Wu also invented a musical instrument for the people to play. Called Sheng, it was made of 13 bamboo pipes stuck on a gourd.

Then came a peaceful and happy age for the world. The people wished to thank Neu Wu, their mother, but she was already riding to the Heavens in a thundercart drawn by a flying dragon. It is said that she remained there forever. She never boasted of her deeds, and the people of the earth never forgot her."

This was the genesis story of the ancient Chinese. I do not feel it degrades my teaching with a child-like type of level. However, it was not considered a holy book or something to stop the growth and intellectual development of the descendants. This story establishes the traditional spirit of the earliest Taoism, which was to assist the free development of mind instead of binding people to be religious minded. I am glad it supports the social position of women in a natural, free society was not limited only to being wives, concubines, servants and captives for slaves.

This story was developed long before history to illustrate the Taoist view of the universe. To sum up this view, here are a few points which were the original concepts of the ancients:

1. At the beginning, the universe was like one lump of energy. It was undistinguishable oneness. It was called "Hun-Tun."

2. Human life was nursed in the universe. The universe was the first existence. Human life was a late-comer and took support from the universe. It also could be viewed as the result of the transformation of the universe.

3. The spirit of life grows within the universe as human life can be viewed. The present physical being of the universe was a result of stretching force internally. Outwardly, this brought about the breaking of the physical limitation of the previous universe.

4. Growing life turns back to be a part of the universe. This means that life and the universe are still one being. They are integrated and inseparable as the big life of the universe.

5. Life in the stage of human beings, as small life, comes from the productivity of the natural femininity, the mystical female. Pang Gu is the universal physical being, while Neu Wu is the spirit of the universe. From her, all lives come about.

6. The survival of human life was conditioned by the battle between water (rain) and fire (sun). When the amount of fire and water (rain and sun) are balanced, harmony occurs and it is a good time for life. If either side wins the war, this causes the suffering of the people. This was the interpretation of earthly climate in the conception of the ancient people. Today, the reality has not changed.

7. To stop the leakage of the sky, Neu Wu had to find a way to stop the hole where water came out. This is a metaphor for spiritual cultivation. Earth means human physical life. Cultivation means to attain the internal balance of water and fire. Water means blood circulation, organ secretions, etc. Fire means the activity of the mind and certain emotions. Particularly, the "hole" which is the depletion of energy by indulging in sex needs to be stopped, otherwise the sky (life spirit) falls. This metaphorically designates the control and transformation of sexual energy. This was the spiritual awakening of early Taoists.

8. The hole could not be stopped up by a stone, which represents a rigid way. The hole could only be stopped by a process of refining, which means to change something to be something else.

9. The thing that could be used for stopping the hole can also be used to produce music in life. One of the interpretations of this is the uplifting emotional joy.

10. The word "Neu" means female. "Wu" is derived from the image of the snail. By their profound developed intuitive knowledge, the ancient developed ones believed the universal movement is a spiral type of movement. A snail with its sensitive antennas breeds strongly. Thus they chose its image for the name of the Universal Mother, Neu Wu. The same spiral movement still makes sense in the framework of today's modern knowledge. For example, modern astronomy has determined that the galaxy in which we live is a spiral. Thus, I feel Neu Wu is safe, even in modern times.

11. Ancient Chinese history was organized by intellectuals of the West Han Dynasty (206 B.C. - 215 A.D). They listed the rulers of different generations. As we have already discussed, the rulers of early times could be viewed as the symbols of progressing stages.

Pre-Heaven. The indistinguishable Hun Tun
Post Heaven. The babyhood of mankind.
Pang Gu, The Universal Being. "People" were at babyhood.
Emperor Heaven. "People" wandered with no direction or
    aim.
Emperor Earth. "People" recognized where they were born
    and where they belonged.
Emperor People. People grew the sense of themselves.
Emperor of Fire-Using. People started to use fire.
Emperor of Shelter-Building. People started to know to
    shelter themselves.
Fu Shi. A stage of developing herdsmanship.
Neu Wu. Spiritual power was exalted.
Shen Nung. A stage of developing agriculture.
Yellow Emperor. A stage of multiple natural cultural
    development.

Following the time of Pang Gu, the word "people" was put inside quotation marks. At that time, humans were not developed like we know them today and looked more like monsters than people. Some ancient scholars amended the formal history to have the following description:

Emperor Heaven, 12 heads, 12 brothers. Reigned up to 18,000 years.

Emperor Earth, 11 heads, 11 brothers. Reigned up to 18,000 years.

Emperor People, 9 Heads, 9 brothers. The earth was divided equally into 9 sections and each brother ruled one section. Each of the nine sections was passed down through 150 generations, totality 45,600 years in reign. (Approximately 300 years per generation).

According to this record, people's heads become less in number and age shorter in number.

This kind of record could not be expected to be accurate. But it gives the sense of how life transformed during this time period.

The emperors' names are also the names of stars in the Big Dipper and of other important stars in the sky.

Some ancient scholars believed that Neu Wu was the sister of Fu Shi. In different records, Neu Wu appears to be the sisterly tribe of Fu Shi, who after Fu Shi's time, continued Fu Shi's social position as the center of ancient society.

The original Immortal Taoism was hidden in this nursery story. I heard it many times from my parents when I was little. The above meaning was given after I was grown.

In human life, the Universal Mother issued forth her male energy to form a man. He carried the mission of breeding. So in a physical sense, one became two. In Taoist cultivation, to realize immortality is to establish internal, not external intercourse. The physical sexual organs of man and woman have differences and are distinguishable one from the other. However, internally, each person, whether man or woman, possesses both yin and yang energy (female and male energy). They exist in proportional amounts; one part is more and one part is less, in either a man or a woman. The mind is the go-between which establishes communication between both to give birth to a new spiritual life.

Thus, this story of Neu Wu contains the highest spiritual truth. I have also interpreted this sacred spiritual reality in the *Story of Two Kingdoms*. It tells the possibility of our physical being becoming a spiritual being by the combination of the two types of energy within each individual. This is not hard to understand, but it is hard to do because we habitually attach ourselves to physical stimulation and pleasure. Thus, this achievement becomes a rare example. In each generation, among a million people in a population, maybe one will be inspired to this achievement. It is the true secret of ancient Taoist immortal teaching. That is different from the later, religious Taoism that was purposed mostly for physical pleasure, and actually encouraged people to reproduce like the prolific snail. But the undeveloped descendants did not see that was a metaphor. Such reproduction only serves to make them go downward in their life evolution.

But the point here is that all human people developed from one mother. Neu Wu was also the name of the first human woman. She symbolized the universal mother, who split herself internally to project the yang energy. She formed man. Then they gave birth to many children. After the children grew, they scattered to live in many different places on the earth. At that time, the earth looked like a big egg; there was only one large continent surrounded by water. Later, a disaster occurred. A big comet shooting directly toward the earth landed on the continent and broke it into pieces. Some of those pieces of land, now known as the seven continents, were inhabited by the original people. The separation produced environmental influences, and the people developed differently, depending upon their way of life and natural environment. For example, the color of their skin changed depending upon how much sunshine they received, bringing about the difference of race, the size of body, temperament, etc. All was affected by the sun's energy and the living natural environment. This is how differences came to exist. So at the beginning, all people were born in an intermediate color and the two extremes developed from there. The variation of color happened from white to black with different middle colors.

Even earlier, when there were no people, life with fins existed in the water. When this life came out of the water to live in the air, the fins transformed to be wings. So now, in a Taoist's vision, we see many different birds flying under the water of the ocean and many different fishes flying overhead in the sky. Fish can be called birds, and birds can be fish. It does not express confusion. It expresses the unique source of all life creatures. All creatures, all lives, come from mother nature. Mother nature was given a name by the ancient Taoists: the mystical universal mother.

Anyway, the variations among the people of the world all have something to do with the position of the sun. Especially, the mentality of people differs by the sun's position. Cold regions are better for the brain. The quality of mind can produce good machines, work and science. By the big attraction of sun, in the hot regions the quality of mind is dreamy type vision which produces religion. In the mild regions, the balanced philosophy can be produced, or go both ways. However, it is not as simple as this, there are too many exceptions and variables can be given. Also, people who are sensitive to this view can give their own contribution in finding the apparent differences of reality. Because each individual life is a small model of nature, the spiritual energy in each individual is the sun energy in personal life. When spiritual energy rises to the top of the head, a balanced view and balanced life is expressed. This is why spiritual cultivation is to nurture the internal sun and to smooth the spiritual energy circulation to reach the top of the head. It is important not to block it in the lower abdomen; that only brings about many descendants.

So the universal mother in each individual person is individual spiritual energy. In this corner of the universe, the universal mother is represented by the energy of the sun. In the vast sphere of the universe, she is the subtle origin of the universe. She is above all. She is prior to all existence and non-existence.

The teaching of the Mother of the Yellow Altar made the mystical universal mother the spiritual focus. You may not be interested in the mythology. However, this teaching continued the ancient spiritual practice, the feminine principle and the principle of spiritual balance. These are all valuable spiritual contributions with perpetual value.

The Mother of Yellow Altar was a title given to the initiating teacher of my mother's spiritual tradition. Mother Chern lived in the time of east Jing Dynasty (317-419 A. D.) At that time, military competition in the northern region of China was strong and brought disaster to all people. Yet in southern China, too many mountains and too much water discouraged military maneuvers. Thus the political center moved to the new region in the south and spread. The new peaceful environment provided people with a suitable environment for spiritual pursuit.

"Yellow Altar" has its esoteric meaning. The teaching is original wisdom. The teaching did not have a purpose of establishing someone to be a social authority or a teacher. The teaching itself cannot be established in any way because it is the way to realize the formless truth. The way itself is as formless as the truth. Each generation has only one student who becomes the spiritual heir to carry or continue the teaching of the Yellow Altar. No person's name is given or recorded; all the teachers remain anonymous. Thus, all teachers in different generations use the same title of "the Mother of Yellow Altar." My mother was the spiritual heir to this teaching, so she was also called the Mother of Yellow Altar. Following the traditional spirit, my mother's personal name was dissolved when she presented the teaching to anyone.

This teaching emphasizes that correct thought, correct language and correct behavior are the spiritual sufficiency of an individual. It does not set certain special rituals, methods of worship or specific concepts as spiritual achievement. The real spiritual achievement is the correct fulfillment in the everyday life of each individual by following the right course of life. In everyday life, effort, cultivation and refinement is required in such achievement. All kinds of self-improvement is needed to achieve oneself to live the right course of life.

According to my personal study, this is golden guidance and is the most sincere teaching in human culture. The teaching of the Mother of Yellow Altar is special. It values the strength and courage to remain with the ordinariness of life with a developed spiritual stature. This is the most respectful power that any person can have. This is one step higher than the life of the "religious people" who think that departing from ordinary life to practice rituals is spiritual. That is an incorrect view of life and reflects trouble in the internals of the practitioners. People who do that become more unbalanced. It is also not healthy for people to be considered special and receive attention or admiration from other people.

The teaching of the Mother of Yellow Altar wishes that all people embrace the valuable spiritual diamond in the ordinariness or normalcy of life. The diamond is a balanced nature. A diamond is valuable no matter where it is.

A spiritual diamond is our own spiritual nature. Poor craftsmanship would devalue the diamond. Poor craftsmanship describes the work of the contorted religious teachings which twist or mishandle the natural organic condition of each person's spiritual nature.

I hope I did not narrow down the teaching of Mother Chern as only being contained in this book. A Taoist views all worlds as one world, and all people of the past, present and future as one person. At least, all people who are spiritually achieved in Tao are one person and one world. All teachers' good teachings describe Mother Chern's teaching. Her teaching also describes all good teaching.

The spiritually achieved ones are not fond of other people using the word "teacher" to address them. Nor do they wish to be highly respected by people. Teaching is the side effect of their lives. Teaching is just like a fragrant tree which naturally gives its sweet scent. This is the true divine nature of those highly spiritually developed ones. This divine nature is missing in general religious promotion.

In this book, my mind has responded to the problem or question of my women students and readers of today. I have especially collected the illustrations that my mother gave me as teaching. I have also given a historical overview to help describe the correct position of man and woman in the world. Particularly, it is my wish to help the modern woman who is not only a pillar of her family, but is also a pillar of society. Clear spiritual vision is essential in the spiritual learning of all people, especially those who are pillars to other human lives.

I wish the teaching of the Mother of Yellow Altar to help further develop your everyday life in these modern times. I hope you are spiritually successful and also achieve well in your individual personal life to join the great life of the Mother of Yellow Altar.

Concluding Discussion

Q: I would like to hear more stories about instances between you and your mother, and interactions between your mother and the rest of the family. They could be useful in showing how your mother did things, type of meals, etc.

Master Ni: My mother was the spiritual heir of Mother Chern. Mother Chern learned spiritually from Master Lan Chi. Master Lan Chi was a family man, not a social teacher. He had a large family, over a hundred children and grandchildren. His main teaching was to realize spiritual virtue towards each individual inside and outside the family. Besides that, because he had an abundant knowledge of herbs, he could instruct and take care of the health of the family members and students.

Mother Chern learned the arts of herbology, spiritual practices and spiritual healing from Master Lan Chi. However, she did not marry. After her father and mother passed away, she remained single. She had a place to live and a small inheritance to maintain her life. She chose to be independent yet she extended her service by teaching people who accepted her. She became quite a recognized teacher at that time. Several influential Taoist Masters were her students. Mother Chern lived in ancient times. When her teaching extended to my mother, many generations had already received her wisdom. Thus, a long lineage of the teaching was established and her main teaching was handed down, complete and intact.

By observing my mother, we know Mother Chern did not feel that one should escape to Heaven because life is disappointing, having a family is a burden, and relationships are not meaningful. Her understanding differed from that type of teaching. Her teaching was to realize your spiritual cultivation or virtue in the present life, wherever and whatever you are, as a daughter, mother or wife. Therefore, my mother's direct relationship with me, my sisters and brothers was close and supportive, because her main training was to realize the meaning or value of life in helpful relationships. She fulfilled her virtue in this way.

In our house, we did not have a fireplace, so during the winters, we usually gathered in the kitchen because it was a little warmer there. We sat there when my mother was doing her chores, like washing the dishes and so forth. My mother used those occasions to teach us. During the summers, we ate outside in our backyard garden. After eating and cleaning up the kitchen, my mother would come out to teach us and converse with us.

She did not have a lot of time for herself. Her life was full of all kinds of activities. In the mornings, after waking, she prepared herself for a busy day. At that time, women made their hair into a bun at the back of their neck. I never saw my mother's hair not dressed neatly. Before she came out from her room, she was clean and dressed, and she immediately started preparing breakfast in the kitchen. After breakfast, she needed to clean the kitchen, and then help my father in the clinic. Of course she made lunch for all of us. In the afternoon, my mother settled down to make clothes and shoes for us. When my sisters were teenagers, she taught them embroidery. She would teach us at any opportunity that arose. I think she could be considered as a good mother of any good Chinese family.

She was very healthy. I never saw her become sick, except I believe she had constipation sometimes. If I did martial arts, she would comment about what needed to be corrected. She also commented on other young men's martial arts performance that was not right. I think my mother used housework as her exercise.

My mother did her spiritual practice in the family shrine whenever she had a little extra time. Occasionally, in good weather, she would visit mountain temples, places that had better spiritual energy. She also sometimes helped my father when he went to teach. My mother would often bring me along to the teaching service.

Q: Something that modern women need to understand more is taking care of ourselves versus nurturing the whole family.

Master Ni: In life, there are two types of activity. One type of activity is external work that requires concentration such as when you drive on the road, communicate with another person for business contact, or work in office. Work at home is the other type of activity. Most modern American or Chinese women still need to do housework after coming home from work. Housework sometimes takes less concentration because it is more routine and can be done kind of automatically. It does not cause high tension. Men need to come home and do work around the house, too. Most of their house or outdoor chores also do not cause lots of tension. Each person always needs to find time to withdraw from outside contact and to re-establish contact with oneself. Even if you live an active life, you need to have time to withdraw from all outside activity. If you do not, your energy will stay scattered. It is healthy to have a balance between the two in daily life. However, whenever you are doing activity in the world or with the public, you should put your full attention to whatever is in front of you. But also, always find time to withdraw that attention back to yourself, be with yourself. That is a fundamental requirement for a person looking for spiritual growth.

If you scatter your energy with all kinds of social activity, without a little time to pull your attention back to yourself, it will weaken your energy. When you are young, you can afford it, but when you are older, you feel exhausted and are worn out much easier. No matter what your age, when you read my books, today should be the day you start to change your life. How? Let me explain. First of all, our attention is always attracted by the outside world. Some things in the outside world are necessary, some are of medium importance, and some are not at all important. The most important thing to learn is to withdraw all the unnecessary attention back to yourself. Forming this habit is the first fundamental step of self-spiritual cultivation. Without doing it, life moves away from you. So you need to devote yourself to nurturing your life. In all activity, you should be still and spiritually centered. Good, effective work that makes a useful contribution can only be made when you are spiritually centered. This is why I make this suggestion.

Q: How to cope with family relationships, including in-laws, stepchildren, aging parents and at the same time, earning money to pay the bills, put children through college, etc.

Master Ni: In the old way of life, each person made a contribution. Even a child had a duty in the family. Of course, it is up to the parents to direct the children to fulfill their duty. In the ancient way of life, the woman was the center of the family, not the man.

Your question expresses that you have much responsibility. As the center of the family, you must manage, conduct or direct each person to fulfill their duty. If all duties fall upon the responsibility of one individual, the person lives an ineffective life and will become exhausted. It is dutiful and healthy for each person living in a family to accomplish their jobs.   In ancient times, in a farmer's family, the woman had in-laws, unmarried brothers and sisters of her husband, and her own children to feed. She had ten hogs and a group of chickens in the back yard to care for, and still needed to send food to the field where her husband works. That was all woman's job. Women of ancient times could do it because they began to learn when they were small, and they fell into the job automatically with no tension.   They were busy, but they were still happy. Generally, all healthy women could do that, it is not special. In my hometown, farmers' families become prosperous, because the center is the woman. Her success was due to how she arranged things. She had energy to be active at anything without feeling the tension. It is not work that makes people's health bad, it is tension. So I suggest - not require - if you live a busy life, you should not worry, reject or resent it. Most important, it is okay to live busily, but try to eliminate all possible tension and pressure. Only pressure and tension, which come from your psychological or emotional creations, will cause your health to decline, your life to become unproductive and you to be unhappy. If you understand this, you will be more fulfilling in a busy life than be nervously watching at the side.

Q: How can modern women deal with their romantic dreams, disappointments and recognition of their limitations?

Master Ni: This is difficult for me to answer.   A dutiful woman will be serious about putting romantic imagination, marriage and family fulfillment together.   Once married, romantic imagination comes most often from the man. Women usually are more concentrated in managing their own energy than men.   I do not know why, maybe because the men are more physically active and therefore are more scattered.   Maybe it is because the woman, once married, decides that "this is my world, this is my life," and she will do her best to feel happiness, achievement and fulfillment.

Q: How can modern women cope with their self-image versus their media image?

Master Ni: What does that mean?

Q: I am not sure.   This is a written question.   I think it means the view people have of women from television.

Master Ni: You do not need to look for that.   If a person lives a decent life, it is not out of anybody's promotion, but from your own spiritual growth.   It is so important to take responsibility for oneself rather than running after social fashion.   Social fashion is a short existence; it is always changing.   If your focus is outside, in buildings, fashions, cars and a social type of life, then you do not live with yourself, you live externally.   This type of life will be shallow. A shallow woman can never be a really spiritual woman. There are lots of women who live that way.   There is a popular singer who is smart enough to sell that type of fashion or model to people.   It is a money-making project, which is different from what people think about it.   They think she is sexy or outrageous, but I think she is totally clear about what she is doing.   She is not making a fool of herself, she is making a fool of other people.   That is my view; maybe I overestimate her.

Her outrageous "personality" is what she sells. Fortunately, most women do not need to live like that. She knows what real happiness is. If she could, she would like to withdraw from all activity.

Q: How can a woman deal with loneliness after her husband's death, divorce, moving and children leaving home? Without their families and familiar surroundings, women suffer from lack of direction.

Master Ni: That is because they do not have any spiritual focus. A long time before anything happens, you need to plant the spiritual seeds in your mind. When you live with many people, that is a chance for you to offer your virtuous service, your help. Living alone is a great opportunity. You have already fulfilled certain obligation, and this gives you a chance to cultivate and nurture yourself.

From both questions, I would like to help you see the reality. In one you have so many people to take care of and still need to pay the bills. Then you do not need to take care of all the people or pay their bills. The reality is that change happens. Sometimes your energy will be more outwardly focused and sometimes it will be more inwardly focused. If you cannot learn to appreciate both, you will never have a good day in your life, so your life will be wasted. If you are widowed, it is a circumstance, it is not a choice. Some parents, after they have spent years putting lots of energy into their children, are delighted to have an opportunity to be alone, nurture themselves and do things they have always wanted to do but never had the time. They can get to know themselves or engage in spiritual cultivation. It is not your choice, but a different life involved with that kind of energy flow. So now that you are alone, why not cultivate yourself? Living alone is a great time to put your attention or focus on your self-achievement. In ancient times, most people with spiritual achievement lived alone. Many widows outlive other people because they start to live alone earlier than other people. Spiritually it is a benefit, not a disadvantage. Your question implies living alone is a disadvantage. That is a totally different direction from achieving emotional or spiritual independence. The question is maybe involved with psychological matters, that require different help. You may be talking about practical matters such as finances, safety, housing, autos, etc., in other words, getting help when you need it.

As a spiritual teacher, I would tell you that this is your time to be yourself, because you have already fulfilled many things that needed to be done. Now it is time to do something for yourself.

Q: Master Ni, what advice can you give regarding women aging in a society that overvalues youth. We see so many examples of people's unwise aging, physically and mentally, and strive to avoid those kinds of mistakes.

Master Ni: This is all good observation. I hope you do not learn from the bad examples but learn to live wisely like the good examples. Much of my work is geared towards helping people with what you describe as aging gracefully, or perhaps it is better to call it anti-aging. One important practice in Taoism is called evergreen or everspring. That is the same term. This practice is done by natural and simple living. A serious Taoist life has no need of health insurance, no need to wait to be ready for your hospitalization, those are all bad things. You should learn first to take care of your health, take care of your life being. This is basic. However, health insurance is still good to have in case of accidents and unforseen trouble. The ancient Taoists did not have automobiles and the other risks of modern life. They could easily live hidden in the mountains. Modern life is different. I do not suggest you let your insurance lapse and your hospital close, but if you are wise, it is your choice to pursue your health. I would like to pass this to individuals who would really like to take care of themselves, live a natural life, without relying upon external establishments.

Q: Could you talk about women's sexual concerns of finding a mate and fear of disease.

Master Ni: I can only respond spiritually. Taoists usually apply their intuitive mind to finding their life direction, mate and place to live. Thus, they do not do anything unnatural. Nor do they do anything from the motive of internal desire caused by hormonal pressure. You still need to apply your spiritual intuitive energy to right circumstance, right opportunity. If there is no such opportunity, the main thing is to cultivate and to nurture your intuitive energy. If your intuitive energy changes to be subconscious desire, that is low. That will direct you to a bad direction, causing disease and early death. That is what makes spiritual life different from worldly life. Spiritual life means in middle age when you are sexually mature, you may have strong sexual desire. Spiritual life is to take no pressure from it, spiritual life knows that this energy is the capital of vital force.   You should not damage it. If you already have children, you do not need to do that any more. In that section of using life, you need to correct that which does not help you.

So the conception of when to do sex is totally different from the world's typical view of doing it whenever possible. There are two different practices. If you are young and your circumstance allows you, like in married life, or if you have a beneficial relationship with a girlfriend or boyfriend, you can have it. If not beneficial, you always need to restrain and discipline yourself not to go in that direction. It is not necessary to be totally celibate, but if there is no good partner or good opportunity, I think you should be wise enough to stay far away from any risky opportunity. Do not take chances for sexual fulfillment.

Q: Could you talk about situations where one spouse loses interest because their expectations of marriage in other areas are not being fulfilled.

Master Ni: The other spouse needs to have patience. Sometimes people have a low cycle and lose interest in sex. Do not push it. Pushing will cause trouble. A total marriage is a combination of many things: emotional, spiritual, psychological and all other things. So one should have your spouse feels less interested in doing that, one should discipline oneself to accommodate the situation. Wait until the cycle changes and your spouse becomes active again. Two individuals who live together as husband and wife will each experience their own, different cycle. So my answer cannot perfectly satisfy each individual, but this is general principle.

You also asked about when other areas make a person feel unfulfilled. If you choose, have patience to not damage the pride of the opposite side.

Q: Could you speak about the general confusion of a woman living in society along with violence, drugs and other abuse?

Master Ni: Keep away from them, totally, absolutely. Do not learn from them, keep away. Concentrate upon your main life activity, with the people you feel safe, and do not go around with people who are unsafe. For example, do not hitchhike. You do not know if the driver is drunk or on drugs, so keep away from unnecessary risk.

Q: What did your mother look like?

Master Ni: She looked like her picture, which is on the cover of this book. In Chinese, there is a proverb that says, "Children never think their mother is ugly." I think my mother is beautiful. She was truly pleasant and presentable in society. Some of my young friends felt their mother was not presentable, especially in a scholarly meeting. But my mother was presentable.

Q: Did she use cosmetics?

Master Ni: She did not use cosmetics for color, like lipstick, but she used them for protection. For example, in winter when her skin was dry, she used lotion for some protection. Or she might use lipstick, but it had no color, because it was to keep her lips from being chapped. She did not use colored cosmetics.

Q: How did she feel about her bound feet?

Master Ni: She did not feel unhappy about it, for two reasons.   One reason is because she was a positive person. The second reason, whatever kind of situation people live under, they still need to be happy.   It is all reason to live as I see.   She did not feel the need to correct the custom, but she did not do that to her daughters.   This custom was stopped in her later years by the new cultural trend.

Q: Did she do T'ai Chi or any martial art?

Master Ni: I did not ever see her doing them, but when I did something with other young men, she would always give suggestions on how they could improve.   I believe she had some knowledge about it.

At that time, there were no spigots in the house for water.   For all the household uses, we needed to carry water from the canal to the water jar in the kitchen.   When I was a little older it was my job to do this.   Usually there was never enough because I was active outside, so she would do it.   She was quite strong.   Usually, when farmers carry water, they balance a pole across their shoulders and hang a bucket on each end.   However, my mother did not use a pole, but carried two buckets in each hand.   With small, bound feet, she could carry them up a steep incline with steps that went down to reach the water in the canal.   When I was a teenager, I helped her do this as part of my kung fu practice.

Q: How did she exercise?

Master Ni: Working.   She worked in the kitchen.   I think she had enough exercise, and did not need to look for other exercise.   She exercised when she worked.

Q: What kind of meals did she cook?

Master Ni: She cooked great meals.   We had ocean and fresh water fish, pork and everything.   The main thing my mother did was serve the children, my sisters and brothers. We were the young gods in the family; when she served us, she cooked great food.

My father and mother ate simply.

In my family, the morning and evening meals had no bloody smell - that means, no meat. Those meals consisted mainly of rice porridge with sweet potatoes. Usually one or two hours after eating, I would notice that my stomach was empty. However, my good times were not when my tummy was full but when my tummy was empty. It was my most effective time for study.

Because the morning and afternoon meals were so watery, nobody in my family was overweight. At noon, the youngsters ate meat and ocean fish but everybody ate vegetables. Meat and fish were given in small amounts. Their purpose in the food was mostly to give flavor. From my observation, the health condition in our family was excellent.

Q: How did Mother Chern enter your mother's life?

Master Ni: Mother Chern lived in ancient times, much earlier than my mother. Her teaching was passed down generation after generation by her spiritual heirs. My mother learned from one of Mother Chern's spiritual heirs. Mother Chern was a spiritually achieved person. I think she ascended, although there was no description of it. Mother Chern did not write books. Her teaching was orally passed down to each generation. Surely I believe my mother had real contact with the spirit of her initiating teacher, Mother Chern.

Q: What was your mother's early training like?

Master Ni: It was just like that of any general Chinese woman. At that time, all women's training came from the mother and father. It was family training. There were schools at that time, but they were closed to women. Women could only learn from their parents or a family teacher.

Q: Mother Chern does not sound like a Chinese name. Can you tell us more about her?

Master Ni: It is not a popular surname. It means sincere or honest. It is a Chinese name. I do not know any other people who carried the same name, because she lived during a different time. However, we know one thing: the spiritual practice she passed down is mostly connected with the *I Ching*. The teaching of Mother Chern is large so I put some of it into this book, *Harmony, the Art of Life,* and *Become the Cloudless Sky*. I introduced her practice in the book, *Taoist Mysticism: God and Humankind United As One*. Even there I did not have enough room to include all her important teaching.

Q: Have I understood correctly that your mother's main practice throughout her day was self-delivery and clear mind?

Master Ni: Originally I wished to organize her practice in this book. It seems too big, therefore it will appear in *Taoist Mysticism - God and Mankind United as One*. Here is what was orally passed about a deep meditation from my parents from their teachers throughout generations:

Tao does nothing.
Tao does all.
This can be known by the accord between mind and truth.
This cannot be known by intelligence.

What does high knowledge mean?
It is to send away all thought by wisdom.
How does one achieve this?
It is attained by the response to nothing.

By making no use of response,
The mind can know all.
By reaching unified oneness,
Nothing else needs to be done.

The one is the root.
The events and phenomenon are the gate.
All events and phenomenon return to the one.
The one is always existent.

The existence of one can be known.
To keep oneness is the way.
By keeping to non-existence,
The enjoyment of all existence can be found.

Q: I was hoping for more material relating to the concerns of today's women. Our lives are so complicated and fragmented that we have little time to reflect on what we are doing.

Master Ni: That is a good question. I can only direct you to cultivate and nurture your spiritual energy. Once you set up your center, you can fix the details of life by yourself. Taoist teaching is not a religious custom. Religious customs are prefabricated, but a Taoist life is not. You construct it as you go along according to circumstance. You can do a thing out of your maturity and feel safe, useful and effective. If those three conditions are not there, you should not do it. It is important to learn the essential things.

Q: Encouraging mothers to expose children to various religious traditions is an excellent idea.

Master Ni: It is also important to tell them the stories from different religions. You do not even necessarily need to take them to all different churches, but all valuable spiritual stories from different customs and faiths should be told. That will broaden their vision, their acceptance of spiritual learning and knowledge will be different. They will look for higher truth and not be limited by one or two stories. Such limitation will formalize the young mind. This is what I experienced when young.

Q: Did your mother do any other spiritual practices?

Master Ni: My mother used a special invocation which she called the six true words. She gave this invocation to many people, and taught them to use beads to practice it. It is helpful when people have random or negative thoughts or are emotionally uneasy because they have an internal struggle. She said that the six true words are the most powerful and truthful words in the entire heritage of all spiritual traditions. They are "Shing chu yuan ming wu nie." Shing means mind, heart or center. Chu means pearl. Yuan means round or smooth rolling or complete in itself. Ming means clear or brightness. Wu means none or no. Nie means obstruction. All together it means, the mind is like a bright pearl which rolls smoothly with no obstruction. She said you do not need to look for the meaning, just say it. My mother believed that all achieved people, whether they lived before or after her, achieved the smoothly moving mind described by this invocation. There is no exception. There is no need for a complicated system or ritual to achieve having a smoothly rolling mind. It can be done any time you are alone, and also when you are watching TV or something and have other people around. If you ever get a chance when you do not have to use your mind, and after you have thought about the important things you need to think about, in your free time you should keep reciting the six true words. They are also called the six words of truth.

Also, she recommended that all people have good faith in the universal mother. All people attain their life from her. A new name for the universal mother is the goddess of boundless blessing. The words of the invocation reflect that the invocation is a spiritual connection with the source of all blessings of life. Nobody can afford to sever this important spiritual connection. My mother taught me once that the name of the universal mother is God of self-blessing. I wondered why she said so. I said to my mother, if I need to bless my life, why should I pray to another individual? My mother smiled and said, "Learning to be modest is a blessing. You need to remember this." She also said that most people who live with all kinds of blessing do not know that they live with blessing. There are two sayings in Chinese about blessings that read as follows: The first one is, he who lives with blessings is ignorant of the blessings. The second one is, People can be blessed by what they do. Therefore, it is meaningful to pray to the God or Goddess of self-blessing too.

This is how you use the beads. You can use any kind of beads or necklace. They can be of any color. Hang the beads or necklace over the fingers of your hand, and use your thumb and index finger to grasp a bead. Say the six truthful words. Then pull the bead gently towards you and grasp the next bead, saying the six truthful words. Continue until you have gone all the way around the necklace. When you say the words, it is good to allow yourself to hear them. Do not say them too loud. The most effective and most useful way to say the words is to think them. You can also sing it or chant it with spiritual clarity and sincerity.

When I was ten years old, I learned to do that practice. I feel it is effective. I improved my impulsive nature by the teaching of "Tai Shan Kan Yin Pien" which is an article I printed in the pamphlet *The Heavenly Way*. It has been reprinted in *The Key to Good Fortune - Refining Your Spirit.* The practice of the six truthful words improved the clarity of my mind. Clarity of mind is achieved by dispersing all kinds of unhealthy or disturbing emotion. That is really useful.

Q: What is your mother's name?

Master Ni: In this book, I promote the spiritual understanding of the universal mother. All good mothers present the reality of the universal mother, as does mine. Therefore, I do not give her name to escape promoting personal worship or adoration. As her traditional practice, she become the Mother of Yellow Altar to give no other name.

Q: Is the practice of the six truthful words related to the mystical pearl?

Master Ni: On many occasions I have described the mystical pearl. Keeping the pearl rolling smoothly is her essential practice. In other words, she kept busy with all kinds of creative work. The work was not monotonous because there were many different kinds of things to do. Her mind responded to her hand, and her hand responded to her mind. In other words, when you contact or work with people, you must keep your spiritual center. Another way to describe it is maintaining spiritual independence from whatever you are experiencing. It means you do not allow any aspect of life to pull you down. Spiritually you are independent of all circumstances. It means you are independent spiritually from any pressure that could be caused by relationship, family, money or job. This is achievement, but it is also a practice.

In other words, the practice of spiritual independence from the circumstances of life is spiritual achievement. The achievement of spiritual independence from all bad situations, unpleasantness, trouble and misery is a practice.

So when you give up the practice, at the same time you give up the achievement. You cannot separately establish your practice aside from the realistic circumstances of life. It is a true way to attain Tao.

Most Taoist lives are like a piece of white clouds or like the life of a wide crane. You do not even know where they stay. You cannot catch them for observation, so it is hard to learn from their example. However, the highly achieved Zen Masters in Chinese history did the same practices as my father and mother.

It is clear that psychological burden is the most harmful thing in people's lives. It makes people age faster and depletes their energy quickly. In order to correct this shortcoming of most people, spiritual liberation means to liberate their spirit from the undevelopment of the mind. If you understand this, you will know the value of purity of mind. I do understand that this is easy to say but not easy to do. All my work and the practices I teach are to help people's understanding to make correct preparation for a powerful spirit and powerful mind. That is most realistic and helpful achievement. Seems all of us need it.

Q: Did your mother learn from Quan Yin?

Master Ni: I believe she took in Quan Yin. Now, I would like
to give a short story to illustrate the type of spirituality that
Quan Yin has.

Once a man who lived with his mother in a small town
made a vow that he would make a pilgrimage to Mount Pu
Tu of the South Sea, the spiritual region of Quan Yin, in
exchange for a wish being granted. During the third spring,
his wish for some business agreements was fulfilled. So he
prepared to make the trip to visit Quan Yin. It would take
several weeks because the mountain was quite far and he
would have to walk. At that time, his mother was not in
good condition, but he believed that he must go because he
made the serious spiritual promise. So he joined the group
of pilgrims.

On the first night, he stayed at an inn. He dreamt that
an old white bird came to him and changed into a dignified
gentleman. He felt sure that it must be a god appearing in
his dream. The god said, "You do not need to go all the way
to the South Sea to see Quan Yin. The magnificent temple
of Mount Pu Tu has a carved jade statue of Quan Yin, that
is all. However, if you immediately go back to your home,
you will see the true Quan Yin. Truthfully, she will appear
in your own home." The man awoke with a clear remem-
brance of the dream, so he said goodbye to his companions
and went back home.

His mother was surprised that her son had returned so
early, but she was glad to have him back. She started to
become busy taking care of him as usual. She prepared the
water for his bath and made his food. She had always
kindly and lovingly taken care of and served her son. He
always deeply appreciated her care.

The son kept expecting the Goddess of Mercy to appear
in the house in person. It did not happen. Yet the son was
an intelligent person, and still felt that the dream had deep
significance. He realized that in the entire world, the most
merciful and selfless person was his own mother. No one
else wholeheartedly took care of him so kindly. She was the
Goddess.

There is a poem I would like to quote to end this short
story.

Buddha lives in a high spiritual mountain.
Yet the mountain is not far from you.
The mountain is truthfully as close as
    your mind and heart.
The mountain is at your mind and heart.
In every mind and heart, there is a pagoda on the
    spiritual mountain.
The wise one practices cultivation under the
    pagoda of the high spiritual mountain.

About Hua-Ching Ni

Hua-Ching Ni is fully acknowledged and empowered by his own spiritual attainment rather than by external authority. He is a teacher of natural spiritual truth and a natural person. He is heir to the wisdom transmitted through an unbroken succession of numberless generations of true masters dating back to the time before written history. As a young boy, he was educated by his family in the foundation of the natural spiritual truth. Later, he learned spiritual arts from various achieved teachers, some of whom have a long traditional background, and fully achieved all aspects of ancient science and metaphysics.

In addition, 38 generations of the Ni family worked as farmers, natural healers and scholars. Master Ni has continued in America with clinics and the establishment of Yo San University of Traditional Chinese Medicine. Master Ni worked as a traditional Chinese doctor and taught spiritual learning on the side as a service to people. He taught first in Taiwan for 27 years by offering many publications in Chinese and then in the United States and other Western countries since 1976. To date, he has published about twenty books in English, made five videotapes of gentle movement and has written some natural spiritual songs sung by an American singer.

Hua-Ching Ni lived in the mountains in different stages. When possible, he stays part-time in seclusion in the mountains and part-time in the city doing work of a different nature. He believes this is better for his nervous system than staying only in one type of environment.

The books that he has written in Chinese include two books about Chinese medicine, five books about self-spiritual cultivation and four books about the Chinese internal school of martial arts. The above were published in Taiwan. He has also written two unpublished books on ancient spiritual subjects related with natural health and spiritual development.

The other unpublished books were written by brush in Chinese calligraphy during the years he attained a certain degree of achievement in his personal spiritual cultivation. He said, "Those books were written when my spiritual energy was rising to my head to answer the deep questions in my mind. In spiritual self-cultivation, only by nurturing your own internal spirit can communication exist between the internal and external gods. This can be proven by your personal spiritual stature. For example, after nurturing your internal spirit, through your thoughts, you contact many subjects which you could not reach in ordinary daily life. Such spiritual inspiration comes to help when you need it. Writings done in good concentration are almost like meditation and are one fruit of your cultivation. This type of writing is how internal and external spiritual communication can be realized. For the purpose of self-instruction, writing is one important practice of the Jing Ming School or the School of Pure Light. It was beneficial to me as I grew spiritually. I began to write when I was a teenager and my spiritual self awareness had begun to grow."

In his books published in Taiwan, Hua-Ching Ni did not give the details of his spiritual background. It was ancient spiritual custom that all writers, such as Lao Tzu and Chuang Tzu, avoided giving their personal description. Lao Tzu and Chuang Tzu were not even their names. However, Master Ni conforms with the modern system of biographies and copyrights to meet the needs of the new society.

Hua-Ching Ni's teaching differs from what is generally called Taoism, conventional religious Taoism or the narrow concept of lineage or religious mixture of folk Taoism. His teaching is non-conventional and differs from the teaching of any other teachers. He teaches spiritual self-sufficiency rather than spiritual dependence.

Master Ni shares his own achievement as the teaching of rejuvenated original spiritual truth, which has its origins in the prehistoric stages of human life. His teaching is the Integral Way or Integral Truth. It is based on the Three Scriptures of ancient spiritual mysticism: Lao Tzu's *Tao Teh Ching, The Teachings of Chuang Tzu* and *The Book of Changes.* He has translated and elucidated these three classics into versions which carry the accuracy of the valuable ancient message. His other books are materials for different stages of learning the truth. He has also absorbed all the truthful high spiritual achievements from various schools to assist the illustration of spiritual truth with his own achieved insight on each different level of teachings.

The ancient spiritual writing contained in the Three Scriptures of ancient spiritual mysticism and all spiritual books of many schools were very difficult to understand, even for Chinese scholars. Thus, the real ancient spiritual teaching from the oriental region is not known to most scholars of later generations, the Chinese people or foreign translators. It would have become lost to the world if Hua-Ching Ni had not rewritten it and put it into simple language. He has practically revived the ancient teaching to make it useful for all people.

BOOKS IN ENGLISH BY MASTER NI

Ageless Guidance for Modern Life - *New Publication!*
Master Ni's work entitled *The Book of Changes and the Unchanging Truth*, contains sixty-four illustrative commentaries. Readers have found them meaningful and useful; they cover a variety of topics and give spiritual guidance for everyday life. Many readers requested the commentaries be printed apart from the big text, so we have put them all together in this one volume. The good directions and principles explained here can guide and enrich your life. Master Ni's delightful poetry and some teachings of esoteric Taoism can be found here as well. 256 pages, softcover, Stock No. BAGUI, $15.95.

The Mystical Universal Mother - *New Publication!*
An understanding of both kinds of energies existing in the universe - masculine and feminine - are crucial to the understanding of oneself, in particular for people moving to higher spiritual evolution. In this book, Master Ni focuses upon the feminine as the Mystical Universal Mother and gives examples through the lives of some ancient and modern women, including a woman Taoist teacher known as Mother Chern or the Mother of Yellow Altar, some famous historical Chinese women, the first human woman called Neu Wu, and Master Ni's own mother. 240 pages, softcover, Stock No. bmyst, $14.95

Moonlight in the Dark Night - New Publication!
In order to attain inner clarity and freedom of the soul, you have to get your emotions under control. It seems that spiritual achievement itself is not a great obstacle, once you understand what is helpful and what is not. What is left for most people is their own emotions, which affect the way they treat themselves and others. This will cause trouble for themselves or for other people. This book contains Taoist wisdom on the balancing of the emotions, including balancing love relationships, so that spiritual achievement can become possible. 168 pages, softcover, Stock No. BBECO, $12.95

Harmony - The Art of Life - *New Publication!*
Harmony occurs when two different things find the point at which they can link together. The point of linkage, if healthy and helpful, brings harmony. Harmony is a spiritual matter which relates to each individual's personal sensitivity and sensitivity to each situation of daily life. Basically, harmony comes from understanding yourself. In this book, Master Ni shares some valuable Taoist understanding and insight about the ability to bring harmony within one's own self, one's relationships and the world. 208 pages, Stock No. BHARM, softcover, $14.95

Attune Your Body With Dao-In: Taoist Exercise for a Long and Happy Life - *New Publication!* - Dao-In is a series of typical Taoist movements which are traditionally used for physical energy conducting. These exercises were passed down from the ancient achieved Taoists and immortals. The ancients discovered that Dao-In exercises not only solved problems of stagnant energy, but also increased their health and lengthened their years. The exercises are also used as practical support for cultivation and the higher achievements of spiritual immortality. 144 pages, BDAOI Softcover with photographs, $14.95

The Key to Good Fortune: Refining Your Spirit - *New Publication!* A translation of Straighten Your Way (Tai Shan Kan Yin Pien) and The Silent Way of Blessing (Yin Chia Wen), which are the main guidance for a mature and healthy life. This amplified version of the popular booklet called The Heavenly Way includes a new commentary section by Master Ni which discusses how spiritual improvement can be an integral part of one's life and how to realize a Heavenly life on earth. 144 pages. Stock No. BKEYT. Softcover, $12.95

Eternal Light - *New Publication!*
In this book, Master Ni presents the life and teachings of his father, Grandmaster Ni, Yo San, who was a spiritually achieved person, a Taoist healer and teacher, and a source of inspiration to Master Ni in his life. Here is an intimate look at the lifestyle of a spiritual family. Some of the deeper teachings and understandings of spirituality passed from father to son are clearly given and elucidated. This book is recommended for those committed to living a spiritual way of life and wishing for higher achievement. 208 pages   Stock No. BETER Softcover, $14.95

Quest of Soul - *New Publication!*
In Quest of Soul, Master Ni addresses many subjects relevant to understanding one's own soul, such as the religious concept of saving the soul, how to improve the quality of the personal soul, the high spiritual achievement of free soul, what happens spiritually at death and the universal soul. He guides the reader into deeper knowledge of oneself and inspires each individual to move forward to increase both one's own personal happiness and spiritual level. 152 pages. Stock No. BQUES Softcover, $11.95

Nurture Your Spirits - *New Publication!*
With truthful spiritual knowledge, you have better life attitudes that are more supportive to your existence. With truthful spiritual knowledge, nobody can cause you spiritual confusion. Where can you find such advantage? It would take a lifetime of development in a correct school, but such a school is not available. However, in this book, Master Ni breaks some spiritual prohibitions and presents the spiritual truth he has studied and proven. This truth may help you develop and nurture your own spirits which are the truthful internal foundation of your life being. Taoism is educational; its purpose is not to group people to build social strength but to help each individual build one's own spiritual strength. 176 pages. Stock No. BNURT Softcover, $12.95

Internal Growth Through Tao - *New Publication!*
Material goods can be passed from one person to another, but growth and awareness cannot be given in the same way. Spiritual development is related to one's own internal and external beingness. Through books, discussion or classes, wise people are able to use others' experiences to kindle their own inner light to help their own growth and live a life of no separation from their own spiritual nature. In this book, Master Ni teaches the more subtle, much deeper sphere of the reality of life that is above the shallow sphere of external achievement. He also shows the confusion caused by some spiritual teachings and guides you in the direction of developing spiritually by growing internally. 208 pages. Stock No. BINTE Softcover, $13.95

Power of Natural Healing - *New Publication!*
Master Ni discusses the natural capability of self-healing in this book, which is healing physical trouble untreated by medication or external measure. He offers information and practices which can assist any treatment method currently being used by someone seeking health. He goes deeper to discuss methods of Taoist cultivation which promote a healthy life, including Taoist spiritual achievement, which brings about health and longevity. This book is not only suitable for a person seeking to improve one's health condition. Those who wish to live long and happy, and to understand more about living a natural healthy lifestyle, may be supported by the practice of Taoist energy cultivation. 230 pages. Stock No. BHEAL Softcover, $14.95

Essence of Universal Spirituality
In this volume, as an open-minded learner and achieved teacher of universal spirituality, Master Ni examines and discusses all levels and topics of religious and spiritual teaching to help you develop your own correct knowledge of the essence existing above the differences in religious practice. He reviews religious teachings with hope to benefit modern people. This book is to help readers to come to understand the ultimate truth and enjoy the achievement of all religions without becoming confused by them. 304 pages. Stock No. BESSE Softcover, $19.95

Guide to Inner Light
Modern life is controlled by city environments, cultural customs, religious teachings and politics that can all divert our attention away from our natural life being. As a result, we lose the perspective of viewing ourselves as natural completeness. This book reveals the development of ancient Taoist adepts. Drawing inspiration from their experience, modern people looking for the true source and meaning of life can find great teachings to direct and benefit them. The invaluable ancient Taoist development can teach us to reach the attainable spiritual truth and point the way to the Inner Light. Master Ni uses the ancient high

accomplishments to make this book a useful resource. 192 pages. Stock No. BGUID. Softcover, $12.95

Stepping Stones for Spiritual Success
In Asia, the custom of foot binding was followed for close to a thousand years. In the West, people did not practice foot binding, but they bound their thoughts for a much longer period, some 1,500 to 1,700 years. Their mind and thinking became unnatural. Being unnatural expresses a state of confusion where people do not know what is right. Once they become natural again, they become clear and progress is great. Master Ni invites his readers to unbind their minds; in this volume, he has taken the best of the traditional teachings and put them into contemporary language to make them more relevant to our time, culture and lives. 160 pages. Stock No. BSTEP. Softcover, $12.95.

The Complete Works of Lao Tzu
Lao Tzu's Tao Teh Ching is one of the most widely translated and cherished works of literature in the world. It presents the core of Taoist philosophy. Lao Tzu's timeless wisdom provides a bridge to the subtle spiritual truth and practical guidelines for harmonious and peaceful living. Master Ni has included what is believed to be the only English translation of the Hua Hu Ching, a later work of Lao Tzu which has been lost to the general public for a thousand years. 212 pages. Stock No. BCOMP. Softcover, $12.95

Order The Complete Works of Lao Tzu and the companion Tao Teh Ching Cassette Tapes for only $23.00. Stock No. ABTAO.

The Book of Changes and the Unchanging Truth
The first edition of this book was widely appreciated by its readers, who drew great spiritual benefit from it. They found the principles of the I Ching to be clearly explained and useful to their lives, especially the helpful commentaries. The legendary classic I Ching is recognized as mankind's first written book of wisdom. Leaders and sages throughout history have consulted it as a trusted advisor which reveals the appropriate action to be taken in any of life's circumstances. This volume also includes over 200 pages of background material on Taoist principles of natural energy cycles, instruction and commentaries. New, revised second edition, 669 pages. Stock No. BBOOK. Hardcover, $35.50

The Story of Two Kingdoms
This volume is the metaphoric tale of the conflict between the Kingdoms of Light and Darkness. Through this unique story, Master Ni transmits the esoteric teachings of Taoism which have been carefully guarded secrets for over 5,000 years. This book is for those who are serious in their search and have devoted their lives to achieving high spiritual goals. 122 pages. Stock No. BSTOR. Hardcover, $14.50

The Way of Integral Life

This book can help build a bridge for those wishing to connect spiritual and intellectual development. It is most helpful for modern educated people. It includes practical and applicable suggestions for daily life, philosophical thought, esoteric insight and guidelines for those aspiring to give help and service to the world. This book helps you learn the wisdom of the ancient sages' achievement to assist the growth of your own wisdom and integrate it as your own new light and principles for balanced, reasonable living in worldly life. 320 pages. Softcover, $14.00, Stock No. BWAYS. Hardcover, $20.00, Stock No. BWAYH

Enlightenment: Mother of Spiritual Independence

The inspiring story and teachings of Master Hui Neng, the father of Zen Buddhism and Sixth Patriarch of the Buddhist tradition, highlight this volume. Hui Neng was a person of ordinary birth, intellectually unsophisticated, who achieved himself to become a spiritual leader. Master Ni includes enlivening commentaries and explanations of the principles outlined by this spiritual revolutionary. Having received the same training as all Zen Masters as one aspect of his training and spiritual achievement, Master Ni offers this teaching so that his readers may be guided in their process of spiritual development. 264 pages. Softcover, $12.50, Stock No. BENLS. Hardcover, $22.00, Stock No. BENLH

Attaining Unlimited Life

The thought-provoking teachings of Chuang Tzu are presented in this volume. He was perhaps the greatest philosopher and master of Taoism and he laid the foundation for the Taoist school of thought. Without his work, people of later generations would hardly recognize the value of Lao Tzu's teaching in practical, everyday life. He touches the organic nature of human life more deeply and directly than that of other great teachers. This volume also includes questions by students and answers by Master Ni. 467 pages. Softcover, $18.00, Stock No. BATTS; Hardcover, $25.00, Stock No. BATTH

Special Discount: Order the three classics Way of Integral Life, Enlightenment: Mother of Spiritual Independence *and* Attaining Unlimited Light *in the hardbound editions, Stock No.* BHARD *for $60.00.*

The Gentle Path of Spiritual Progress

This book offers a glimpse into the dialogues of a Taoist master and his students. In a relaxed, open manner, Master Ni, Hua-Ching explains to his students the fundamental practices that are the keys to experiencing enlightenment in everyday life. Many of the traditional secrets of Taoist training are revealed. His students also ask a surprising range of questions, and Master Ni's answers touch on contemporary psychology, finances, sexual advice, how to use the I Ching as well as the telling of some fascinating Taoist legends. Softcover, $12.95, Stock No. BGENT

Spiritual Messages from a Buffalo Rider, A Man of Tao
This is another important collection of Master Ni's service in his worldly trip, originally published as one half of The Gentle Path. He had the opportunity to meet people and answer their questions to help them gain the spiritual awareness that we live at the command of our animal nature. Our buffalo nature rides on us, whereas an achieved person rides the buffalo. In this book, Master Ni gives much helpful knowledge to those who are interested in improving their lives and deepening their cultivation so they too can develop beyond their mundane beings. Softcover, $12.95, Stock No. BSPIR

8,000 Years of Wisdom, Volume I and II
This two volume set contains a wealth of practical, down-to-earth advice given by Master Ni to his students over a five year period, 1979 to 1983. Drawing on his training in Traditional Chinese Medicine, Herbology, Acupuncture and other Taoist arts, Master Ni gives candid answers to students' questions on many topics ranging from dietary guidance to sex and pregnancy, meditation techniques and natural cures for common illnesses. Volume I includes dietary guidance; 236 pages; Stock No. BWIS1 Volume II includes sex and pregnancy guidance; 241 pages; Stock No. BWIS2. Softcover, Each Volume $12.50

Special discount: Both Books I and II of 8,000 Years of Wisdom, Stock No. BWIS3, for $22.00.

The Uncharted Voyage Towards the Subtle Light
Spiritual life in the world today has become a confusing mixture of dying traditions and radical novelties. People who earnestly and sincerely seek something more than just a way to fit into the complexities of a modern structure that does not support true self-development often find themselves spiritually struggling. This book provides a profound understanding and insight into the underlying heart of all paths of spiritual growth, the subtle origin and the eternal truth of one universal life. 424 pages. Stock No. BUNCH. Softcover, $14.50

The Heavenly Way
A translation of the classic Tai Shan Kan Yin Pien (Straighten Your Way) and Yin Chia Wen (The Silent Way of Blessing). The treaties in this booklet are the main guidance for a mature and healthy life. The purpose of this booklet is to promote the recognition of truth, because only truth can teach the perpetual Heavenly Way by which one reconnects oneself with the divine nature. 41 pages. Stock No. BHEAV. Softcover, $2.50

Special Discount: Order the Heavenly Way in a set of 10 - great for gifts or giveaways. (One shipping item). BHIV10 $17.50.

Footsteps of the Mystical Child
This book poses and answers such questions as: What is a soul? What is wisdom? What is spiritual evolution? The answers to these and many other questions enable readers to open themselves to new realms of understanding and personal growth. There are also many true examples about people's internal and external struggles on the path of self-development and spiritual evolution. 166 pages. Stock No. BFOOT. Softcover, $9.50

Workbook for Spiritual Development
This book offers a practical, down-to-earth, hands-on approach for those who are devoted to the path of spiritual achievement. The reader will find diagrams showing fundamental hand positions to increase and channel one's spiritual energy, postures for sitting, standing and sleeping cultivation as well as postures for many Taoist invocations. The material in this workbook is drawn from the traditional teachings of Taoism and summarizes thousands of years of little known practices for spiritual development. An entire section is devoted to ancient invocations, another on natural celibacy and another on postures. In addition, Master Ni explains the basic attitudes and understandings that are the foundation for Taoist practices. 224 pages. Stock No. BWORK. Softcover, $12.95

Poster of Master Lu
Color poster of Master Lu, Tung Ping (shown on cover of workbook), for use with the workbook or in one's shrine. 16" x 22"; Stock No. PMLTP. $10.95

Order the Workbook for Spiritual Development *and the companion Poster of Master Lu for $18.95.* Stock No. BPWOR.

The Taoist Inner View of the Universe
This presentation of Taoist metaphysics provides guidance for one's own personal life transformation. Master Ni has given all the opportunity to know the vast achievement of the ancient unspoiled mind and its transpiercing vision. This book offers a glimpse of the inner world and immortal realm known to achieved Taoists and makes it understandable for students aspiring to a more complete life. 218 pages. Stock No. BTAOI. Softcover, $14.95

Tao, the Subtle Universal Law
Most people are unaware that their thoughts and behavior evoke responses from the invisible net of universal energy. The real meaning of Taoist self-discipline is to harmonize with universal law. To lead a good stable life is to be aware of the actual conjoining of the universal subtle law with every moment of our lives. This book presents the wisdom and practical methods that the ancient Chinese have successfully used for centuries to accomplish this. 165 pages. Stock No. TAOS. Softcover, $7.50

MATERIALS ON TAOIST HEALTH, ARTS AND SCIENCES

BOOKS

The Tao of Nutrition by Maoshing Ni, Ph.D., with Cathy McNease, B.S., M.H. - Working from ancient Chinese medical classics and contemporary research, Dr. Maoshing Ni and Cathy McNease have compiled an indispensable guide to natural healing. This exceptional book shows the reader how to take control of one's health through one's eating habits. This volume contains 3 major sections: the first section deals with theories of Chinese nutrition and philosophy; the second describes over 100 common foods in detail, listing their energetic properties, therapeutic actions and individual remedies. The third section lists nutritional remedies for many common ailments. This book presents both a healing system and a disease prevention system which is flexible in adapting to every individual's needs. 214 pages. Stock No. BNUTR. Softcover, $14.50

Chinese Vegetarian Delights by Lily Chuang
An extraordinary collection of recipes based on principles of traditional Chinese nutrition. Many recipes are therapeutically prepared with herbs. Diet has long been recognized as a key factor in health and longevity. For those who require restricted diets and those who choose an optimal diet, this cookbook is a rare treasure. Meat, sugar, diary products and fried foods are excluded. Produce, grains, tofu, eggs and seaweeds are imaginatively prepared. 104 pages. Stock No. BCHIV. Softcover, $7.50

Chinese Herbology Made Easy - by Maoshing Ni, Ph.D.
This text provides an overview of Oriental medical theory, in-depth descriptions of each herb category, with over 300 black and white photographs, extensive tables of individual herbs for easy reference, and an index of pharmaceutical and Pin-Yin names. The distillation of overwhelming material into essential elements enables one to focus efficiently and develop a clear understanding of Chinese herbology. This book is especially helpful for those studying for their California Acupuncture License. 202 pages. Stock No. BCHIH. Softcover, 14.50

Crane Style Chi Gong Book - By Daoshing Ni, Ph.D.
Chi Gong is a set of meditative exercises that was developed several thousand years ago by Taoists in China. It is now practiced for healing purposes, combining breathing techniques, body movements and mental imagery to guide the smooth flow of energy throughout the body. This book gives a more detailed account and study of Chi Gong than the videotape alone. It may be used with or without the videotape. Includes complete instructions and information on using Chi Gong exercise as a medical therapy. 55 pages. Stock No. BCRAN. Spiral bound $10.50

VIDEO TAPES

Physical Movement for Spiritual Learning: Dao-In Physical Art for a Long and Happy Life (VHS) - by Master Ni. Dao-In is a series of typical Taoist movements which are traditionally used for physical energy conducting. These exercises were passed down from the ancient achieved Taoists and immortals. The ancients discovered that Dao-In exercises not only solved problems of stagnant energy, but also increased their health and lengthened their years. The exercises are also used as practical support for cultivation and the higher achievements of spiritual immortality. Master Ni, Hua-Ching, heir to the tradition of the achieved masters, is the first one who releases this important Taoist practice to the modern world in this 1 hour videotape. Stock No. VDAOI VHS $59.95

T'ai Chi Chuan: An Appreciation (VHS) - by Master Ni - Different styles of T'ai Chi Ch'uan as Movement have different purposes and accomplish different results. In this long awaited videotape, Master Ni, Hua-Ching presents three styles of T'ai Chi Movement handed down to him through generations of highly developed masters. They are the "Gentle Path," "Sky Journey," and "Infinite Expansion" styles of T'ai Chi Movement. The three styles are presented uninterrupted in this unique videotape and are set to music for observation and appreciation. Stock No. VAPPR. VHS 30 minutes $49.95

Crane Style Chi Gong (VHS) - by Dr. Daoshing Ni, Ph.D.
Chi Gong is a set of meditative exercises developed several thousand years ago by ancient Taoists in China. It is now practiced for healing stubborn chronic diseases, strengthening the body to prevent disease and as a tool for further spiritual enlightenment. It combines breathing techniques, simple body movements, and mental imagery to guide the smooth flow of energy throughout the body. Chi gong is easy to learn for all ages. Correct and persistent practice will increase one's energy, relieve stress or tension, improve concentration and clarity, release emotional stress and restore general well-being. 2 hours Stock No. VCRAN. $65.95

Eight Treasures (VHS) - By Maoshing Ni, Ph.D.
These exercises help open blocks in a person's energy flow and strengthen one's vitality. It is a complete exercise combining physical stretching and toning and energy conducting movements coordinated with breathing. The Eight Treasures are an exercise unique to the Ni family. Patterned from nature, its 32 movements are an excellent foundation for Tai Chi Chuan or martial arts. 1 hour, 45 minutes. Stock No. VEIGH. $49.95

Tai Chi Chuan I & II (VHS) - By Maoshing Ni, Ph.D.
This exercise integrates the flow of physical movement with that of integral energy in the Taoist style of "Harmony," similar to the long form of Yang-style Tai Chi Chuan. Tai Chi has been practiced for thousands of years to help both physical longevity and spiritual cultivation. 1 hour each. Each Video Tape $49.95. Order both for $90.00. Stock Nos: Part I, VTAI1; Part II, VTAI2; Set of two, VTAI3.

AUDIO CASSETTES

Invocations: Health and Longevity and Healing a Broken Heart - By Maoshing Ni, Ph.D. *Updated with additional material!* This audio cassette guides the listener through a series of ancient invocations to channel and conduct one's own healing energy and vital force. "Thinking is louder than thunder." The mystical power by which all miracles are brought about is your sincere practice of this principle. 30 minutes. Stock No. AINVO. $8.95

Chi Gong for Stress Release - By Maoshing Ni, Ph.D.
This audio cassette guides you through simple, ancient breathing exercises that enable you to release day-to-day stress and tension that are such a common cause of illness today. 30 minutes. Stock No. ACHIS. $8.95

Chi Gong for Pain Management - By Maoshing Ni, Ph.D.
Using easy visualization and deep-breathing techniques that have been developed over thousands of years, this audio cassette offers methods for overcoming pain by invigorating your energy flow and unblocking obstructions that cause pain. 30 minutes. Stock No. ACHIP. $8.95

Tao Teh Ching Cassette Tapes
This classic work of Lao Tzu has been recorded in this two-cassette set that is a companion to the book translated by Master Ni. Professionally recorded and read by Robert Rudelson. 120 minutes. Stock No. ATAOT. $15.95

Order Master Ni's book, The Complete Works of Lao Tzu, and Tao Teh Ching Cassette Tapes for only $25.00. Stock No. ABTAO.

This list of Master Ni's books in English is ordered by date of publication for those readers who wish to follow the sequence of his Western teaching material in their learning of Tao.

1979: *The Complete Works of Lao Tzu*
      The Taoist Inner View of the Universe
      Tao, the Subtle Universal Law
1983: *The Book of Changes and the Unchanging Truth*
      8,000 Years of Wisdom, I
      8,000 Years of Wisdom, II
1984: *Workbook for Spiritual Development*
1985: *The Uncharted Voyage Towards the Subtle Light*
1986: *Footsteps of the Mystical Child*
1987: *The Gentle Path of Spiritual Progress*
      Spiritual Messages from a Buffalo Rider, (originally
             part of *Gentle Path of Spiritual Progress*)
1989: *The Way of Integral Life*
      Enlightenment: Mother of Spiritual Independence
      Attaining Unlimited Life
      The Story of Two Kingdoms
1990: *Stepping Stones for Spiritual Success*
      Guide to Inner Light
      Essence of Universal Spirituality
1991: *Internal Growth through Tao*
      Nurture Your Spirits
      Quest of Soul
      Power of Natural Healing
      *Attune Your Body with Dao-In: Taoist Exercise for a Long and
             Happy Life*
      Eternal Light
      Harmony: The Art of Life
      The Key to Good Fortune: Refining Your Spirit
      Become the Cloudless Sky

In addition, the forthcoming books will be compiled from his lecturing and teaching service:

*Golden Message: The Tao in Your Daily Life (by Daoshing and
       Maoshing Ni, based on the works of Master Ni, Hua-Ching)*
Learning Gentle Path Tʻai Chi Chuan
Learning Sky Journey Tʻai Chi Chuan
Learning Infinite Expansion Tʻai Chi Chuan
Learning Cosmic Tour Ba Gua
The Mystical Universal Mother
Taoist Mysticism: God and Mankind United As One
Life and Teachings of Two Immortals, Volume I: Kou Hong
Life and Teachings of Two Immortals, Volume II: Chen Tuan

How To Order

Name: _____

Address: _____

City: _____ State: _____ Zip: _____

Phone - Daytime: _____ Evening: _____

(We may telephone you if we have questions about your order.)

Qty.	Stock No.	Title/Description	Price Each	Total Price

Total amount for items ordered_____

Sales tax (CA residents only, 7%)_____

Shipping Charge (See below)_____

Total Amount Enclosed_____

Visa _____ Mastercard _____ Expiration Date _____

Card number:_____

Signature:_____

Shipping: In the US, we use UPS when possible. Please give full street address or nearest crossroads. All packages are insured at no extra charge. If shipping to more than one address, use separate shipping charges. Remember: 1 - 10 copies of Heavenly Way, Tao Teh Ching audio tapes and each book and tape are single items. Posters (up to 5 per tube) are a separate item. Please allow 2 - 4 weeks for US delivery and 6 - 10 weeks for foreign surface mail.

By Mail: Complete this form with payment (US funds only, No Foreign Postal Money Orders, please) and mail to: Union of Tao and Man, 117 Stonehaven Way, Los Angeles, CA 90049

Phone Orders: (213) 472-9970 - You may leave credit card orders anytime on our answering machine. Please speak clearly and remember to leave your full name and daytime phone number. We will call only if we have a question with your order, there is a delay or you specifically ask for phone confirmation.

Inquiries: If you have questions concerning your order, please refer to the date and invoice number on the top center of your invoice to help us locate your order swiftly.

Shipping Charges -
   Domestic Surface: First item $3.25, each additional, add $.50.
   Canada Surface: First item $3.25, each additional, add $1.00.
   Canada Air: First item $4.00, each additional, add $2.00.
   Foreign Surface: First Item $3.50, each additional, add $2.00.
   Foreign Air: First item $12.00, each additional, add $7.00.

For the Trade: Wholesale orders may be placed direct to publisher, or with NewLeaf, BookPeople, The Distributors, Inland Books, GreatWay in US or DeepBooks in Europe.

Thank you for your order

Spiritual Study Through the College of Tao

The College of Tao and the Union of Tao and Man were established formally in California in the 1970's. This tradition is a very old spiritual culture of mankind, holding long experience of human spiritual growth. Its central goal is to offer healthy spiritual education to all people of our society. This time tested tradition values the spiritual development of each individual self and passes down its guidance and experience.

Master Ni carries his tradition from its country of origin to the west. He chooses to avoid making the mistake of old-style religions that have rigid establishments which resulted in fossilizing the delicacy of spiritual reality. Rather, he prefers to guide the teachings of his tradition as a school of no boundary rather than a religion with rigidity. Thus, the branches or centers of this Taoist school offer different programs of similar purpose. Each center extends its independent service, but all are unified in adopting Master Ni's work as the foundation of teaching to fulfill the mission of providing spiritual education to all people.

The centers offer their classes, teaching, guidance and practices on building the groundwork for cultivating a spiritually centered and well-balanced life. As a person obtains the correct knowledge with which to properly guide himself or herself, he or she can then become more skillful in handling the experiences of daily life. The assimilation of good guidance in one's practical life brings about different stages of spiritual development.

Any interested individual is welcome to join and learn to grow for oneself. You might like to join the center near where you live, or you yourself may be interested in organizing a center or study group based on the model of existing centers. In that way, we all work together for the spiritual benefit of all people. We do not require any religious type of commitment.

The learning is life. The development is yours. The connection of study may be helpful, useful and serviceable, directly to you.

- -

Mail to: Union of Tao and Man, 117 Stonehaven Way, Los Angeles, CA 90049

_____ I wish to be put on the mailing list of the Union of Tao and Man to be notified of classes, educational activities and new publications.

Name:_____

Address:_____

City:_____State:_____Zip:_____

Herbs Used by Ancient Taoist Masters

The pursuit of everlasting youth or immortality throughout human history is an innate human desire. Long ago, Chinese esoteric Taoists went to the high mountains to contemplated nature, strengthen their bodies, empower their minds and develop their spirit. From their studies and cultivation, they gave China alchemy and chemistry, herbology and acupuncture, the I Ching, astrology, martial arts and T'ai Chi Chuan, Chi Gong and many other useful kinds of knowledge.

Most important, they handed down in secrecy methods for attaining longevity and spiritual immortality. There were different levels of approach; one was to use a collection of food herb formulas that were only available to highly achieved Taoist masters. They used these food herbs to increase energy and heighten vitality. This treasured collection of herbal formulas remained within the Ni family for centuries.

Now, through Traditions of Tao, the Ni family makes these foods available for you to use to assist the foundation of your own positive development. It is only with a strong foundation that expected results are produced from diligent cultivation.

As a further benefit, in concert with the Taoist principle of self-sufficiency, Traditions of Tao offers the food herbs along with the Union of Tao and Man's publications in a distribution opportunity for anyone serious about financial independence.

Send to: Traditions of Tao
             c/o 117 Stonehaven Way
             Los Angeles, CA 90049

❑ Please send me a Traditions of Tao brochure.

❑ Please send me information on becoming an independent distributor of Traditions of Tao herbal products and publications.

Name _____

Address_____

City_____State_____Zip_____

Phone (day)_____(night)_____

Yo San University of Traditional Chinese Medicine

"Not just a medical career, but a life-time commitment to raising one's spiritual standard."

Thank you for your support and interest in our publications and services. It is by your patronage that we continue to offer you the practical knowledge and wisdom from this venerable Taoist tradition.

Because of your sustained interest in Taoism, we formed Yo San University of Traditional Chinese Medicine, a non-profit educational institute in January 1989 under the direction of founder Master Ni, Hua-Ching. Yo San University is the continuation of 38 generations of Ni family practitioners who handed down knowledge and wisdom from fathers to sons. Its purpose is to train and graduate practitioners of the highest caliber in Traditional Chinese Medicine, which includes acupuncture, herbology and spiritual development.

We view Traditional Chinese Medicine as the application of spiritual development. Its foundation is the spiritual capability to know life, to know a person's problem and how to cure it. We teach students how to care for themselves and others, and emphasize the integration of traditional knowledge and modern science. We offer a complete Master's degree program approved by the California State Department of Education that provides an excellent education in Traditional Chinese Medicine and meets all requirements for state licensure.

We invite you to inquire into our school about a creative and rewarding career as a holistic physician. Classes are also open to persons interested only in self-enrichment. For more information, please fill out the form below and send it to:

Yo San University,
12304 Santa Monica Blvd. Suite 104,
Los Angeles, CA 90025

❏ Please send me information on the Masters degree program in Traditional Chinese Medicine.

❏ Please send me information on health workshops and seminars.

❏ Please send me information on continuing education for acupuncturists and health professionals.

Name _____

Address_____

City_____State_____Zip_____

Phone(day)_____(night)_____